"An excellent description of the methods, means of recruitment, way of life and generally dismal ends of the pirates who flourished from the 16th to the end of the 18th century."
—BOSTON GLOBE

"Folks who began reading about pirates in their childhood (remember Long John Silver and Captain Hook?) have no reason to stop now. UNDER THE BLACK FLAG provides a satisfying and salty overview of nautical badmen (and a few women too) going back some 500 years." —PARADE

"Revisionist history backed by captivating accounts of thuggery and buggery." —ESQUIRE

"Cordingly has written a wonderfully entertaining history of pirates and piracy ... that for all its scrupulosity about facts can't help but be a rip-roaring read. ... [His] descriptions of pirate life are fascinating and unexpected."
—MEN'S JOURNAL

"A vivid account of the glory days of buccaneers . . . It reminds us that the London of Handel and Dr. Johnson was a place where the decomposing bodies of executed men were hung in public places and that life in Britain's imperial outposts was closer to HEART OF DARKNESS than to Colonial Williamsburg." —CIVILIZATION

"Entirely engaging and informative . . . A witty and spirited book."
—Jonathan Yardley, WASHINGTON POST BOOK WORLD

"If you've ever been seduced by the myth of the cutlass-wielding pirate, consider David Cordingly's UNDER THE BLACK FLAG. This lively history explores the sources of the myths, including Robert Louis Stevenson's wildly influential TREASURE ISLAND."
—USA TODAY, "Best Bets"

"Engagingly told . . . A tale of the power of imaginative literature to re-create the past." —LOS ANGELES TIMES

Under the Black Flag

The Romance and the Reality of Life Among the Pirates

David Cordingly

A HARVEST BOOK   HARCOURT BRACE & COMPANY

San Diego   New York   London

This Harvest edition published by arrangement with Random House.

Library of Congress Cataloging-in-Publication Data
Cordingly, David.
Under the black flag: the romance and reality of life
among the pirates / David Cordingly. —1st Harvest ed.
p.   cm. —(A Harvest book)
Originally published: New York: Random House, c1996.
Includes bibliographical references and index.
ISBN 0-15-600549-2
1. Pirates.   I. Title.
[G535.C635   1997]
910.4′5—dc21   97-15048

Book design by Carole Lowenstein
Printed in the United States of America
First Harvest edition 1997

K M N L J

For Matthew and Rebecca

Preface and Acknowledgments

In May 1992 an exhibition entitled *Pirates: Fact and Fiction* opened at the National Maritime Museum in London. It was scheduled to last four months but proved so popular that it remained open for three years. The exhibition was organized by my colleague John Falconer and myself, with help from many members of the museum staff and support from a great number of contributors. Exhibits included artifacts from the sunken pirate city of Port Royal, Jamaica; Captain Kidd's privateering commission from the Public Record Office; fine portraits of Robert Louis Stevenson and William Dampier from the National Portrait Gallery; Byron's manuscript copy of *The Corsair;* the Peter Pan costume worn by Pauline Chase in the 1909 London production, and the pirate costumes worn by Dustin Hoffman and Bob Hoskins in Steven Spielberg's film *Hook;* W. S. Gilbert's annotated prompt copy of *The Pirates of Penzance;* pieces of eight, ducats, and doubloons from the British Museum; and charts, weapons, logbooks, ship models, and buccaneer journals from the National Maritime Museum.

As a result of the widespread publicity which accompanied the opening of the exhibition I was approached by Suzanne Gluck of the New York literary agents ICM, and urged to write a book which contrasted the fictional image of piracy with the reality. I would like to thank Suzanne for starting me on a most enjoyable project, and to record my debt to Ann Godoff, my editor at Random House, who persuaded me to transform my first manuscript into a book which will, I hope, have a wider appeal beyond those interested in maritime history. I am grateful to Alan Samson and Andrew Gordon at Little, Brown, my publishers in England, for helping me to clarify my thoughts in a number of areas. I would also like to record my thanks to Giles O'Bryen, Clinton Black, Gillian Coleridge, John Falconer, Enrica Gadler, William Gilkerson, Alec Herzer, Helga Houghton, Kevin McCarey, David Marley, Julia Millette, Dian Murray, Peter Neill, Richard Pennell, Linda Silverman, and Norman Thrower, as well as the staff at the Library of Congress, the British Library, the Institute of Jamaica, the London Library, the Public Record Office, and my former colleagues at the National Maritime Museum. Above all I would like to thank my wife and family for their encouragement, advice, and numerous suggestions during the preparation of this book and the exhibition which preceded it.

The sources used in the text are given in the Notes and Bibliography at the end, but I would like to acknowledge my particular debt to four books which I would recommend to anyone wishing to pursue the subject in more depth. The first is Robert Ritchie's book *Captain Kidd and the War Against the Pirates,* which must be the most thoroughly researched and documented book on the life of a pirate ever written. The second is Marcus Rediker's *Between the Devil and the Deep Blue Sea.* Apart from its revelations about the life of the ordinary seaman, this contains a penetrating analysis of the Anglo-American pirates in the early eighteenth century. The third is *The Sack of Panama* by Peter Earle, which features a vivid and balanced account of Sir Henry Morgan's expeditions, and is based on research in the Spanish archives. The fourth is Nicholas Rodger's *The Wooden World.* This scarcely mentions pirates but provides an extraordinary insight into how the Royal Navy worked and what went on above and below deck. In quoting from seventeenth- and eighteenth-century manuscripts and printed books, I have followed Rodger's example and used modern spelling, punctuation, and capitalization. I have only broken this rule when it seemed to me that the original spelling and use of abbreviations provided additional information about the writer and the circumstances under which the document was written.

D.C.
Brighton, Sussex
February 1995

Contents

CONTENTS

x

List of Maps

Introduction

Pirates have always been elusive figures. They came out of the blue. They attacked, they looted, and they vanished. They left no memorials or personal belongings behind. A few journals provide glimpses of pirate life, but the woodcuts and engravings which illustrate the early histories of piracy are as fictitious as the many stories of buried treasure. And yet the lack of physical evidence has not lessened their mysterious attraction. Reason tells us that pirates were no more than common criminals, but we still see them as figures of romance. We associate them with daring deeds on the Spanish Main, with rakish black schooners and tropical islands and sea chests overflowing with gold and silver coins.

Most of us will never meet any pirates, and yet we know, or we think we know, exactly what they looked like. We learned about them when we were children. We have seen them on the stage and screen. They are as recognizable as cowboys, and like cowboys, they have acquired a legendary status. They have inspired some of the finest writers of the English language, and two pirate stories in particular, *Treasure Island* and *Peter Pan,* have become literary classics.

Over the years fact has merged with fiction. Inevitably some of the stories vanish into thin air when they are examined. Most people assume that pirates made their victims walk the plank because that is the fate which Captain Hook was planning for the Lost Boys, but real pirates had no time for such ceremonies. Seamen who resisted a pirate attack were hacked to death and thrown over the side. The typical plunder was not chests full of doubloons and pieces of eight, but a few bales of silk and cotton, some barrels of tobacco, an anchor cable, some spare sails, the carpenter's tools, and half a dozen black slaves.

Not all the images associated with pirates prove to be fictitious. The popular view of what they looked like is surprisingly close to reality: pirates really did tie scarves or large handkerchiefs around their heads, and they did walk around armed to the teeth with pistols and cutlasses. The common practice in theatrical productions and films of dressing pirate captains in the frock coats and full-bottom wigs of the Stuart period also makes sense because it was in the reign of King Charles II that the buccaneers of the Caribbean were at their most active.

The aim of this book is to examine the popular image of pirates today, to find out where this image came from, and to compare it with the real world of the pirates. The picture which most of us have turns out to be a blend of historical facts overlaid with three centuries of ballads, melodramas, epic poems, romantic novels, adventure stories, comic strips, and films. In the process, the pirates have acquired a romantic aura which they never had in the seventeenth century and which they certainly never deserved. Pirates were not maritime versions of Robin Hood and his Merry Men. Piracy, like rape, depended on the use of force or the threat of force, and pirate attacks were frequently accompanied by extreme violence, torture, and death. John Turner, who was chief mate of the ship *Tay*, was captured by Chinese pirates in 1806 and held prisoner for five months. He was beaten and kicked and imprisoned at night belowdecks in a space eighteen inches wide and four feet long; but this was nothing compared with the treatment meted out to officers of the Chinese navy who had also been captured. Turner described how one man was nailed to the deck through his feet with large nails, "then beaten with four rattans twisted together, till he vomited blood; and after remaining some time in this state, he was taken ashore and cut to pieces." The pirates disemboweled another officer, cut out his heart, soaked it in spirits, and ate it.[1]

Similar horror stories emerge from the Mediterranean and the West Indies. One of the most poignant accounts of a pirate attack was written by Miss Lucretia Parker, a young woman captured by Cuban pirates in 1825. She was traveling from St. Johns to Antigua in the sloop *Eliza-Ann* under the command of an Englishman, Captain Charles Smith. On the eleventh day of the voyage they were intercepted by a small schooner whose decks were crowded with heavily armed pirates. After a brief fight the pirates captured the *Eliza-Ann*, looted her, and sailed both vessels to a small island off the coast of Cuba. All the victims were rowed ashore. Miss Parker later described their fate in a letter to her brother George who lived in New York:

> Having first divested them of every article of clothing but their shirts and trousers, with swords, knives, axes, &c, they fell on the unfortunate crew of the *Eliza-Ann* with the ferocity of cannibals! In vain did they beg for mercy and intreat of their murderers to spare their lives! In vain did poor Capt. S. attempt to touch their feelings and to move them to pity by representing to them the situation of his innocent family—that he had a wife and three small children at home wholly dependent on him for support! but, alas, the poor man entreated in vain! his appeal was to monsters possessing hearts callous to the feelings of humanity! having received a heavy blow from one with an axe, he snapped the cords with which he was bound, and attempted an escape by flight, but was met by another of the ruffians, who plunged a knife or dirk to his heart! I stood near him at this moment and was covered with his blood—on receiving the fatal wound he gave a single groan and fell lifeless at my feet. . . . Dear brother, need I attempt to paint to your imagination my feelings at this awful moment![2]

Miss Parker expected to become the next victim, but it soon became clear that the pirate captain was keeping her for himself. Her virtue was saved by the appearance of a British warship on the horizon. The pirates abandoned the *Eliza-Ann* and fled. They were later captured and taken to Jamaica, where Miss Parker identified them. They were all hanged.

There has been piracy since the earliest times. There were Greek pirates and Roman pirates, and centuries of piracy when the Vikings and Danes were ravaging the coasts of Europe. The southern shores of England were infested with smugglers and pirates during Tudor times. A group of Dutch pirates called the Sea Beggars, or *Watergeuzen*, played a small but critical role in the history of the Netherlands.

In 1571 and 1572 they temporarily abandoned their plundering raids and joined the forces of William of Orange to help liberate their country from the Spanish. In the Mediterranean, pirates took part in the holy war which was waged between the Christians and the Muslims for several centuries: Barbary corsairs intercepted ships traveling through the Strait of Gibraltar or coming from the trading ports of Alexandria and Venice, swooping down on the heavily laden merchantmen, in their swift galleys powered by oars and sails. They looted their cargoes, captured their passengers and crews, and held them to ransom or sold them into slavery.

The French played a major part in the history of piracy. Many of the most successful and most fearsome of the buccaneers who prowled the Spanish Main came from French seaports. Corsairs based at Dunkirk menaced the shipping in the English Channel in the mid-seventeenth century. Their most famous leader was Jean Bart, who was responsible for the capture of some eighty ships. He later joined the French navy and was ennobled by King Louis XIV in 1694.

The Red Sea and the Persian Gulf were always notorious for pirates, and the Malabar coast on the western shores of India was home to the Maratha pirates, led by the Angria family, who plundered the ships of the East India Company during the first half of the eighteenth century.

In the Far East there was piracy on a massive scale. The Ilanun pirates of the Philippines roamed the seas around Borneo and New Guinea with fleets of large galleys manned by crews of forty to sixty men, launching savage attacks on shipping and coastal villages until they were stamped out by a naval expedition in 1862. But the most formidable of all, in terms of numbers and cruelties, were the pirates of the South China Sea. Their activities reached a peak in the early years of the nineteenth century, when a community of around forty thousand pirates with some four hundred junks dominated the coastal waters and attacked any merchant vessels which strayed into the area. From 1807 these pirates were led by a remarkable woman called Mrs. Cheng, a former prostitute from Canton.

Although the Chinese pirates and the Barbary corsairs will appear in some of the ensuing chapters, this book concentrates on the pirates of the Western world, and particularly on the great age of piracy, which began in the 1650s and was brought to an abrupt end around 1725, when naval patrols drove the pirates from their lairs and mass hangings eliminated many of their leaders. It is this period which has inspired most of the books, plays, and films about piracy, and has been largely responsible for the popular image of the pirate in the West today. The period opens with the emergence of the buccaneers in the Caribbean. It includes the savage raids of Henry Morgan on Portobello and Panama, and the unfortunate life and miserable death of Captain Kidd. It reaches a peak around 1720, when some two thousand pirates were terrorizing ships on both sides of the Atlantic and seriously threatening the trade of the American colonies.

BEFORE PROCEEDING any further, we need to be clear about the difference between piracy and privateering, and the use of the words "corsair" and "buccaneer."

A pirate was, and is, someone who robs and plunders on the sea. According to a law against piracy which was passed in the reign of King Henry VIII, the term not only applied to robbery on the high seas but also to felonies, robberies, and murders committed in any haven, river, creek, or place where the Lord High Admiral had jurisdiction.

A privateer was an armed vessel, or the commander and crew of that vessel, which was licensed to attack and seize the vessels of a hostile nation. The license was issued in the form of a document known as a "letter of marque and reprisal." Originally the license was granted by the sovereign to enable a merchant whose ship or cargo had been stolen or destroyed to seek reprisals by attacking the enemy and recouping his losses, but by the sixteenth century the system was being used by maritime nations as a cheap way of attacking enemy shipping in time of war. By issuing letters of marque to private ships, the sovereign was saved the cost of building and maintaining a large standing navy.

The letter of marque was an impressive-looking certificate written in ponderous legal phrases and decorated with elaborate pen-and-ink flourishes. The privateer captain was expected to keep a journal and to hand over all ships and goods seized to an Admiralty Court to be assessed and valued. A proportion of the value went to the sovereign; the rest went to the ship's owners, her captain and crew. In theory, an authorized privateer was recognized by international law and could not be prosecuted for piracy, but the system was wide open to abuse and privateers were often no more than licensed pirates.

Pirates based in the Mediterranean were called corsairs. The most famous were those of the Barbary Coast, who operated from Algiers, Tunis, Salé, and other ports along the northern shores of Africa, and they were authorized by the rulers of the Muslim countries to attack the ships of Christian countries. Less well known were the corsairs of Malta. They were sent out to loot shipping by the Knights of St. John, a military order created during the Crusades to fight the Muslim infidels on behalf of the Christian nations. As far as the captains and crews of the merchant ships sailing the Mediterranean were concerned, all the corsairs were pirates. Occasionally one of the European nations would send a squadron of warships to combat the corsair menace, but it was not till Algiers was bombarded by the guns of a massive allied fleet in 1816 that the corsairs ceased to be a serious threat to shipping.

Buccaneers were pirates who operated in the Caribbean and around the coast of South America during the seventeenth century. Nowadays the term is used very loosely to include lawless adventurers who preyed on any ships which fell into their hands, as well as men like Henry Morgan who made war on the Spanish with a commission from the English Governor of Jamaica. The original buccaneers were hunters in the woods and valleys of Hispaniola, the mountainous Caribbean island which is now Haiti and the Dominican Republic. They were mostly French, and they lived off the herds of cattle and pigs which had been introduced by the first Spanish settlers. They cooked and dried strips of meat over open stoves or barbecues in the fashion of the Arawak Indians, and it was the French word for this process, *boucaner* (meaning to smoke-dry, or cure), which gave these wild and uncouth men their name. They dressed in leather hides and, with their butchers' knives and bloodstained appearance, looked and smelled like men from a slaughterhouse.

During the 1620s, the huntsmen drifted from the inner regions of Hispaniola to the north coast and particularly to the offshore island of Tortuga, which became a base for piratical attacks on passing merchant ships and Spanish galleons heading home with treasure from Mexico and Peru. At first there was little organization among the buccaneers, but they soon developed a loose confederation which became known as the Brethren of the Coast. At intervals they came together for a combined raid on a major target, the most famous being the attack on Panama in 1671 which was led by Henry Morgan and resulted in the sacking and burning of the Spanish city.

Many of the pirate captains were formidable characters, and some of the events which took place during the great age of piracy were as dramatic as any fiction. If it were not for the details contained in the logbooks of the naval officers concerned, it would be hard to believe the story of Blackbeard and his final stand among the shallows on the coast of Carolina. Scarcely less spectacular was the battle between the pirate ships of Bartholomew Roberts and the British warship HMS *Swallow*, which was fought on the other side of the Atlantic. The engagement began in a rising gale off Africa, with rain sweeping across the stormy seas. As the seamen struggled to load and fire their guns on the pitching decks of their ships, a tropical storm unleashed its full force and thunder and lightning filled the air. The battle was to prove a turning point in the war against the pirates.

Trial documents, naval logbooks, reports from colonial governors, and the depositions of captured pirates and their victims are the principal sources of information for the great age of piracy. The other source, which has been much plundered by writers and film directors, is a remarkable book published within two or three years of many of the events described within its pages. It is entitled *A General History of the Robberies and Murders of the Most Notorious Pyrates,* and its author was Captain Charles Johnson. The first edition was published on May 14, 1724, and was so popular that other editions followed in rapid succession. Johnson took most of his information from the transcripts of pirate trials and from the reports in contemporary newspapers such as the *London Gazette* and the *Daily Post*. The vivid detail of places and conversations suggests that he also interviewed seamen and former pirates. He shows a familiarity with the use of seaman's language which indicates that he may have been a sea captain, although his name could be the nom de plume of a professional writer or journalist.

In 1932 the American scholar John Robert Moore announced at a literary meeting that the real author of the *General History of the Pirates* (as it is usually known) was none other than Daniel Defoe.[3] He devoted several years to proving his theory and published his conclusions at length in *Defoe in the Pillory and Other Studies.* Moore's arguments were persuasive. He showed that the style of the language used and the frequent inclusion of moral reflections was typical of Defoe, and pointed out that Defoe was clearly fascinated by pirates: the year after publishing *Robinson Crusoe,* Defoe had written *Captain Singleton,* a work of fiction presented as the true autobiography of a pirate. He had also published a biography of Captain Avery entitled *The King of the Pirates,* and an account of the Scottish pirate John Gow.

Professor Moore's reputation as the foremost Defoe scholar of his generation persuaded most of the libraries of the world to recatalog the *General History of the Pirates* under the name of Defoe. But in 1988 two academics, P. N. Furbank and W. R. Owens, demolished Moore's theory in their book *The Canonisation of Daniel Defoe.* They showed that there was not a single piece of documentary evidence to link Defoe with the *General History of the Pirates,* and pointed out that there were too many discrepancies between the stories in the book and the other works on pirates attributed to Defoe. So convincing are their arguments that there seems no alternative but to abandon the attractive theory that Defoe wrote the *General History of the Pirates* and to return the authorship of the work to the mysterious Captain Johnson. Whatever the identity of the author, the book has had a far-reaching effect on the popular view of pirates. It is the prime source for the lives of many pirates of what is often called the Golden Age of Piracy. It publicized a generation of villains, and gave an almost mythical status to men like Blackbeard and Captain Kidd, who subsequently became the subject of ballads and plays.

As the threat of piracy receded and attacks on merchant shipping in the Caribbean and along the American seaboard became few and far between, the public perception of pirates underwent a change. Instead of being regarded as common murderers and robbers they began to acquire the status of romantic outlaws. This image was given a major boost with the publication of an epic poem by Lord Byron in the early years of the nineteenth century. It was entitled *The Corsair* and described the adventures of Conrad, a proud and tyrannical pirate leader. With his pale and gloomy countenance and his air of doom, the corsair combined the vices of a Gothic villain with the ideals of the noble outlaw. Byron tells how Conrad rescues a lovely slave girl from the harem of the Turkish Pacha. She brings him a dagger so that he may kill his enemy the Pacha while he is sleeping. Conrad decides against such a cowardly act, whereupon the slave girl murders the Pacha herself. They escape to Conrad's pirate island. There Conrad learns that Medora, the love of his life, is dead from grief in the mistaken belief that he has been killed. Conrad is in despair. He sails away and is never heard of again.

Byron had visited the Mediterranean during an extended grand tour, and he based Conrad and his crew on the corsairs who operated around the Greek islands and the Turkish coast at that time. He had already achieved fame with the publication of *Childe Harold's Pilgrimage* and the public was eager for more. When *The Corsair* was published in February 1814 it took London by storm. John Murray, the publisher, told Byron that he could not recollect any work which had excited such a ferment. "I sold on the day of publication—a thing perfectly unprecedented—10,000 copies; and I suppose thirty people, who were purchasers (strangers) called to tell the people in the shop how much they had been delighted and satisfied."[4] In the following month, seven more editions were printed. Apart from becoming a best-seller in England, Byron's poem had a considerable following on the Continent. Among the many works inspired by its piratical theme were Verdi's opera *Il Corsaro* of 1848 and the overture *Le Corsaire* by Berlioz.

Fictional works about pirates blossomed during the nineteenth century. Walter Scott wrote a historical novel, *The Pirate,* based on the life of a notorious Scottish pirate called John Gow. Captain Marryat published an adventure story which was also called *The Pirate,* and R. M. Ballantyne included pirates in *Coral Island,* the most enduring of his many stories for boys. But it was Robert Louis Stevenson who was to bring the distant world of pirates to life with a slim volume about a sea cook, a treasure map, and a schooner called the *Hispaniola.*

UNDER THE BLACK FLAG

I

WOODEN LEGS AND PARROTS

ROBERT LOUIS STEVENSON was thirty years old when he began writing *Treasure Island*. It was his first success as a novelist, and although *Dr. Jekyll and Mr. Hyde* and *The Master of Ballantrae* are considered finer works by many critics, it is the book with which his name is indelibly associated. The first fifteen chapters were written at Braemar among the Scottish mountains in August and September 1881.[1] The late summer weather was atrocious, and Stevenson and his family huddled around the fire in Miss Mcgregor's cottage while the wind howled down the Dee valley and the rain beat on the windows. There were five of them staying there: Stevenson's parents, his American wife, Fanny, and her twelve-year-old son, Lloyd Osbourne, who was Stevenson's stepson. To pass the time, Lloyd painted pictures with a shilling box of watercolors. One afternoon Stevenson joined him and drew a map of an island. He was soon adding names to the various hills and inlets. Lloyd later wrote, "I shall never forget the thrill of Skeleton Island, Spyglass Hill, nor the heart-stirring climax of the three red crosses! And the greater climax still when he wrote down the words 'Treasure Island' at the top right-hand corner! And he seemed to know so much about it too—the pirates, the buried treasure, the man who had been marooned on the island."[2] In an essay which he wrote in the last year of his life, Stevenson revealed how the future character of the book began to appear to him as he studied the map. It was to be all about buccaneers, and a mutiny, and a fine old Squire called Trelawney, and a sea cook with one leg, and a sea song with the chorus "Yo-ho-ho and a bottle of rum."

Within three days he had written three chapters, and as he wrote each chapter he read it out to the family, who, apart from Fanny, were delighted with the results and added their own suggestions. Lloyd insisted that there should be no women in the story. Stevenson's father devised the contents of Billy Bones' sea chest, and suggested the scene where Jim Hawkins hides in the apple barrel. During the course of the next two weeks Stevenson had a visit from Dr. Alexander Japp, who was equally enthusiastic and took the early chapters along to the editor of *Young Folks* magazine. He agreed to publish the story in weekly installments, but after fifteen chapters Stevenson abruptly ran out of inspiration and could write no more. The holiday in Scotland came to an end, and he moved south to Weybridge, where he corrected the proofs of the early chapters and despaired at what still remained to be done. Stevenson was the victim all his life of a chronic bronchial condition which racked him with coughing fits and hemorrhages. These frequently threatened his life and led to constant travels in search of a healing climate. He had not been well in Scotland, and it was therefore planned that he should pass the winter with Fanny and Lloyd at Davos in Switzerland. They traveled there in October, and the change of scene worked wonders. "Arrived at my destination, down I sat one morning to the unfinished tale; and behold! it flowed from me like small talk; and in a second tide of delighted industry, and again at a rate of a chapter a day, I finished *Treasure Island*." [3]

When it was first published in weekly installments in *Young Folks* magazine (from October 1881 to January 1882), it failed to attract any attention, or indeed to sell any additional copies, but when published separately as a book in 1883, it soon proved popular. The Prime Minister, Gladstone, was reported to have stayed up till two in the morning in order to finish it, and it was widely praised by literary critics and by other writers. Henry James thought it a delightful story, "all as perfect as a well-played boy's game," [4] and Gerard Manley Hopkins wrote, "I think Robert Lewis Stevenson shows more genius in a page than Scott in a volume." [5] G. K. Chesterton particularly admired Stevenson's evocative style: "The very words carry the sound and the significance. It is as if they were cut out with cutlasses; as was that unforgettable chip or wedge that was hacked by the blade of Billy Bones out of the wooden sign of the 'Admiral Benbow.' "[6]

Treasure Island was intended as a book for boys, and has an immediate appeal as an exciting adventure story; but like *Robinson Crusoe* and *Alice in Wonderland*, it has been enjoyed by adults as much as by children. The subtle observation of character, the vivid imagery of the language, and the disturbing undercurrents running beneath the surface of the story have fascinated readers and provoked endless study of the text. The story was adapted for the stage, and every year in London and elsewhere well-known actors and less well known parrots are auditioned for productions. There have been at least five films based on the story. In 1920 a silent version featured a woman (Shirley Mason) playing the part of Jim Hawkins. The 1934 version had Jackie Cooper cast as Jim and Wallace Beery as Long John Silver. In 1950 the Walt Disney corporation sponsored a lavish production with Bobby Driscoll as Jim and Robert Newton giving a definitive performance as Long John Silver. Orson Welles played the same part in the 1971 version, and in 1990 Charlton Heston played Silver and his son played a somewhat older than usual Jim Hawkins.

Thanks to Stevenson's illuminating letters and essays, we know a great deal about the various sources which inspired him during the writing of the book, as well as the models for some of the principal characters. The catalyst was the treasure map, but he also drew on his memories of the works of Daniel Defoe, Edgar Allan Poe, and Washington Irving. He took the Dead Man's Chest from *At Last* by Charles Kingsley, and admitted his debt to "the great Captain Johnson's History of the Notorious Pirates." Interestingly, he was scathing about Captain Marryat's *The Pirate*, which he thought was an arid and feeble production.

The dominating personality in *Treasure Island* is, of course, Long John Silver. He is better known than any of the real pirates of history and, together with Captain Hook, has come to represent many people's image of a pirate. He is tall and powerful and has a wily character which alternates between jovial good humor and utter ruthlessness in the pursuit of gold. His left leg was cut off after he had been hit by a broadside when serving as quartermaster of Captain Flint's ship off Malabar. He does not have a wooden leg but carries a crutch, "which he managed with great dexterity, hopping around on it like a bird." In Captain Johnson's *General History of the Pirates* there is a memorable description of "a fellow with a terrible pair of whiskers, and a wooden leg, being stuck around with pistols, like the man in the Almanack with darts, comes swearing and vapouring upon the quarter-deck."[7] It is possible that Stevenson had this figure in the back of his mind when he came up with Long John Silver, but he always said that his sea cook was based on his friend W. E. Henley, a writer and poet who made a considerable impression on everyone who met him. Lloyd Osbourne described him as "a great, glowing, massive-shouldered fellow with a big red beard and a crutch; jovial, astoundingly clever, and with a laugh that rolled out like music. Never was there such another as William Ernest Henley; he had an unimaginable fire and vitality; he swept one off one's feet."[8]

Henley was the son of a Gloucester bookseller and contracted tubercular arthritis as a boy, which crippled him and led to his having one foot amputated. He traveled to Edinburgh to see the eminent Professor Lister about his condition, and while in the Scottish capital he was introduced to Stevenson. Henley had little talent as a writer, but he became a forceful and independent editor of several magazines and anthologies. In a letter to Henley from Switzerland shortly after completing *Treasure Island,* Stevenson wrote, "I will now make a confession. It was the sight of your maimed strength and masterfulness that begot John Silver in *Treasure Island.* Of course he is not in any other quality or feature the least like you; but the idea of the maimed man, ruling and dreaded by the sound, was entirely taken from you."[9] Stevenson later expanded on this and explained that his aim had been to take an admired friend and to deprive him of his finer qualities, leaving him with nothing but his strength and his geniality, and to try and express these traits in the person of a rough seaman.

What is so striking about *Treasure Island* in terms of piracy is that the characters and the maritime details are totally convincing. Unlike Captain Marryat, who must have met a few pirates but could only produce stage characters in his book, Stevenson had never come across any pirates in his life, and yet he was able to create a cast of vicious and murderous men and to conjure up an authentic atmosphere of double-dealing and casual violence. The murder of Tom Morgan by Long John Silver is carried out with a practiced ease which leaves Jim

Hawkins fainting with horror. Jim's confrontation with the evil Israel Hands is the stuff of nightmares. Equally effective are the descriptions of the *Hispaniola* at sea, rolling steadily before the trade winds and "dipping her bowsprit now and then with a whiff of spray." In 1890 W. B. Yeats told Stevenson that *Treasure Island* was the only book in which his seafaring grandfather had ever taken any pleasure, and it is easy to see why. Not only does Stevenson use seaman's language with conviction, but he also understands the finer points of sailing and ship handling. This can be explained by his upbringing. His father and his grandfather were both distinguished lighthouse engineers and frequently voyaged around the Scottish coasts and islands on tours of inspection. It was originally intended that Stevenson should follow in their footsteps, and he did spend three years training as an engineer, sometimes passing the summer vacations cruising in the yachts of the Lighthouse Commission. In June 1869 he accompanied his father in the yacht *Pharos* on a visit to the Orkney Islands, and in 1870 inspected lighthouses on the Pentland Firth and in the Hebrides. Although he abandoned plans for a career in the lighthouse service, he continued to travel extensively, frequently by sea. In the summer of 1874 he voyaged around the Inner Hebrides in the yacht *Heron* with two friends, and in 1876 he traveled by canoe through the rivers and canals of northern France (later to be written up in *An Inland Voyage*). Two years before writing *Treasure Island* he made a return voyage across the Atlantic, though not in vessels in any way resembling the schooner *Hispaniola:* the outward journey from the Clyde was in the passenger ship *Devonia* and the return voyage was in the Royal Mail liner *City of Chester*. Several years later, when he had become an established writer, he voyaged extensively among the Pacific islands.

The effect of *Treasure Island* on our perception of pirates cannot be overestimated. Stevenson linked pirates forever with maps, black schooners, tropical islands, and one-legged seamen with parrots on their shoulders. The map with a cross marking the location of the buried treasure has become one of the most familiar piratical props, and is such an appealing concept that it has joined the repertoire of children's party games and become a regular feature of dozens of adventure stories. Yet it is an entirely fictional device which owes its popularity to that spidery drawing of Treasure Island which is usually reproduced as the frontispiece of Stevenson's book.

Wooden legs and parrots were not fictional devices, however. Pirates, like the wounded seamen who ended their days in Greenwich Hospital, were always vulnerable to serious injury when working a ship in a storm or when attacking another vessel. In 1684 Robert Dangerfield was among the crew of a pirate ship on the coast of West Africa when they attacked a Dutch merchant ship. Broadsides were fired by both ships, which resulted in two pirates being killed and five wounded, "two of them losing each one leg." [10] Captain Skyrm, who was commander of one of Bartholomew Roberts' pirate ships, had his leg shot off in the battle with HMS *Swallow*. Israel Hynde, boatswain of Roberts' ship *Ranger,* lost his arm in the same action. [11] The treatment of such wounds was often rough and ready. When William Phillips was wounded in his left leg during a skirmish between two pirate ships, there was no surgeon on board either vessel and it was decided that the ship's carpenter was the most suitable man to tackle the job. The carpenter produced the largest saw from his tool chest and went to work "as though he were cutting a deal board in two and soon the leg was separated from the body of the patient." [12] To cauterize the wound, the carpenter heated his broadax, but he proved less skilled with this tool and burned more of the flesh than was necessary. Miraculously Phillips survived the operation.

Stevenson knew what he was doing when he cast Long John Silver as a cook. It was standard practice in the Royal Navy to select the cook from among disabled seamen. In his irreverent account of shipboard life in the early eighteenth century, Ned Ward described the cook as "an able fellow in the last war, and had been so in this too, but for a scurvy bullet at L'Hogue, that shot away one of his limbs, and so cut him out for a sea-cook." [13] Thomas Rowlandson, the celebrated caricaturist and painter of Georgian England, was responsible for a charming series of watercolors illustrating the various ranks and trades in the navy. His picture of the sea cook shows him balanced on a wooden leg as he stirs a steaming cauldron with a long spoon.

The popular association of pirates with parrots can also be traced back to *Treasure Island*. Long John Silver kept his parrot in a cage in the galley of the *Hispaniola,* but the bird also accompanied him when he went ashore. The parrot, called Cap'n Flint, was reported to be two hundred years old, and had been at Madagascar and Portobello. Arthur Ransome reinforced the link between pirates and parrots in his adventure stories about children on their summer holidays in the English Lake District and elsewhere. These stories have lost some of their appeal for children today but were immensely popular with English boys and girls in the 1930s, 1940s, and 1950s. In *Swallows and Amazons,* first published in 1930, Nancy and Peggy Blackett play the part of pirates and fly the Jolly Roger from the mast of their thirteen-foot sailing dinghy. They have an uncle who is a retired pirate and lives on a houseboat. Ransome makes clear his debt to *Treasure Island* by calling the uncle Captain Flint and providing him with a green parrot. At one point Peggy Blackett remarks, "We were teaching the parrot to say 'Pieces of Eight' so that it would be a good pirate parrot to take with us to Wild Cat Island. It only says 'Pretty Polly.' That's no use to anyone." Captain Flint and his parrot appear in several of the subsequent stories, notably in *Peter Duck,* which describes a voyage to the Caribbean in search of buried treasure.

It was common for seamen who traveled in the tropics to bring back birds and animals as souvenirs of their travels. Parrots were particularly popular because they were colorful, they could be taught to speak, and they were easier to look after on board ship than monkeys and other wild animals. They also commanded a good price in the bird markets which were such a feature of eighteenth-century London. In September 1717 Michael Bland put an advertisement in *The Post-Man* which announced that "Parrotkeets with red heads from Guiney, and 2 fine talking Parrokeets from Buenos Ayres, and several young talking Parrots" were being sold at The Leopard and Tyger at Tower Dock near Tower Hill. In the next issue of *The Post-Man,* David Randall went one better: he announced the sale at the Porter's Lodge, Charing Cross, of "Parrokeets which talk English, Dutch, French, and Spanish, Whistle at command, small Parrokeets with red heads, very tame and pretty."[14]

Parrots were sometimes used as presents to bribe officials or to obtain their goodwill. Clinton Atkinson, a notorious Elizabethan pirate, gave parrots to the deputies of the vice admiral of Dorset in 1583. The pirate captain Stephen Haynes gave two parrots to a servant of Sir Christopher Halton in 1582, and gave another two parrots to the Lord Admiral's cook.[15] There are several references to parrots in Woodes Rogers' book of 1712, *A Cruising Voyage Round the World,* but the most interesting account of how the buccaneers collected and kept parrots appears in William Dampier's description of his second voyage to South America. In 1676 he was in the Bay of Campeche near Vera Cruz and noted that the tame parrots found there were the largest and fairest birds of their kind in the West Indies:

> Their colour was yellow and red, very coarsely mixed; and they would prate very prettily and there was scarce a man but what sent aboard one or two of them. So that with provision, chests, hen-coops and parrot-cages, our ships were full of lumber, with which we intended to sail.[16]

Who exactly were the pirates, and where did they come from? The overwhelming majority were seamen: a sample of seven hundred men indicted for piracy between 1600 and 1640 shows that 73 percent described themselves as mariners or sailors.[17] The proportion was even higher in the 1720s, during the great age of piracy. Marcus Rediker's analysis of the Anglo-American pirates operating in the western Atlantic and Caribbean at that time shows that 98 percent were formerly seamen in the merchant service or the Royal Navy or had served in privateers.[18] Most were merchant seamen who had volunteered to join the pirates when their ships were captured.

The fact that almost all pirates were professional seafarers explains a great deal about them. It explains their ability to make the long voyages which frequently took them from the American coast to Africa and the Indian Ocean. It explains how they were able to find their way among the treacherous reefs and shoals of the Caribbean, and why they were able to give the navy the slip so often. It also helps to explain much of their behavior and their attitude to life.

Seamen in the days of sail were a race apart. They spoke a language that was so filled with technical expressions that it was nearly incomprehensible to a landsman. We are all familiar with phrases such as "Avast there" and "All hands aloft" from shipboard scenes in the movies, but not many of us would be able to carry out the following instructions:

> Lift the skin up, and put into the bunt the slack of the clews (not too taut), the leech and foot-rope, and body of the sail; being careful not to let it get forward under or hang down abaft. Then haul your bunt well up on the yard, smoothing the skin and bringing it down

well abaft, and make fast the bunt gasket round the mast, and the jigger, if there be one, to the tie.

This is taken from *The Seaman's Manual* by R. H. Dana of 1844. Even more baffling are some of the phrases used by sailors in the seventeenth century. Here is an extract from a book by the former pirate Sir Henry Mainwaring:

> If the ship go before a wind, or as they term it, betwixt two sheets, then he who conds uses these terms to him at the helm: *Starboard, larboard, the helm amidships.* . . . If the ship go by a wind, or quarter winds, they say *aloof,* or *keep your loof,* or *fall not off, wear no more, keep her to, touch the wind, have a care of the lee-latch;* all these do imply the same in a manner, and are to bid him at the helm to keep her near the wind.[19]

As well as using phrases and expressions peculiar to life at sea, sailors looked different. Their faces and arms were burned and weathered to the nut-brown color of Robert Louis Stevenson's sea captain Billy Bones. They were liable to have scars and injuries from handling sails and gear in heavy weather. Months of keeping their balance on a heaving deck gave them a rolling gait. Above all they were distinguished by their clothes. In the early years of the eighteenth century most landsmen wore long coats and long waistcoats over knee breeches and stockings. Seamen on the other hand wore short blue jackets, over a checked shirt, and either long canvas trousers or baggy "petticoat breeches," which somewhat resembled culottes. In addition, they frequently wore red waistcoats, and tied a scarf or handkerchief loosely around the neck.[20]

Most pirates wore variations of this traditional costume, which was hard-wearing and practical, though some wore more exotic clothes stolen from captured ships, or made from the silks and velvets which they plundered. Kit Oloard dressed "in black velvet trousers and jacket, crimson silk socks, black felt hat, brown beard and shirt collar embroidered in black silk."[21] John Stow noted that two pirates facing execution in 1615 gave away their fancy clothes, including breeches of crimson taffeta, velvet doublets with gold buttons, and velvet shirts with gold lace. Pirate captains seem to have adopted the clothes of naval officers or merchant sea captains, which at this period followed the style of English gentlemen. When he fought his last sea battle in 1722, the pirate captain Bartholomew Roberts was, according to Captain Johnson, "dressed in a rich crimson damask waistcoat and breeches, a red feather in his hat, a gold chain round his neck, with a diamond cross hanging to it." [22]

The men who became pirate leaders were not the clean-cut heroes portrayed by Errol Flynn and Douglas Fairbanks, Sr., in the movies, nor were they the jovial rogues of Gilbert and Sullivan's *The Pirates of Penzance*. They were tough and ruthless men capable of savage cruelty and murder. They were elected by the votes of the crew and could be replaced as captain if they failed to satisfy the majority of the men under their command. They were expected to be bold and decisive in action, and skilled in navigation and seamanship. Above all they had to have the force of personality necessary to hold together an unruly bunch of seamen. The pirates who operated in the West Indies were drawn from a number of seafaring nations and many were black slaves, so there was no sense of national identity to unite them. Most pirates were by nature rebellious and lazy. They were notorious for foul language, and for prolonged bouts of drinking, which frequently led to quarrels and violence. They came together in an uneasy partnership, attracted by the lure of plunder and the desire for an easy life.

There are surprisingly few detailed descriptions of what the pirate leaders looked like, and those we do have are rarely flattering. When the *Beckford Galley* was captured by pirates off Madagascar in 1698, the ship's owners issued the following description: "Ryder the Pyrate, at present Commander of the Beckford Galley is a middle siz'd man of a swarthy complexion, inclinable by his aspect to be of a churlish constitution, his own hair short and brown and apt when in drink to utter some Portuguese or Moorish words." [23]

The Scotsman Captain Alexander Dolzell, executed for piracy in 1715, was described by the chaplain of Newgate Prison as "a seaman by profession, a pernicious and dangerous person; of a morose, stubborn, and ill disposition by nature." [24]

Equally unpleasant was Philip Lyne, who made a habit of torturing and killing the captains of the ships which he captured. He confessed to the killing of thirty-seven masters of vessels and an unspecified number of able seamen. The *Boston Gazette* of March 28, 1726, printed a graphic account of the appearance of Lyne and his crew as they walked to their trial in Barbados after being captured off the coast of South America:

> The commander went at the head, with about 20 other pirates, with their black silk flag before them, with the representation of a man in full proportion, with a cutlass in one hand, and a pistol in the other, extended; as they were much wounded and no care taken in dressing, they were very offensive, and stunk as they went along, particularly Line the commander; he had one eye shot out, which with part of his nose, hung down on his face.

The most memorable description of any pirate is that of Blackbeard in Captain Johnson's *General History of the Pirates*. It is often quoted, but worth repeating because Blackbeard became a legend and, together with such fictional characters as Captain Hook, Long John Silver, and Byron's Corsair, was largely responsible for the image of the pirate which became popular over the years.

> Captain Teach assumed the cognomen of Black-beard, from that large quantity of hair, which, like a frightful meteor, covered his whole face, and frightened America more than any comet that has appeared there a long time.
>
> This beard was black, which he suffered to grow of an extravagant length; as to breadth, it came up to his eyes; he was accustomed to twist it with ribbons, in small tails, after the manner of our Ramilies wigs, and turn them about his ears: in time of action, he wore a sling over his shoulders, with three brace of pistols, hanging in holsters like bandoliers; and stuck lighted matches under his hat, which appearing on each side of his face, his eyes naturally looking fierce and wild, made him altogether such a figure, that imagination cannot form an idea of a fury, from Hell, to look more frightful.[25]

This fearsome picture was not entirely drawn from Johnson's imagination. Henry Bostock, master of the sloop *Margaret*, was attacked by Blackbeard at dawn on December 5, 1717. He later described him as "a tall spare man with a very black beard which he wore very long."[26] Lieutenant Maynard, the naval officer who led the expedition against Blackbeard and fought him to the death on the deck of his ship, noted in a letter to a fellow officer that Captain Teach "went by the name of

Blackbeard, because he let his beard grow, and tied it up in black ribbons."[27]

The practice of going into action armed to the teeth is confirmed by numerous accounts of pirate attacks. The carrying of several pistols was not simply to frighten the enemy but was a wise precaution. Flintlock pistols were unreliable at sea, and if one failed to fire because of a damp charge, a second might save the day. When he went into battle against the forty-gun warship HMS *Swallow*, Bartholomew Roberts had two pairs of pistols hanging at the end of a silk sling, slung over his shoulders "according to the fashion of the Pirates."[28] There is interesting confirmation of this among the artifacts recovered from the sunken pirate ship *Whydah:* at the stern of the wreck, an elegantly designed pistol with ornate brass scrollwork was discovered, and tied around its handle was three feet of silk ribbon. Pirates were also in the habit of wearing their weapons when they were off duty. Robert Drury visited one of the pirate settlements at Madagascar in 1716 and found the men living in some style on their plantations. One of these men was a Dutchman named John Pro, who spoke good English. "He was dressed in a short coat with broad, plate buttons, and other things agreeable, but without shoes or stockings. In his sash stuck a brace of pistols, and he had one in his right hand. The other man was dressed in an English manner, with two pistols in his sash and one in his hand, like his companion."[29]

Like their fellow seamen, pirates were mostly young men in their twenties. The average age of a pirate in the early eighteenth century was twenty-seven, which was exactly the same as the average age of a merchant seaman in the eighteenth century, and similar to the average age of seamen in the Royal Navy.[30] The youthfulness of the crews was largely necessitated by the physical demands of working a sailing ship in all weathers. This required agility, fitness, stamina, a certain amount of physical strength, and an ability to put up with extreme discomfort above and below deck. Apart from the obvious perils of heaving in wet, flapping canvas one hundred feet above a pitching deck, there was a constant requirement to haul on ropes at all hours of the day and night, and the likelihood of being cold and wet for days on end.

Pirates operating in the West Indies and American seaboard came from several seafaring countries. In the seventeenth century most of the men in the buccaneer ships were French or British, but all crews tended to be multinational. Of the five hundred men who took part in buccaneer Henry Morgan's attack on the Spanish treasure port of Portobello in 1668, forty were Dutchmen, several were French, Italian, Portuguese, mulatto, or black, and the remainder were British.[31] The majority of attacks in the Caribbean during the early years of the eighteenth century were made by French privateers, and in the years after 1725 the governors of the colonies reported numerous attacks by the Spanish coastguardsmen (*guardo del costa*), who exceeded their brief to defend Spanish possessions and took to piracy. But the pirates who terrorized the Caribbean from around 1715 to 1725, and used the island of Providence in the Bahamas as a base, were overwhelmingly from the English-speaking nations. By far the largest number, around 35 percent, were native Englishmen; next came men born in the American colonies, around 25 percent of the total; 20 percent came from the West Indian colonies, mostly Jamaica, Barbados, and the Bahamas; 10 percent of the pirates were Scottish; 8 percent were Welsh; and there was a scattering of Swedish, Dutch, French, Spanish, and Portuguese.[32]

It is not surprising to find that most pirates hailed from seaports. The majority of the English pirates, for instance, were born in London; others were born in Bristol or the West Country. American pirates came from Boston, Charleston, Newport, New York, Salem, and other east coast ports.

A considerable number of the men on the pirate ships were black. Christian Tranquebar was on a ship attacked by two vessels commanded by Bartholomew Roberts in 1721, and reported that Roberts' ship was manned by 180 white men and 48 French Creole blacks; his consort (companion ship), a brigantine, was manned by 100 white men and 40 French blacks.[33] When Captain Chaloner Ogle rounded up the men on board Roberts' ships after the battle off Cape Lopez on the African coast, he noted that 187 white men and 75 black men were found alive. The same pattern emerges for other pirate ships. Governor Phenney reported from New Providence that the pirate brigantine *Good Fortune,* commanded by Anstead, had a crew of 60 white men and 19 blacks when she attacked a Bristol ship near Jamaica in June 1721.[34] Edward England, William Moody, and Richard Frowd were all reported as having crews of whites and blacks, and the crew of Augustin Blanco was reported to consist of "English, Scots, Spaniards, Mulattoes, and Negroes."[35]

What is not clear is the precise status of the black men on these pirate ships. It has been suggested that the democratic nature of pirates, and their defiance of the usual customs of the day, led them to welcome the blacks as equal partners on board. It is also said that runaway slaves from the West Indian plantations joined pirate ships because they would find refuge on board, and also to achieve their freedom. This is a romantic idea, but it is not borne out by the facts. The pirates shared the same prejudices as other white men in the Western world. They regarded black slaves as commodities to be bought and sold, and they used them as slaves on board their ships for the hard and menial jobs: working the pumps, going ashore for wood and water, washing and cleaning, and acting as servants to the pirate captain. Robert Dangerfield's account of his two years on a pirate ship includes a description of an attack on a French ship on the west coast of Africa. The pirates plundered the ship of fifty tons of iron, twenty-five pipes of brandy, several bales of linen, and 16 blacks. They later sold the blacks to the English Governor on the coast at Gambo.[36] When William Dampier set off on a buccaneering expedition in 1681, he described the company as having 44 white men, a Spanish Indian, and 2 Moskito Indians, all of whom carried weapons, "and 5 slaves taken in the South Seas, who fell to our share."[37] That the slaves did not carry weapons is an indication of their status as servants to the rest of the company. The buccaneer leaders L'Ollonais and Henry Morgan regarded slaves as part of their booty when they raided Spanish towns in Central America. When Morgan died a wealthy man in Jamaica, his estate included 109 black slaves.

Robert Ritchie's detailed study of Captain Kidd makes it clear that slaves were used to carry out the heavy work on Kidd's ship, though in the Indian Ocean Lascars rather than black slaves were used for this purpose because they were more readily available in that part of the world. An earlier example of a similar practice appears in the journal of Basil Ringrose. He describes the capture of a Spanish merchant ship by the buccaneers in 1679. They take prisoners from the ship, including "twelve slaves, of whom we intended to make good use to do the drudgery of our ship."[38] During the peak period of pirate activity in the West Indies in the years around 1720, there were numerous reports of pirates capturing slave ships, and even going ashore to steal black slaves from the islands. In 1724 a group of merchants trading to Jamaica wrote to the Council of Trade and Plantations in London and complained that pirates were responsible for "the havoc and destruction of the ships employed in the negro trade on which the being of our Colonies chiefly depends."[39]

A COMMON FEATURE of many pirate films, and a number of novels, is the portrayal of the pirate captain as an aristocrat, or as an educated man of some standing in society, who has taken to piracy as the result of some misfortune in his recent past. The hero of the film *Captain Blood* is a handsome English physician, played by Errol Flynn, who has been sentenced to slavery in the West Indies because he was caught attending to a wounded rebel soldier. He escapes, captures a ship, and becomes a pirate captain. In *The Black Pirate*, Douglas Fairbanks, Sr., is a duke who has joined the pirates in order to seek out and avenge himself on the pirates who murdered his father. There were, in fact, no aristocrats among the Anglo-American pirates of the early eighteenth century, but there were several in the previous century. The most interesting was Sir Henry Mainwaring, who took his degree at Brasenose College, Oxford, in 1602, studied law at the Inner Temple, and after a spell in the army, bought a ship from the famous shipwright Peter Pett and went to sea as a pirate. Between 1613 and 1615 he plundered Spanish ships in the English Channel and on the coast of Spain. He returned to England, received a pardon, and embarked on a successful career as a naval commissioner, a Member of Parliament, and a writer on maritime subjects. One of his works was a treatise entitled "Of the Beginnings, Practices, and Suppression of Pirates."[40]

Less successful was Sir Francis Verney, who left England after an argument with his stepmother over his inheritance. He joined the corsairs in the Mediterranean, "making havoc of his own countrymen, and carrying into Algiers prizes belonging to the merchants of Poole and Plymouth." He was later captured by Sicilian corsairs and served two years as a galley slave. He died at the age of thirty-one in the

Hospital of St. Mary of Pity at Messina. William Lithgow visited him shortly before he died, and reported that Verney "in the extremest calamity of extreme miseries entreated death."[41]

There were several aristocrats and wealthy landowners in the Elizabethan period who were closely involved with the pirates and smugglers operating around the British coastline and who profited from their activities. These included Sir Richard Edgecumbe, Sir Robert Rich, Sir Richard Bulkely of Beaumaris in Wales, and Sir John Killigrew and his wife, Lady Killigrew, of Pendennis Castle in Cornwall.

It may have been Lady Killigrew who provided the inspiration for Daphne du Maurier's novel *Frenchman's Creek*. The Frenchman who is the hero of the story is one of the most romantic of all the fictional pirates. He has a fine house in Brittany and has taken to piracy simply for the sense of danger and excitement which it gives him. He has a beautiful ship called *La Mouette* in which he carries out daring raids on the coast of Cornwall. He is charming to Lady St. Colomb, the lovely heroine of the story, who is much impressed that he reads the poetry of Ronsard and spends hours drawing waterbirds. It has to be said that he bears no resemblance to the majority of uncouth men who plagued the Atlantic shipping lanes in the early eighteenth century. But there were a few educated pirates, notably Major Stede Bonnet. At his trial in Charleston, South Carolina, the judge described him as "a Gentleman that have had the advantage of a liberal education, and being generally esteemed a Man of Letters." Bonnet had lived in comfortable circumstances on the island of Barbados until he suddenly tired of his life there. At his own expense he fitted out a sloop with ten guns, assembled a crew of seventy, and embarked on a career as a pirate. He plundered a succession of ships off the coast of Virginia and Carolina, and then joined up with Blackbeard and his crew. Bonnet's problem was that he had no seafaring experience and was therefore not equipped to command a ship. He was persuaded by Blackbeard to hand over his sloop, and an experienced seaman took over as captain. The *Boston News Letter* of November 11, 1717, reported that Bonnet had been observed on Blackbeard's ship, and that he "has no command, he walks about in his morning gown, and then to his books of which he has a good library aboard."

Bonnet's background and education were held against him at his trial and provided the judge with an opportunity to make a lengthy and moralizing speech. Bonnet was totally stricken by the death sentence passed on him. "His piteous behaviour under sentence very much affected the people of the Province, particularly the women."[42] He wrote a pathetic letter to the Governor from prison, but to no avail. He was hanged from a gallows set up on the waterfront of Charleston harbor.

Apart from Long John Silver, the most memorable of all the pirates of fiction is Captain Hook, the villain of J. M. Barrie's play *Peter Pan.* Although he is not always portrayed as an aristocrat onstage, Barrie's text makes it clear that Captain Hook has had the benefit of the very best education. His most alarming feature is, of course, the hook which replaces the hand bitten off by the crocodile, but he is distinguished from the rest of his crew by "the elegance of his diction, even when he was swearing," and by his clothes, which are modeled on those of Charles II, the rakish Stuart king he was told he strangely resembled. In 1927, many years after the first production of *Peter Pan,* Barrie revealed in a talk to the boys of Eton College that Captain Hook had been educated at Eton and Balliol. The books he borrowed from the library of his Oxford college included poetry, mostly of the Lakeland School. "These volumes may still be occasionally picked up at secondhand bookstalls with the name 'Jacobus Hook' inserted as the owner."

Unlike Robert Louis Stevenson, who was little known outside a small literary circle until the appearance of *Treasure Island,* his fellow Scotsman J. M. Barrie was already a celebrated author and playwright when he wrote *Peter Pan.*[43] His third novel, *The Little Minister,* had been hailed as a work of genius, and a number of long-running plays, including *The Admirable Crichton* of 1902, had brought him wealth and acclaim. His reputation undoubtedly helped to overcome the difficulties posed by the stage production of *Peter Pan.* When the famous actor-manager Herbert Beerbohm Tree was first shown the script he thought Barrie had taken leave of his senses and turned it down, but the American producer Charles Frohman had a very different reaction. When Barrie read the play to him he immediately sensed a winner and agreed to give it his full backing.

Beerbohm Tree's misgivings were understandable. A whimsical story about a boy who never grew up and a cast which included a large dog, mermaids, Lost Boys, Red Indians, a crew of bizarre pirates, and a crocodile with a ticking clock inside it were bad enough. More formidable were the staging requirements, which involved extended flying sequences, elaborate scenery, and a giant reducing lens to miniaturize the actress who played the part of Tinker Bell. However, the producer and playwright were determined to overcome all obstacles. George Kirby's Flying Ballet Company were taken on to devise a new form of flying equipment, costumes were commissioned from the artist William Nicholson, and the cast was led by Gerald du Maurier, who played the parts of Mr. Darling and Captain Hook, and by Nina Boucicault, who played Peter Pan.

The rehearsals were chaotic, and Barrie had to alter and rewrite the script as they went along. The first performance was scheduled for December 22, 1904, but had to be postponed because the machinery for raising the Little House to the treetops was not ready, and there were major problems over the installation of the set of the pirate ship in the third act. Rumors about the lavish production of Barrie's new play had circulated around London and led to an unusually expectant audience arriving to watch the first performance on December 27. The reception was ecstatic, and Barrie was able to send a relieved telegram to Charles Frohman in New York: "Peter Pan all right. Looks like a big success."[44] It was more than all right. The children were bewitched and fell in love with Peter and Wendy. The critics were full of praise, especially for Barrie's "marvellous fertility in humorous and pathetic touches." And everybody enjoyed the flying sequences and the spirited acting of a talented cast.

Although the pirates are only one element in the plot, it is evident that Barrie enjoyed devising them. He makes several references to *Treasure Island* (he was a friend and admirer of Stevenson) and to the historical pirates he had read about in Captain Johnson's *General History*. Hook's ship is moored in Kidd's Creek, and we are told that Hook himself was Blackbeard's bosun and "the worst of them all." Barrie also has fun with mock nautical phrases, often stringing them together in a nonsensical way: "Avast, belay, yo ho, heave to, A-pirating we go." No adult is likely to believe that real pirates resembled Bosun Smee, with his glasses and his sewing machine, or Gentleman Starkey, "once an usher in a public school," but Captain Hook is another matter. He is a larger-than-life character who has become one of the best-loved villains of stage and screen. The part is a gift to an actor and has been played by a host of famous names, including

Charles Laughton, Boris Karloff, Alastair Sim, Donald Sinden, and Dustin Hoffman. Over the years a Peter Pan industry has grown up. Every Christmas holiday there are stage performances of *Peter Pan* in theaters and church halls throughout Britain and the United States. There are dozens of illustrated versions of the book available. There are Peter Pan playgrounds and theme parks. Walt Disney made a cartoon version of the story, and Steven Spielberg devised and directed *Hook*, a star-studded epic with stunning visual effects and costumes and a magnificent pirate ship. It is little wonder that many children first learn about pirates through seeing some version of the Peter Pan story.

IF EVER THERE WAS a typical pirate, Henry Avery would fill the bill. He was not aristocratic. He was not notoriously cruel. And, like so many of his kind, his career as a pirate was surprisingly short. He is not so well known today as Captain Kidd and Blackbeard, and he ended his days in obscurity, but during his lifetime he became a legend. A play entitled *The Successful Pirate*, which was inspired by his career, ran for several years at Drury Lane Theatre, and Daniel Defoe wrote a book called *The King of the Pirates* which seems to have been based on interviews with him.

Henry Avery (also known as John Avery, Long Ben, and Captain Bridgeman) did not conform to any of the popular images we have of pirates today. He was of middle height, rather fat, with a dissolute appearance and what was described as a jolly complexion. According to Defoe, he was born in Plymouth in 1653 and spent some years in the Royal Navy, serving as a midshipman on HMS *Kent* and HMS *Rupert*.[45] In 1694 he was second mate of the *Charles*, a privateer which had been hired to raid the Spanish colonies. The ship spent several months in the port of Corunna, where the crew grew restless because their pay was delayed. On May 7, while the ship's captain was laid low with drink, Avery and a number of his companions seized the ship.

"I am captain of this ship now," Avery announced, "I am bound to Madagascar, with the design of making my own fortune, and that of all the brave fellows joined with me."

They renamed the ship the *Fancy* and sailed south. They plundered three English ships in the Cape Verde Islands, and captured two Danish ships on the west coast of Africa near the island of Principe. After rounding the Cape of Good Hope, they headed for the northeast corner of Madagascar, where they dropped anchor and went ashore for much needed provisions. Avery's plan was to intercept the ships of the pilgrim fleet which sailed every year from the Indian port of Surat across to Mocha at the mouth of the Red Sea and then up to Mecca. The fleet was almost as attractive a target for pirates as the Spanish treasure ships were for the buccaneers in the Caribbean, because merchants traveled with the pilgrims so that they could trade spices and cloth for gold and coffee. The emperor of the Mogul Empire in India, who was known as the Great Mogul, also sent his own ships with the fleet.

In September 1695 Avery was cruising off the mouth of the Red Sea in the *Fancy*, which was now armed with forty-six guns and had a crew of 150 men. He was joined by a number of other pirate ships, including the *Pearl* and the *Portsmouth Adventure* from Rhode Island and the *Amity* from New York. The first ship in the pilgrim fleet to fall into the pirates' hands was the *Fath Mahmamadi*, which was looted of gold and silver worth more than £50,000. A few days later Avery sighted the ship which was to make his fortune and whose capture was to create his legend. The *Ganj-i-Sawai* (or *Gunsway*, as she was later called) was the largest of the ships belonging to the Great Mogul. She had forty guns, and her captain, Muhammed Ibrahim, had four hundred rifles to defend her against attack, which made the ship a formidable opponent.

Avery had luck on his side. As his flotilla of pirate ships approached the *Ganj-i-Sawai,* one of his first shots brought down the Muslim ship's mainmast. Then one of her cannon exploded, causing carnage and confusion on deck. The fight lasted two hours, but when the pirates came alongside and boarded her, they met with little resistance. The Indian historian Khafi Kahn wrote that the captain of the *Ganj-i-Sawai* dressed up some Turkish girls as men and urged them to fight while he fled belowdecks and hid himself in the hold.

According to the stories which circulated afterward, one of the Great Mogul's daughters was on the ship, together with her attendants, a number of slave girls, and many wealthy merchants. Avery claimed that no harm was done to the women, but one of the pirate crew later confessed at his trial that "the most horrid barbarities" were committed.[46] All the evidence suggests that the pirates embarked on an orgy of rape, torture, and plunder which lasted several days as the ships lay becalmed in the Arabian Sea. Huge quantities of gold and silver were looted, including 500,000 rials, which, when divided among the pirates, produced at least £1,000 for every man with a full share.

With the taking of this prize Avery wisely decided to retire from his brief career as a pirate. He abandoned the other pirate ships which had sailed with him and headed for the West Indies. He bribed the Governor of New Providence to allow his men to come ashore and presented him with his ship and £1,000 worth of ivory tusks. The pirates went their separate ways, some heading for Carolina and others for England. Six of Avery's crew were eventually caught. In October 1696 they were tried at the Old Bailey in London, amid considerable public excitement, and sentenced to death.

Back in India the Great Mogul was outraged by the attack on his ship and threatened to drive the East India Company and all Englishmen out of his empire. Only by much diplomacy, and by promising to bring Avery and his crew to justice, were the British authorities able to repair the damage caused by this single act of piracy. But Avery himself was never caught. The popular belief was that he lived out his days in luxury on a tropical island, but it seems that he was swindled of most of his riches by merchants in the West Country and that he ended his days in poverty at the village of Bideford in Devon, "not being worth as much as would buy him a coffin."[47]

It was the play based on Avery's life which did much to foster the legend of the pirate as a brave outlaw, and certainly encouraged the belief that Avery and his kind made their fortunes from their piratical exploits. *The Successful Pirate* was first performed at the Theatre Royal in Drury Lane in 1713. Avery, thinly disguised as Arviragus, King of the island of Madagascar, was portrayed as a heroic character, who had once commanded a fire ship in the Dutch Wars but had subsequently declared war on mankind and become a pirate. He had established himself as a Royal Outlaw, and ruler over "a Race of Vagabonds, the Outcasts of the Earth." In the first scene we learn that a ship from India has been captured and brought into the port of Laurentia. The ship is full of jewels and gold, and has on board the lovely Zaida, granddaughter of the Great Mogul, and a host of female retainers. Arviragus decrees that the spoils from the ship must be divided among his sailors, who have "ranged the globe with me, burnt, froze, starved. . . ." Zaida is in love with Aranes, a young man of noble birth in her company, but Arviragus wants her for himself. The situation is neatly solved at the end of the play when we learn that Aranes is the long-lost son of Arviragus. This gives Arviragus the opportunity to give up his throne to Aranes and Zaida, and "to quit Imperial sway and die a private man, as I was born."

The author of *The Successful Pirate* was Charles Johnson (not to be confused with the author of the *General History of the Pirates*), a second-rate dramatist whose regular output of a play a year for nineteen years was ridiculed by Alexander Pope and other writers of the time. He was accused of plagiarism and mocked for "the fatness of his person" and his habit of spending his days at Buttons Coffee House. In 1733 he married a rich young widow and took over a tavern in Covent Garden. He died on March 11, 1748, at the age of sixty-nine.[48]

The Successful Pirate was the first in a long line of popular melodramas with piratical themes which entertained the theatergoing public in London during the course of the next 150 years. Some, like *Blackbeard, or The Captive Princess* of 1798, were based loosely on historical characters. Others were pure fiction. *The Red Rover, or The Mutiny of the Dolphin,* which opened at the Adelphi Theatre on February 9, 1829, was based on one of the adventure stories of James Fenimore Cooper, and was adapted for the London stage by the hack playwright Edward Fitzball. One critic described the play as "arrant trash," but it was generally agreed that the imperfections of the script were redeemed by the spirited acting of Frederick Yates, who played the part of the Red Rover. Yates was a former soldier who became manager of the Adelphi. His bold and athletic performance was ideally suited to the part of the pirate villain who terrorizes the seas and dies dramatically in the last scene, shot by his mutinous crew.

Douglas Jerrold, author of the hugely popular *Black Ey'd Susan,* contributed a melodrama entitled *Descart, The French Buccaneer,* and Edward Fitzball produced another piratical piece entitled *False Colours: or The Free Trader,* which featured a pirate called Hawkset. The combined effect of all these works was to establish the pirate as a theatrical villain, alongside other stock villains such as brigands and bandits.

Gilbert and Sullivan parodied these melodramas when they created

The Pirates of Penzance. For copyright reasons this was first performed in New York on December 30, 1879,[49] with the London premiere held at the Opera Comique in the Strand on April 3, 1880. With its witty libretto, colorful costumes, and some of Arthur Sullivan's most memorable songs and choruses, *The Pirates of Penzance* immediately established itself as a favorite in the Gilbert and Sullivan repertoire. The story is sheer nonsense and revolves around the mistake made by Ruth, "a pirate maid of all work," when she apprentices Frederick, the hero, to a pirate instead of to a pilot. The pirates themselves are as genial and ineffective as the policemen who are sent to catch them, but a complicated plot ends happily with Frederick marrying the Major General's pretty daughter, Mabel, and the pirates revealed as patriotic noblemen who will no more go a-pirating. In spite of its lighthearted approach to the subject, *The Pirates of Penzance* has had a considerable influence on the way many people view pirates today. For more than a hundred years it has been performed by amateur and professional companies around the world, and its cast of hearty and good-natured fellows have contributed to the illusion that pirates were really misunderstood ruffians who never meant to harm anyone.

2

PLUNDERING
THE
TREASURE PORTS

HOMBRE DE DIOS lies in the corner of a bay on the Isthmus of
Panama. In the 1570s it was one of the principal treasure ports
on the Spanish Main, that hot and humid stretch of the American
coast which curves around the southern rim of the Caribbean Sea.
Twice a year a fleet of Spanish galleons anchored in the bay and loaded
up with gold and silver which had been carried thousands of miles by
ship and by mule trains from the distant mountains of Peru and Bolivia.

Unlike Panama and Cartagena and some of the other Spanish cities
of Central America, Nombre de Dios had no fine buildings. It was a
shantytown. Some two hundred houses and sheds, roughly constructed of wooden planks, crouched along the waterfront at the edge
of the jungle. When the treasure ships arrived, the town swarmed with
seamen and slaves and officials. At other times most of the houses lay
empty.[1] During the rainy season there were thunderstorms and tropical
downpours. Mosquitoes, fevers, and tropical diseases flourished in the
damp heat.

Francis Drake, who was later to make his name as the greatest British
seaman of the Elizabethan age, had paid a reconnaissance visit to the
town in 1571. Disguised as a Spanish merchant, he inspected the
harbor and noted the location of the King's treasure-house. He had
found a sheltered cove nearby which would provide a safe anchorage

for any future expedition. He also made contact with some of the escaped black slaves called Cimaroons who lived in the surrounding jungle and were always ready to revenge themselves on the hated Spanish. In July 1572 he returned to Nombre de Dios.[2] He had two small ships, the *Pasco* and the *Swan,* and a total of seventy-three men. He anchored his ships behind a headland to the east of the town. During the night he transferred his men into small pinnaces or canoes, and they set off around the headland and across the bay. They beached the canoes at 3:00 A.M. and made for the shore battery, which consisted of six guns and was guarded by one man. Having silenced the guns, Drake split his force in two. One group, led by his brother John, headed for the western side of the town to create a diversion, while Drake himself led the attack from the east and marched into the town with beating drums and the sounding of trumpets. There was panic from the inhabitants, who imagined they were being attacked by a huge force.

But then things started to go wrong. A group of Spanish soldiers opened fire, killing an English trumpeter and hitting Drake in the thigh. He ignored the pain and led his men to the treasure-house on the waterfront, but the blood was pouring from his wound, and he left a trail behind him which, his companions later recalled, filled his footprints. They were preparing to force the doors of the treasure-house when a thunderstorm broke out, and as the full force of a tropical downpour deluged the streets, the attacking force had to take shelter. When the rain ceased, many of Drake's men found that their guns and bows were useless because powder, matches, and bowstrings were soaked. Some of the men were inclined to give up, but Drake had no time for doubts: "I have brought you to the treasure house of the world," he told them. "If you leave without it you may henceforth blame nobody but yourselves."[3] His resolution was in vain. When the doors of the treasure-house were opened, it was found to be empty. The last treasure fleet had sailed only six weeks before and the next batch of treasure would not be brought from Panama until another fleet arrived in several months time. Drake was now so weak from loss of blood that he collapsed and had to be carried back to the pinnaces on the beach. The attack was a total failure.

A lesser man than Drake would have abandoned the enterprise, but it was characteristic of his indomitable spirit that he decided to wait for the next Spanish fleet and make good use of the intervening weeks. Having recovered from his wound, he organized raids along the coast, and explored inland with the assistance of native guides. On February 11, 1573, he climbed a ridge at the top of which the Cimaroons had built a platform. From this vantage point Drake was able to take his first look at the distant Pacific Ocean. He prayed aloud that God would spare him to sail in an English ship upon that glistening sea.

He and his men traveled on through the swamps and jungle until they came in sight of Panama City. They saw the treasure ships from Peru arrive, and they waited while the treasure was unloaded and checked and packed onto the mules. Drake prepared an ambush some way along the mule trail, but again things went wrong. One of his men had got drunk and made a premature attack on a few donkeys carrying goods of no value, which warned off the mule train carrying the treasure. Five months of waiting had come to nothing.

Drake refused to give up. He raided the town of Venta Cruces on the banks of the river Sagres. Then at last his luck turned. In March he met a group of French Huguenots led by Captain le Testu, a privateer from Le Havre, who informed him that three caravans of 190 mules were heading for Nombre de Dios. In the undergrowth some twenty miles from the town, the combined force of Englishmen, Frenchmen, and blacks pounced on the mule train. They found that every mule was carrying 300 pounds weight of silver. It was a massive haul, and exactly what Drake needed to restore the morale of his men and to justify the months of fighting through the jungle and surviving battles on land and at sea. Escaping the clutches of a Spanish flotilla which was cruising off the coast, Drake headed back to England with his plunder. The treasure he captured from the mule train and his other raids amounted to some fifteen tons of silver ingots and around £100,000 in gold coins.

Drake was not a pirate in the sense that Blackbeard and Bartholomew Roberts were pirates, but he committed numerous acts of piracy. Like Nelson, he was intensely patriotic, and shared his passionate hatred for England's enemies. In Nelson's case the enemy was France, but for Drake it was Spain. When Drake attacked a Spanish ship or a Spanish town, he did so in the name of Queen Elizabeth and flew the English flag of St. George at the masthead of his ships. Ambitious and piratical by nature, he plundered and looted every Spanish vessel he could lay his hands on and made himself a rich man. He was bold and decisive in action, and yet displayed a remarkable sensitivity in his dealings with his men, who adored him, and with captured enemies, who regarded him with admiration. Coming from a family of seamen and farmers in Devon, he inevitably appeared a rough provincial among the polished courtiers who surrounded his Queen, but he overcame his humble beginnings by his unrivaled skills as a seaman and navigator, and by his extraordinary exploits on the Spanish Main.

Drake sailed with his cousin John Hawkins on his voyages to Africa and the West Indies, and shared in his successes and failures, but it was the raid on the mule train which made his name. Three years after his return from Nombre de Dios, Drake embarked on a voyage which was to take him all around the world. He sailed on December 13, 1577, in the *Pelican*, later to be renamed the *Golden Hind*. She was a small galleon, only one hundred feet in length overall and eighteen feet in the beam, but she was described by her pilot as a good sailer and "in a great measure stout and strong."⁴ Four other vessels made up the fleet which set sail from Plymouth that winter. It took them two months to reach the South American coast near the river Plate. By the time they had weathered the Strait of Magellan in September 1578, three of the ships accompanying the *Golden Hind* had been abandoned or lost, and the fourth had lost contact with Drake during a storm and headed back to England.

Drake pressed on, and as he cruised north along the coast of Chile, he made a series of raids on Spanish settlements and shipping. Off the port of Valparaiso he took a Spanish ship whose cargo included £8,000 in gold and 1,770 jars of wine. Further prizes (a "prize" was a ship captured by force, or threat of force, at sea or in harbor) yielded 4,000 ducats of silver, a chest of bullion, and an emerald-encrusted crucifix. And then on March 1, 1579, he intercepted the treasure ship *Nuestra Señora de la Concepción*, which was en route from Lima to Panama. From his coastal raids he had learned that this great ship was a floating treasure store, laden with silver and gold from Peru. She was so heavily armed that she had acquired the nickname *Cacafuego*, which is usually translated as "Spitfire" but literally means "Shitfire."

Drake had offered a reward of a gold chain to the man who first spotted the Spanish galleon. The reward was won by his young nephew John, who was on the lookout in the maintop or crow's nest of the

Golden Hind. Drake decided to employ a tactic much used by pirates throughout the ages, which was to disguise his ship as a slow, harmless merchantman. His crew were ordered to battle stations, and all sail was set, but he reduced the speed of his ship by towing astern cables and mattresses and a line of heavy pots. San Juan de Antón, the captain of the *Cacafuego,* was completely fooled. When the ships came within hailing distance, as was traditional when two ships met at sea, he demanded to know the name and destination of Drake's ship. "Strike sail" was the shout across the water, "or we will send you to the bottom." The Spanish captain naturally refused to strike and ordered the Englishman to come aboard and surrender. A trumpet sounded from the *Golden Hind,* and a line of armed men appeared above her deck rail. The first bombardment from her guns brought down the mizzenmast of the Spanish ship, and this was followed by a withering fire of arrows and musket shot which enabled the English ship's pinnace to come alongside the *Cacafuego* with a boarding party. The Spanish captain was taken prisoner and surrendered his ship. He was treated with courtesy by Drake, who told him not to distress himself, for such were the fortunes of war.

Drake took his prize to a secluded stretch of coast where he and his men took stock of the *Cacafuego*'s cargo. The ship's hold was packed with treasure. According to one contemporary report, there was "a great quantity of jewels and precious stones. 13 chests of royals of plate, 80 lb of gold, and 26 tons of uncoined silver."[5] In the ship's register, the gold and silver listed in the name of the King of Spain and other individuals was valued at 362,000 pesos. There was also a large quantity of unregistered treasure which the Spanish captain valued at 400,000 pesos. The total sum of 762,000 pesos would be worth nearly £12 million today. Drake had captured one of the richest prizes of all time. It took his men six days to transfer the treasure to the *Golden Hind,* and while this was being done, he invited San Juan and his passengers to dine with him, showed them around his ship, and proudly displayed the charts and drawings which he and his officers had made of the coasts they had navigated. He told San Juan de Antón that he had come "to rob by command of the Queen of England and carried the arms she had given him and her commission."[6]

Before he parted from the *Cacafuego,* Drake gave a letter of safe conduct to her captain and distributed gifts to him and his men. This was a generous gesture toward a beaten enemy, but did nothing to lessen the rage and alarm of the Spanish authorities when they learned the full scale of the damage inflicted by the English pirate. Up and down the coast of America, Spanish ships were on the lookout for him, and Drake wisely decided to call an end to his looting and headed west into the vastness of the Pacific Ocean. He miraculously survived storms, attacks by hostile islanders, and the grounding of his ship on a coral reef among the islands of Indonesia, and arrived back at Plymouth on September 26, 1580, after a voyage lasting two years and nine months.

The *Golden Hind* was the second ship in history to sail around the world, and since Magellan died during his pioneering voyage, Drake was the first commander to complete the circumnavigation. It was an epic achievement, and Drake became a national hero. The Spanish Ambassador demanded compensation for "the plunders committed by this vile corsair," but his protests were ignored. Drake spent six hours with Queen Elizabeth at Richmond Palace, recounting the details of his voyage, and was later knighted by her on the deck of his ship at Deptford. Although an official inventory was taken of Drake's plunder and some five tons of silver were deposited in the Tower of London, it is difficult to calculate the total value of the treasure which was looted during those months on the coast of South America. The Queen authorized Drake to keep £10,000 for himself and to distribute £8,000 among his crew. The shareholders who had backed the voyage (and they included the Queen) received a handsome return on their investment. The total value of the treasure in 1580 was probably around £500,000, which would be worth more than £68 million today.

WHEN DRAKE made his first raid in the Caribbean, the Spanish had been sending gold and silver back to Europe for nearly fifty years. The saga of Spain's conquest of the New World had begun with Christopher Columbus. On October 12, 1492, he had stepped ashore on an island in the Bahamas after a voyage of seventy days across the Atlantic. From the Bahamas he sailed south to Cuba and east to Hispaniola (now Haiti) before sailing back to Spain to report on his discoveries. His second voyage took him to Dominica and along the chain of

West Indian islands to Puerto Rico, Hispaniola, and Jamaica, where he landed in St. Ann's Bay on May 5, 1494. The mountainous islands of Jamaica and Hispaniola were to become the principal bases for buccaneer raids, and would play a key role in the history of piracy.

With his third and fourth voyages, Columbus traveled along the coast of South America and up the Gulf of Darien, constantly searching for a sea passage to India and the East. He failed in the mission which he had set himself, but his voyages changed the map of the known world. The Spanish authorities were not slow to exploit his discoveries. In 1502 a permanent settlement was established on Hispaniola, and another Spanish colony was set up by Balboa on the American mainland near Panama. But it was the expedition which followed which was to transform the European vision of the New World and lead to two centuries of plunder, privateering, and piracy on the Spanish Main.

In 1519 a small force of six hundred soldiers landed on the coast of Mexico near the site of what is now the town of Vera Cruz. They were armed with swords, pikes, and crossbows and had brought with them sixteen horses, a few small cannon, and thirteen muskets. Led by Hernán Cortés, the men marched inland through the steamy jungles of the coast and up through mountain passes to the high plateau of Central Mexico. As they traveled, Cortés used a combination of diplomacy and force to obtain food and assistance from the villages they passed through. He learned that the country was ruled by the Aztecs, a warlike people who exacted tribute and forced labor from the villagers.[7] The Aztecs had not learned the use of the wheel and did not use horses or oxen, but they had created a civilization which was remarkable for its highly developed agricultural system, its sculpture and hieroglyphs, and its impressive buildings, particularly the awe-inspiring temples. These temples were the scene of human sacrifices which had a horrible, pagan fascination for the invading army. Even more fascinating for Cortés and his men was the discovery that the country was rich in gold and silver, which the Aztec craftsmen fashioned into marvelous jewelry and ornaments.

Within two years of landing in Mexico, Cortés had conquered the country. He had besieged and taken the Aztec capital of Tenochtitlán, which was built on islands along the shore of an inland lake. He reduced the houses to rubble and began the building of what was to become Mexico City. Montezuma, the Aztec ruler, was stoned to

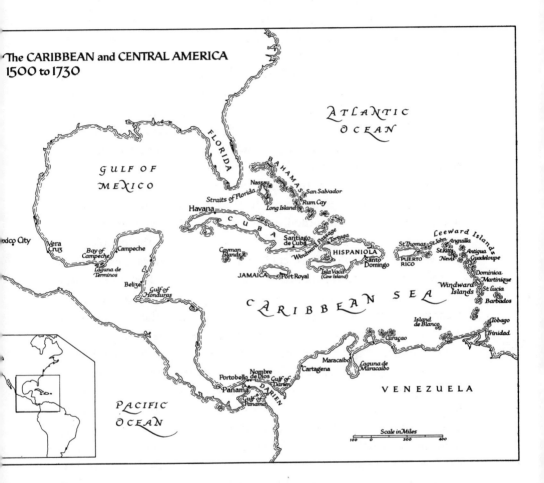

The CARIBBEAN and CENTRAL AMERICA
1500 to 1730

death by his own people, and in his place was established the kingdom of New Spain, which exacted tribute from the subject people in much the same way as the Aztecs had done. During the course of the 1520s, chests full of Aztec gold and jewels were shipped back to the King of Spain in ever-increasing quantities.

Meanwhile, rumors of another rich empire in the vast continent to the south of Mexico began to reach the Spanish explorers and settlers in Panama, or what was then called Darien. The land ruled by the Incas of Peru extended for some two thousand miles across the mountains and valleys of the Andes. The religious and political centers were on remote sites at heights of more than ten thousand feet, but the Incas had established an amazing network of mountain tracks and rope bridges which enabled the rulers to control the scattered population of farmers and peasants. In many respects the Inca civilization was similar to that of the Aztecs: they had no wheeled vehicles and their only beast of burden was the llama, but they had an effective political system which enabled them to extract tribute from the people, and they were skillful builders and craftsmen. Like the Aztecs, they worked in gold and silver, and produced magnificent personal ornaments and images of their gods. In 1532 a group of Spaniards led by Francisco Pizarro set out from Panama to conquer Peru and the Inca peoples. The tiny force consisted of 180 soldiers and twenty-seven horses.

Pizarro lacked the diplomatic skills of Cortés—he was illiterate and came from a humble peasant family—but he was shrewd and ambitious, and a bold and ruthless soldier. At Cajamarca in northern Peru he encountered Atahualpa, the ruler of the Inca Empire. He double-crossed him, and mounted a surprise attack of astonishing bravado, capturing Atahualpa and murdering most of his retinue. Soon afterward he was joined by reinforcements which swelled his army to around six hundred men, and headed south for the Inca capital of Cuzco. Deprived of their leader, the Inca forces were unable to resist the onslaught of the Spanish conquistadores. In November 1533 Pizarro's men sacked the ancient city of Cuzco. A roomful of gold jewelry and ornaments, which had been collected from far and wide as a ransom to buy the freedom of Atahualpa, was melted down and, together with treasure looted from the inhabitants, was distributed among the Spanish soldiers. One fifth of the gold was retained for sending back to the King of Spain. As a final act of brutality, Pizarro ordered the execution of Atahualpa.

Within another ten years Spain effectively controlled most of South and Central America, and with it one of the world's major sources of precious metals. In addition to the Aztec and Inca treasure, a further source of riches was discovered in 1545. At Potosí in what is now Bolivia was a mountain which contained massive quantities of silver. It was 15,381 feet high, and within a few years of the discovery of its hidden treasure, it was riddled with mine shafts. A colonial town was established at the foot of the mountain, and hundreds of native Americans were drafted in by the Spanish to dig out the silver ore and to work the mills which were built to process the ore. Mule trains were loaded with the silver and dispatched over the mountain passes and through the jungle paths to the ports of Cartagena and Portobello. At first the Aztec gold from Mexico and the silver from the Potosí silver mountain was sent back to Spain in the form of bars and crude ingots, but the Spanish rulers soon established mints for converting the precious metals into coins. A mint was established at Mexico City in 1536, another at Lima in 1565, and a third at Potosí in 1574. The total value of the gold and silver produced by these mints and shipped back to Spain was astounding. Between 1596 and 1600, Spain imported treasure from the New World worth 34,428,500 pesos.[8] In today's terms that would be the equivalent of £516 million or $774 million.

The most famous of the coins associated with the New World were the "pieces of eight," or pesos. They were shipped back to Spain in huge quantities to finance the operations of the ever-growing Spanish Empire, and became the common currency for trading in South and Central America and the West Indies. For more than a hundred years the pieces of eight circulating in the New World were crudely struck silver coins of a type called cobs.[9] They were roughly the size of the fifty-pence piece currently in use in Britain, and were sometimes so roughly fashioned that they were almost square in shape rather than round. The pieces of eight produced in Spain, and those produced from 1732 onward in Mexico, were more finely made and smoothly rounded. Both types usually had the Spanish coat of arms on one side and a design representing the pillars of Hercules on the other. The twin pillars symbolized the limits of the ancient world at the Strait of

Gibraltar, and in the early designs they were depicted rising out of the sea. In later designs two hemispheres representing the Old and New World were added in the space between the pillars. The pieces of eight were so familiar and so widespread that the twin pillars were eventually turned into the dollar sign used today. In 1644 one piece of eight was valued in England at four shillings and sixpence. That would be the equivalent of about £15 or $23 today.

Although familiarly known as pieces of eight, or pesos, the proper name for these coins was "eight reales." All the silver coins struck by the mints in Spain and her overseas empire were called reales, while the gold coins were "escudos." Several denominations of escudos and reales were struck, but it was the piece of eight and the doubloon which became particularly associated with Spanish treasure and pirates. The doubloon, which was the gold eight-escudo coin, was the highest-value Spanish coin in circulation. It was slightly larger than the modern fifty-pence piece, and had the King of Spain's head on one side and the Spanish coat of arms on the other. A handful of doubloons would have been worth a small fortune to any pirate. Ducats, which are often referred to in pirate literature, were originally Venetian coins, and were the principal trading currency of the Mediterranean region in the days of the Barbary corsairs. There were gold and silver ducats, the gold coins being worth about seven shillings in the English money of the day and the silver ducats about five shillings.

Spain's rivals and enemies were alerted to the scale of the wealth flowing from the New World by the activities of French corsairs cruising the shipping lanes on the approaches to the ports of Europe. In 1523 Jean Fleury was sailing off Cape St. Vincent on the southern shores of Portugal when he sighted three heavily laden Spanish caravels. The ships were under the command of Captain Quiñones and were nearing the end of the long voyage from Mexico. Fleury and his men captured two of the ships and were astonished by what they found on board. They had stumbled on several tons of the treasure plundered by Cortés: there were three huge cases of gold ingots; 500 pounds weight of gold dust in bags; Aztec pearls weighing 680 pounds; and emeralds, topazes, golden masks set with gems, Aztec rings and helmets, and feathered cloaks.[10] Jean Fleury was in the employment of the Viscount of Dieppe, and it was not long before news of his rich prizes reached the courts of western Europe. The King of France,

Francis I, issued commissions to sea captains, and during the next forty years it was the French privateers and buccaneers who led the attacks on the Spanish treasure ships and treasure ports.

One of the first on the scene was Captain François le Clerc, more picturesquely known as Jambe de Bois because of his wooden leg. In 1553 he set sail with a squadron of three royal ships and a number of privateers. Cruising along the coasts of Hispaniola and Puerto Rico, he captured a succession of merchant ships. In 1554 he launched an attack on Santiago de Cuba, which was then the principal Spanish settlement on the great island of Cuba. With a force of eight ships and three hundred men he swept into the harbor, and spent thirty days looting and sacking the town and causing so much destruction that it took years to recover. The following year Jacques de Sores, who had sailed out from France with le Clerc, captured the city of Havana on the north coast of Cuba. When he failed to obtain the ransom which he had demanded, he proceeded to burn the city to the ground. He followed this by setting fire to all the ships in the harbor and laying waste to the countryside around the town. As a final act of vandalism his soldiers desecrated the church and stole the priests' vestments, which they put to use as cloaks.

It was now the turn of the English to challenge Spain's claim to the riches of the New World. Sir Francis Drake was the most famous of the English "Sea Dogs," and was certainly the most feared by the Spanish, but it was John Hawkins who showed the way and taught Drake his trade. Hawkins came from a seafaring family in Plymouth and made himself one of the richest men in England by the success of his trading voyages.[11] He was tough and resourceful, and though his activities incurred the wrath of the Spanish, he was a merchant and a privateer rather than a pirate. His instructions to his sailors would have been laughed to scorn by the crew of a pirate ship: "Let every man serve God daily, love one another, preserve your victuals, beware fire, and keep good company."[12]

His first voyage in 1562 took him from Plymouth to the African coast of Guinea, where he loaded his three ships with three hundred black slaves. Crossing the Atlantic, he sold the slaves for a handsome profit to the plantation owners on Hispaniola. The success of the venture secured him backing from the highest quarter for his second voyage. Queen Elizabeth authorized the use of the 700-ton warship

Jesus of Lubeck as flagship of the squadron, and the Navy Board and the merchants of the City of London were among the investors.

The squadron sailed from Portsmouth in October 1564 and made a series of raids on the African coast which resulted in the rounding up of four hundred slaves. When he arrived off South America, he found that the Spanish authorities had warned all their settlements against trading with him. Undaunted, Hawkins sailed from port to port, and by a combination of shows of force and much haggling, he eventually sold his human consignment as well as his cargo of wine, flour, cloth, and linen in return for gold, silver, and pearls. He sailed home via Hispaniola and the Straits of Florida, and arrived back in England in September 1565. The expedition had cost about £7,000 to mount, and the total profit on the original outlay was around 60 percent. Hawkins had shown that Spain's monopoly on trade with the New World could be breached. The Spanish Ambassador in London was outraged, and when he learned that Hawkins was planning a third voyage, he sent an urgent warning to King Philip of Spain.

Hawkins' third expeditionary force consisted of six ships and sailed from Plymouth in October 1567. His young cousin Francis Drake accompanied him on the voyage and was later given command of one of the vessels. They spent several months on the African coast and had the utmost difficulty in procuring slaves. When they crossed the Atlantic, they found that the King of Spain's instructions had preceded them: "We coasted from place to place making our traffic with the Spaniards as we might, somewhat hardly, because the King had straitly commanded all his governors in those parts by no means to suffer any trade with us."[13] Again Hawkins used a combination of force and diplomacy to sell his cargo, but following a storm in the Gulf of Mexico he was driven to seek shelter at San Juan de Ulúa, the treasure port of Vera Cruz. He promptly captured the fort overlooking the harbor. The next day the Spanish treasure fleet arrived accompanied by two warships, and Hawkins found himself negotiating not with local officials but with the newly appointed Viceroy of New Spain.

In the middle of the negotiations and without warning the Spanish Viceroy ordered his men to attack the British ships, and a full-scale battle broke out. Hawkins and Drake were lucky to escape alive. Drake's homeward journey was uneventful, but Hawkins had a nightmare journey and arrived back in Plymouth with only fifteen men still alive. An acute shortage of food and water caused one hundred of Hawkins' crew to plead with him to be put ashore on the coast of Mexico. Many of these died from sickness and malnutrition, but a number of them surrendered to the Spanish authorities: two were executed, and the rest were given two hundred lashes each and condemned to serve eight years as galley slaves.

The Battle of San Juan de Ulúa and its aftermath showed Hawkins and his countrymen that peaceful trade with the Spaniards in the West Indies was no longer possible. Drake never forgot the treachery of the Spanish Viceroy and henceforth devoted himself to plunder and war against Spain.

Exasperated by the attacks of English and French privateers, the Spanish had taken extensive measures to protect their hoards of gold and silver. At the treasure ports of Vera Cruz, Cartagena, Portobello, and Havana they built massive forts to defend the towns from attack by sea. Soldiers were sent out from Spain to man the forts and their gun batteries. To protect the treasure ships from attack they organized them into convoys. Twice a year a fleet of up to thirty ships came out from Spain with goods for the settlers. Anchored under the guns of the forts, the ships unloaded their domestic products and equipment, and then took on board the sealed chests of silver and gold before making the return journey to Seville accompanied by heavily armed warships.

While such precautions prevented looting by small-time thieves, they were not always effective against the attacks of the more determined privateers, and particularly the bands of privateers and adventurers who came to be known as the buccaneers. Driven out of their inland hunting grounds on Hispaniola by Spanish soldiers, the uncouth men who had lived there on the wild cattle and pigs migrated to the north coast of Hispaniola. There they were joined by a mixed bunch of runaway slaves, deserters, escaped criminals, and religious refugees. Around 1630 a number of buccaneers settled on the small, rocky island off the north coast of Hispaniola which had been discovered by Columbus and named Tortuga because its humped shape resembled a turtle. It had a good harbor and commanded the shipping lanes through the Windward Passage. One of the first buccaneer chiefs on Tortuga was Jean le Vasseur, a French Huguenot refugee who had been a military engineer. He built a fort on the rocky outcrop above the harbor and armed it with twenty-four guns. For several years Fort de Rocher successfully defended the buccaneer stronghold from Spanish attempts to take the island.

The most vivid account of the activities of the buccaneers is contained in a remarkable book by Alexander Exquemelin entitled *The Buccaneers of America*. The book contains bloodthirsty stories of buccaneer raids, torture, and pillage and also includes evocative descriptions of the landscapes, fauna, and flora of the West Indies. Exquemelin went out to Tortuga in 1666 on a ship of the French West India Company and later joined the buccaneers as a surgeon. He lived among them for more than twelve years and witnessed many of their raids. Careful comparison of his stories with the events described in Spanish documents of the period has shown that he gets most of the facts right but is often mistaken about place-names and dates.[14] Some of his wilder stories appear to be secondhand accounts which he probably heard in taverns, but it is clear that he took part in a number of buccaneer expeditions up to and including Henry Morgan's sacking of Panama City in 1671.

The reception of Exquemelin's classic work gives some idea of its impact. It was written in Dutch, and first published in Amsterdam in 1678 under the title *De Americaensche Zee-Rovers*. In 1681 a Spanish edition was printed, and translations into other European languages followed. The first English translation was published in London in 1684 and within three months a second edition followed. As the publisher wrote: "The first edition of this History of the Buccaneers was received with such general applause of most people, but more especially of the learned, as to encourage me towards obliging the public with this second impression."[15]

Exquemelin's book is so packed with detail about the lives and customs of the buccaneers that it is not surprising it proved popular. It has provided the basis for all serious histories of the buccaneers and, in spite of some inaccuracies, remains the standard work on the subject. Exquemelin devoted the first part of his book to the exploits of some of the more colorful buccaneers: Bartholomew Portugues, who captured a Spanish treasure ship, was taken prisoner and escaped by using earthenware jars as buoyancy aids; Roche Brasiliano, a Dutch buccaneer who was notorious for his drunken debauches and for roasting Spaniards alive on wooden spits; and the French buccaneer Francis

L'Ollonais, who sacked Maracaibo and captured a Spanish ship carrying 40,000 pieces of eight and jewels worth 10,000 pieces of eight. L'Ollonais also specialized in barbaric cruelties. According to Exquemelin, "It was the custom of L'Ollonais that, having tormented any persons and they not confessing, he would instantly cut them in pieces with his anger, and pull out their tongues."[16]

Exquemelin devoted nearly half his book to the life of Henry Morgan, a Welshman whose exploits on the Spanish Main became legendary. Whether Morgan was a pirate, a corsair, or a privateer is a matter of debate. The Spanish regarded him as a corsair, and since some of his most spectacular raids were carried out when England was at peace with Spain, those actions, like those of Francis Drake, were acts of piracy. But Morgan always carried a commission from the Governor of Jamaica so that technically he was a privateer. He no doubt simply regarded himself as a soldier fighting the enemies of his country on behalf of the King of England. The one label we can give him is that of buccaneer, that romantic-sounding word which applied to several generations of fortune hunters who roamed the Caribbean looking for plunder. They included soldiers and seamen, deserters and runaway slaves, cutthroats and criminals, religious refugees, and a considerable number of out-and-out pirates.

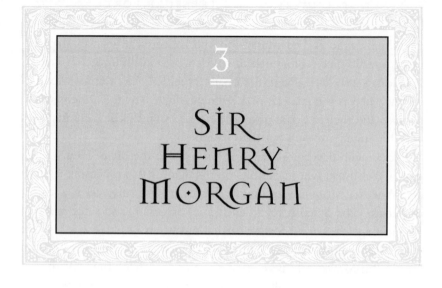

SİR
HEПRY
MORGAП

ON AUGUST 25, 1688, the greatest of the buccaneers died at home on his estate in Jamaica. When the news reached the Governor's house, the Duke of Albemarle immediately ordered a state funeral. Across the harbor at Port Royal the commander of HMS *Assistance,* Captain Wright, noted in his log, "This day about eleven hours morning, Sir Harry Morgan died."[1] Morgan's body was brought to the King's House at Port Royal, where it lay in state to enable friends and relations and drinking partners to pay their last respects. The coffin was placed on a gun carriage, and the funeral procession moved slowly through the hot, dusty streets to the church of St. Peters. Morgan had been one of the wealthy benefactors whose money had gone toward building the church some years earlier. The stone tower was the tallest building in the town and provided an excellent lookout across the approaches to the harbor. Dr. Longworth led the service in the church, and then led the procession back through the streets to the cemetery at the Palisadoes on the edge of the town. As the coffin was laid to rest, Captain Wright gave the order to the gun crews on the *Assistance* to fire a twenty-two-gun salute. The regular booming of the guns was echoed by the guns of the other warship in the harbor, HMS *Drake.* There was a pause as the noise of the last gun died away, and then all the merchant ships at anchor and moored along the busy wharves fired their guns in a deafening barrage of explosions.

It was a remarkable send-off for a buccaneer, but then Henry Morgan was no ordinary buccaneer.[2] He had received a knighthood and been appointed Lieutenant Governor of Jamaica by King Charles II. He had purchased several thousand acres on the island and set up his own sugar plantations. He was happily married for more than twenty years, and described his wife in his will as "my very well and entirely beloved wife Dame Mary Elizabeth Morgan."[3] He was well connected and influential: when he was arrested and sent back to London following his sacking of Panama City, Major General Bannister, who commanded the land forces in Jamaica, wrote on Morgan's behalf to Lord Arlington, telling him that Morgan had received high praise from the Governor and the Council for his proceedings against the Spanish. "I hope without offence I may say he is a very well deserving person, and one of great courage, who may, with his Majesty's pleasure, perform good public service at home or be very advantageous to this island if war should break forth with the Spaniard."[4] During his enforced stay in London, Morgan was welcomed in the drawing rooms of high society. John Evelyn, the diarist, met him at Lord Berkeley's and talked to him about his gallant exploits, and he paid frequent visits to the London house of the Duke of Albemarle, who was a Member of Parliament, and a friend of the King.

It is a pity that there are no descriptions of Morgan's appearance as a buccaneer leader, because he must have had considerable charisma to impose his will on the ragbag of pirates, hunters, and adventurers who carried out the daring raids on Portobello, Maracaibo, and Panama under his command. The only physical descriptions we have of him are restricted to the last few years of his life, when he was in his fifties and was suffering from the accumulated effects of tropical fevers, dropsy, and alcoholism. Hans Sloane, the physician and naturalist, attended him during his last few months and described Morgan as "lean, sallow-coloured, his eyes a little yellowish and belly jutting out or prominent."[5] Despite his precarious health, Morgan refused to abandon his dissolute lifestyle. "Not being able to abstain from company, he sat up late at night drinking too much, whereby he had a return of his first symptoms. . . ."[6]

Henry Morgan came from a good family in the county of Monmouth in Wales, and later in life insisted that he was a gentleman's son. He was born around 1635, and though little is known of his parents, we do know that two of his uncles were distinguished soldiers: one of them was Major General Sir Thomas Morgan, and the other was Colonel Edward Morgan, who was briefly Lieutenant Governor of Jamaica and died while leading an expedition to Curaçao.[7] At an early age Morgan decided to follow in the footsteps of his uncles and become a soldier. He later wrote, "I left school too young to be a great proficient in that or other laws, and have been more used to the pike than the book."[8] He joined the expeditionary force under General Venables and Admiral Penn which was dispatched from Britain in 1654 with the aim of capturing Hispaniola. An army of nearly seven thousand men landed at Santo Domingo on the south side of the island, but was compelled to withdraw, defeated by a combination of fierce Spanish resistance, incompetent leadership, and the deadly effects of tropical diseases.

Having failed to achieve the objective of the expedition, Penn and Venables decided to attack Jamaica, which was defended by only a few Spanish soldiers. This time the superior numbers assured success, and they captured the island, which henceforth became a British settlement and an important base for the operations of the Royal Navy and for privateers. Morgan spent the next few years taking part in raids on Spanish towns in Central America. In two of the successful attacks led by Captain Myngs, the records show that Morgan was one of the ship's captains given commissions by the Governor of Jamaica. Morgan himself led a raid in 1663 which resulted in the sacking of Villahermosa, and the plundering of Gran Granada in Nicaragua. He returned to Jamaica in 1665, having established himself as a formidable military leader. When Edward Mansfield, the leader of the privateers, was put to death by the Spaniards in Havana, Morgan was the natural successor. At the age of thirty-two he became Admiral of the Brethren of the Coast, that loose association of privateers and pirates which made up the body of men who came to be known as buccaneers.

In the years following Drake's attack on the mule train in 1572, the Spanish had abandoned Nombre de Dios as a treasure port and transferred their operations to Portobello, a few miles along the coast. Lionel Wafer, the buccaneer surgeon who visited the place in 1680, described it as having "a very fair, large and commodious harbour, affording good anchoring and good shelter for ships, having a narrow mouth and spreading wider within. The galleons from Spain find good riding here during the time of their business in Portobel; for from hence they take in such of the treasures of Peru as are bought thither over land from Panama."[9] The Spanish built two castles to command each side of the bay, and a third was in the process of construction at the inner end of the harbor. There were two churches, a hospital, stables and warehouses, and 150 houses built for the merchants and officials. In spite of its impressive appearance, the town suffered from the same humid atmosphere and fevers as Nombre de Dios. At low tide the receding sea exposed an expanse of shore, "which having a black, filthy mud, it stinks very much and breeds noisome vapours, through the heat of the climate."[10]

Morgan had learned that the forts which defended the town from the sea were poorly manned, and he calculated that a surprise attack from the landward side would overwhelm them. In July 1668 he sailed with a fleet of twelve small ships to the Bay of Boca del Tora to the west of Portobello. There he transferred his attacking force of five hundred men into twenty-three canoes, which he had commandeered in Cuba. Under cover of darkness the buccaneers rowed the canoes along the coast until they were within three miles of the town. Around midnight they beached the canoes at Estera Long Lemos and marched across country, arriving outside Portobello half an hour before dawn on July 11.

The first task was to capture the lookout post on the outskirts of the town. It was defended by five men who bravely opened fire on the advancing buccaneers. They were quickly overwhelmed, but the shots were heard in the town and alerted the sentries in the castles. The alarm was also given by some men in a canoe who had spotted Morgan's invading force and raced into the harbor shouting, "To arms, to arms!" and firing their guns in the air.[11] There was confusion and terror as the citizens woke in the darkness: some fled the town, some cowered in their houses. The soldiers meanwhile ran to join the garrison in Santiago Castle. Morgan had lost the advantage of total surprise, but gave the order to charge. Shouting and screaming, his men ran across the open ground in front of the castle. They expected to be at the mercy of the guns of the castle, but only one shot was fired and the cannonball sailed harmlessly over their heads and splashed into the sea. Within a few minutes one group of buccaneers had passed out of range of the castle guns and was running into the town. Yelling and firing and slashing at anyone who attempted resistance, they herded the terrified men, women, and children into one of the churches. The other group of buccaneers mounted the hill overlooking the town and began picking off the soldiers on the castle walls with their long-barreled muskets.

As the early morning sun illuminated the rooftops, the buccaneers found themselves in possession of the town. The next task was to capture the forts. The half-built Fort of San Geronimo was situated on a small island near the quay, and at first the soldiers manning it refused to surrender. They changed their minds as a group of ferocious-looking buccaneers waded out toward them. Santiago Castle was a more formidable target, and Morgan made a ruthless decision. The Mayor, several women and old men, and some friars and nuns were dragged from the church and forced to precede the advancing bucca-neers as a human shield. The soldiers in the castle fired a cannon loaded with chain shot, killing one of Morgan's men and wounding two friars. There were no more shots from the castle, and the bucca-neers reached the main gate without further casualties. Meanwhile another group of buccaneers had found some ladders and managed to scale the walls of the castle on the seaward side. They hoisted a red flag, and on seeing this, the buccaneers on the hill ran down to join in the attack. In spite of the overwhelming numbers of the attackers, many of the men in the castle refused to surrender, and forty-five of the eighty soldiers in the garrison were killed before the castle was captured. The constable of artillery, humiliated by his incompetent efforts to defend the castle, pleaded to be shot. One of the buccaneers obligingly executed him with his pistol. The rest of the day was spent in looting and drinking. According to Exquemelin's account, "all the prisoners were brought inside the town, the men and women being housed separately, and a guard set to look after them. The rovers brought their own wounded into a house near by. Having put every-thing in order, they began making merry, lording it with wine and women." [12]

Next morning Morgan sent two of his men across the harbor to the Castle of San Phelipe and demanded its surrender. The commander of the garrison had forty-nine men and plenty of ammunition, but no food because this was normally sent over each day from the town. At first he determined to hold out, but was shaken to see two hundred buccaneers, armed to the teeth, advancing across the harbor in canoes. They landed to the east of the castle and took up positions among the rocks. After several hours of desultory firing on both sides, the commander decided to parley with the English attackers. His officers refused to agree to this, and while they were arguing, some of the buccaneers sneaked inside the castle and flung open the main gates. The remaining buccaneers swarmed inside and the Spanish garrison surrendered. Morgan ordered the English flag to be flown above the ramparts, and at this signal his squadron of ships, which had been waiting outside the bay, set sail. The four warships and eight smaller craft swept into the harbor and dropped anchor.

Having captured the town, Morgan sent a letter to the President of Panama. He told him that he would burn Portobello to the ground if he did not receive a ransom payment of 350,000 pesos. Don Agustín rejected the demand out of hand: "I take you to be a corsair and I reply that the vassals of the King of Spain do not make treaties with inferior persons."[13] Morgan retorted with a letter which began, "Although your letter does not deserve a reply, since you call me a corsair, I write you these few lines to ask you to come quickly. We are waiting for you with great pleasure and we have powder and ball with which to receive you."[14] The Spanish sent an army of eight hundred men from Panama, but they were demoralized by the journey through the swamps, by the torrential rain, and by the shortage of food and powder. Most of all they were daunted by the fire from the buccaneers' muskets and the guns of the English ships when they approached Portobello.

Negotiations dragged on for three weeks, but in the end Don Agustín capitulated. On August 3 two mule trains left Panama with the ransom. Morgan and his men were soon in possession of 40,000 pesos in silver coins, 4,000 pesos in gold coins, several chests of silver plate, and twenty-seven bars of silver worth 43,000 pesos. Together with the treasure already looted from the town, the buccaneers' haul amounted to around 250,000 pesos. Morgan set sail for Jamaica and arrived in Port Royal to a hero's welcome. For the next few weeks the town was the scene of spectacular orgies of drinking, gambling, and womanizing as the buccaneers blew their money in the taverns and whorehouses.

The capture of Portobello was one of the most successful amphibious operations of the seventeenth century. For sheer boldness it was comparable with De Ruyter's attack on the British fleet anchored in the Medway the previous summer: De Ruyter had burned several warships, towed the British flagship *Royal Charles* back to Holland, and caused panic in the towns and villages of the lower Thames and Medway. This humiliating defeat had followed hard on the heels of the Fire of London and the Great Plague, so that news of Morgan's exploit delighted the hard-pressed citizens of London. The fact that Britain had signed a peace treaty with Spain a few months before made little difference. King Charles listened politely to the protests of the Spanish Ambassador, but refused to recall the Governor of Jamaica, who had authorized the raid, or return the booty plundered by Morgan and his men.

The buccaneers soon ran out of money and began demanding that their captains put to sea again. In October 1668 Morgan let it be known that he was planning another raid and sailed to Isla Vaca (Cow Island) on the southwestern coast of Hispaniola. There he was joined by several French buccaneers from Tortuga and by the thirty-four-gun warship HMS *Oxford,* which had been sent out to Jamaica to help in the defense of the island. By January 1669 there were ten ships and eight hundred men gathered at the rendezvous. Morgan transferred his flag to the *Oxford* and held a council of war to discuss the next objective. It was agreed that the first expedition would be a raid on the city of Cartagena, which was one of the treasure ports on the Spanish Main. The night after this decision was taken a rowdy dinner was held in the cabin of the flagship. As was usual with buccaneer parties, the drinks and toasts were punctuated with the firing of the ship's guns. At some point during the drunken proceedings, the gunpowder in the magazine was set alight and the ship was blown apart. Morgan, who seems to have had a charmed life, was picked up from the water and was one of only ten people on board to survive the blast.

The loss of the *Oxford,* and some two hundred men, put an end to the ambitious plan to raid Cartagena. Morgan sailed instead to Maracaibo on the coast of Venezuela. None of the forts or towns around the great lagoon of Maracaibo were well defended, so the buccaneers spent an easy week plundering and carousing. But word of their arrival had reached Don Alonzo de Campos y Espinosa, who was Admiral of Spain's West Indian fleet. He took his three warships to the entrance of the lagoon and set a trap for Morgan. He repaired the guns of the fort, which Morgan's men had spiked, and anchored his warships so they blocked the channel. When Morgan learned what was happening, he devised an ingenious series of deceptions. A Cuban merchant ship which he had captured in the lagoon was disguised as a powerful warship. Additional gunports were cut in her sides, and logs were used to simulate cannon. The decks of the ship were lined with more logs, which were roughly painted and clothed to look like seamen. The ship was then loaded with barrels of gunpowder fitted with fuses. With Morgan's flag at her masthead the merchant ship led the attack, accompanied by two small frigates. They headed straight at the largest of the anchored Spanish ships, the *Magdalena* of 412 tons. The merchant ship was sailed alongside the *Magdalena* and secured to her with grappling irons. The fuses were lit and the twelve buccaneers on board escaped in the boats. Within a few minutes the merchant ship exploded and the flames swept across to the *Magdalena,* which was soon reduced to a burning hulk. One of the other Spanish ships hastily weighed anchor and headed for the protection of the fort but ran aground on a sandbank. The third warship was chased by Morgan's ships and captured.

The fort still controlled the entrance to the harbor, and there were now several hundred soldiers and seamen manning the guns which commanded the channel. Morgan opened negotiations with Don Alonzo, but when these broke down, he came up with another plan. He hoodwinked the Spanish into thinking that he was going to make a land attack by sending boats ashore filled with armed men. The boats returned to the anchored fleet with the men lying hidden below the thwarts. The Spanish were so convinced that Morgan was planning a land assault that a number of guns were moved to cover the landward approaches to the fort. In the middle of the night Morgan's fleet weighed anchor and drifted silently past the fort with the tide. By the time the Spanish spotted them they were out of range of the guns.

Once again Morgan returned to Port Royal in triumph, though the plunder was on a smaller scale than previously and, according to one reliable authority, amounted to half the booty from the Portobello raid.[15] While the buccaneers repaired to the taverns to spend their loot, Morgan reported to the Governor, Sir Thomas Modyford. He learned that Modyford had just received a letter from Lord Arlington informing him that hostilities with Spain must stop. This was bad news for the buccaneers, but for Morgan it provided a breathing space. It gave him the opportunity to spend time with his wife, to look up his many friends and relations in Jamaica, and to buy some real estate. He had already bought one plantation and he now purchased 836 acres in the parish of Clarendon near Chapelton village. The area is still called Morgan's Valley today.

At around the time that the news reached Jamaica that there must be no more raids against Spanish ships or settlements, the Governor of Cartagena received a letter from the Queen of Spain authorizing war against the English in the Indies. The challenge was taken up by a Portuguese corsair called Captain Rivero, who raided the Cayman Islands and then attacked a Jamaican privateer ship off Cuba. In June 1670 he landed thirty men at Montego Bay on Jamaica's north coast and destroyed most of the houses in the settlement. A month later he raided a coastal village on the south coast and burned two houses. Rivero was never a serious threat to Jamaica, but his attacks naturally provoked demands for retaliation. News then came from the Dutch Governor of Curaçao that Spain had officially declared war on Jamaica. The Council of Jamaica assembled and agreed that "a commission be granted to Admiral Henry Morgan to be Admiral and Commander in Chief of all the ships of war belonging to this harbour,"[16] and authorizing him to assemble a fleet "and to attack, seize and destroy all the enemy's vessels that shall come within his reach." He also had authority to land in the enemy's country and to take and destroy anything that would "tend to the preservation and quiet of this island."

Morgan received his commission on August 1, 1670, and once again sailed to Isla Vaca to rendezvous with the buccaneers. By the end of September no less than thirty-eight ships and around two thousand men had joined Morgan's flagship. On December 12, 1670, a council of war was held aboard the flagship, and it was agreed that the city of Panama was to be the target. A week later the biggest buccaneer fleet ever seen in the Caribbean set sail and headed for San Lorenzo at the mouth of the river Chagres. The castle at the river entrance put up a fierce resistance, and it took three assaults and the loss of many men before it was captured. Not till the English flag was flying over the battlements could Morgan's fleet sail past the silenced guns and head upriver. When they were several miles upstream, the buccaneers transferred into small boats and canoes. These took them a few miles further, but then it was time to leave the river and begin the march through the jungle.

Panama was the principal treasure port on the Pacific coast of Central America for the gold and silver which was brought by ship from Peru and Potosí. It had a population of around six thousand, most of whom were black slaves. The President of the city's council (*Audiencia*) was Don Juan Pérez de Guzmán, who had made strenuous efforts to improve Panama's defenses. He had ensured that there was a good supply of weapons and ammunition and had done his best to increase the city's garrison. When Morgan and his men emerged from the jungle and onto the plain in front of Panama, they saw that Don Juan had stationed his troops across the road so that they blocked the way into the city. There were about twelve hundred defenders on foot and some four hundred horsemen, but the majority of them were inexperienced recruits and were no match for Morgan's battle-hardened buccaneers.

At 7:00 A.M. on January 28, 1671, Morgan gave the order for his men to advance. They were in four squadrons and carried red and green banners which billowed out in the fresh breeze blowing across the plain. As he approached the waiting army, Morgan decided that a frontal assault would be costly and therefore ordered one of his squadrons to wheel aside and capture the hill to the right of the city. Don Juan's men thought the buccaneers were retreating and charged forward; the Spanish horsemen also charged. The buccaneers, finding themselves facing a disorganized rabble of men and horses, stood their ground and fired with deadly accuracy into the advancing hordes. The leading horses were shot down by French sharpshooters who were in the buccaneer vanguard, and the surviving horsemen turned around and headed back to Panama. The men on foot were at the mercy of a devastating volley from the main body of the buccaneers, which killed around a hundred men and caused the remainder to turn tail and run. Don Juan's secret weapon had been two herds of oxen which were to be stampeded toward the buccaneers by black cowboys. The oxen lumbered onto the battlefield, but were simply shooed away by the buccaneers and sent back to the city. Morgan's men now charged at the fleeing army, hacking and slashing their way across the plain. By midmorning some five hundred men lay dead or wounded under the tropical sun. The buccaneers lost only fifteen men in the action.

Don Juan had made sure that if the battle was lost, the buccaneers would be left with an empty city. Much of Panama's treasure had been loaded onto ships while Morgan's men were still hacking their way through the jungle. Barrels of gunpowder had been placed in many of the houses, and the captain of artillery had orders to blow up the ammunition store if the buccaneers advanced on the city. As the fleeing army ran through the streets, the captain lit the fuses and the resulting blast could be heard six miles away. The gunpowder barrels were then ignited, and as they exploded, they began the fires which would soon burn most of the buildings to the ground. For several hours there was chaos as angry buccaneers ran from house to house looking for gold and valuables, and blacks darted here and there with flaming torches, carrying out Don Juan's orders to set fire to all the wooden buildings. By nightfall the whole of the central part of the city was in flames, and by morning only the stone tower of the cathedral and some of the public buildings built of stone were still standing.

"Thus was consumed the famous and ancient city of Panama, the greatest mart for silver and gold in the whole world," [17] wrote Morgan in his report to Modyford. His men searched the smoking ruins and the surrounding countryside for treasure, and even raided the islands which lay offshore. The inhabitants were savagely tortured to reveal where they had hidden their money, and by the end of February a considerable pile of plunder had been assembled. Morgan gathered his army and headed back through the jungle to his ships. According to Exquemelin, the buccaneers took with them 175 mules loaded with silver plate and coin, and six hundred prisoners. Morgan later reported that the total value of their plunder was £30,000. When divided among so many men, this amounted to little more than £15 per head. There was much anger, and many of the buccaneers suspected Morgan of cheating them out of their share. Exquemelin was among the disappointed buccaneers, and this may explain why he painted such a black picture of Morgan and portrayed him as a cruel and unscrupulous villain.

When the English edition of Exquemelin's book was printed in London by two publishers, Morgan was sent copies and decided to sue both publishers for libel. He was particularly outraged at being called a pirate, and strongly objected to the passage which said that he had first gone out to the West Indies as an indentured servant. He insisted that he "never was a servant to anybody in his life, unless to his Majesty."[18] The matter was settled out of court. Subsequent editions were amended and Morgan received £200 damages in the King's Bench Court against each of the publishers. Unfortunately for Morgan, the earlier editions continued to circulate and are still quoted today in many histories of piracy.

Morgan hurried home to Jamaica, leaving the buccaneers to disperse in different directions. Most of the French contingent, who made up nearly one third of the army, returned to Hispaniola and the offshore island of Tortuga. Many buccaneers headed north along the coast to Honduras and the Bay of Campeche to join the growing settlements of logwood cutters. Some followed Morgan to Jamaica and joined the crew of trading sloops or fishing boats, or settled down to a more peaceful life ashore. The sack of Panama was the last major action of the buccaneers. Piracy continued, of course, and was to become an increasing menace to trade in the West Indies, but the pirates who followed in the wake of Morgan were freelance raiders who attacked the ships of all nationalities and rarely carried commissions authorizing their activities.

Πews of the Panama expedition was well received in Jamaica. "I think we are pretty well revenged for their burning our houses on ye north and south side of this island,"[19] wrote Modyford's brother with masterly understatement, and the Council of Jamaica met on June 10, 1671, and publicly thanked Morgan for carrying out his commission. The authorities in London were not so pleased. In spite of the Queen of Spain's letter of April 1669 and the subsequent raids by Spanish corsairs, England was officially at peace with Spain. Sir Thomas Modyford had no authority from London to issue a commission to Morgan giving him carte blanche to attack and destroy anything in reach. The Spanish authorities in the New World and in Madrid were humiliated and outraged by the destruction of Panama. The news threw the Queen of Spain "in such a distemper and excesse of weeping and violent passion as those about her feared it might shorten her life."[20]

The British endeavored to distance themselves from "ye late accident in America" by blaming it all on a bunch of privateers who had got out of hand. It was decided that Modyford must be replaced as Governor, and Sir Thomas Lynch was sent out in his stead with secret orders to arrest Modyford and send him back England. On his arrival in London, Modyford was sent to the Tower of London. This was clearly a propaganda exercise to appease the Spanish. He was treated like a gentleman, and after two years' confinement was allowed to rejoin London society; eventually he was sent back to Jamaica as Chief Justice. The Spanish were not appeased and continued to demand that the British take action against the infamous corsair who had led the attack on Panama. In April 1672 Henry Morgan was arrested and sent home to England in the frigate HMS *Welcome*. He had been very ill with fever for several months and there was much sympathy for his plight. Even Lynch wrote on his behalf: "To speak the truth of him, he's an honest, brave fellow, and had both Sir T. M. and the Council's commission and instructions. . . ."[21] Morgan spent two years in London waiting to learn his fate. He was never imprisoned and was free to visit friends and relations. He used his time well, and was even asked by Lord Arlington to submit a memorandum to the King on how the defenses of Jamaica might be improved.

Governor Lynch had been sending a constant stream of letters to London. He was worried by the increasing activities of pirates, and was concerned that the French might attempt an attack on Jamaica. It was felt that he was no longer the right man for the job, and in January 1674 Lord Arlington informed the Council of Trade and Plantations that Lynch was being replaced as Governor of Jamaica by Lord Vaughan. He was to be assisted by Henry Morgan, who was to be appointed to the post of Lieutenant Governor. Before he left England, Morgan was given a knighthood by King Charles II. Whether this was conferred on him because of the dignity of his new office or in recognition of his exploits against the Spanish is not clear. Certainly he had many friends at court, and was widely admired as a brilliant and courageous commander.

Morgan traveled out to the West Indies on the ship *Jamaica Mer-*

chant and was shipwrecked on the shores of Isla Vaca, the place he had used as a rendezvous before the attacks on Maracaibo and Panama. Everyone got ashore safely in the boats, but the *Jamaica Merchant* sank, taking to the bottom the cannon which Morgan was bringing with him to boost the defenses of Port Royal. Before too long the passengers and crew of the wrecked ship were picked up by a passing merchant ship and taken to Jamaica, where they landed on March 6, 1676.

The qualities which made Morgan such an effective buccaneer leader were not those required in the role of Lieutenant Governor. He attended meetings of the Assembly, acquired more land, and spent much of his time supervising his estates. He did not get on well with Lord Vaughan, who complained of his "imprudence and unfitness to have anything to do with the civil government"[22] and his habit of drinking and gaming in the taverns of Port Royal. But he came into his own when Vaughan was recalled and he was left as Acting Governor. A powerful French fleet commanded by Comte d'Estrées was reported off Curaçao and was considered a serious threat to Jamaica. Morgan declared martial law, mobilized the militia, and ordered the building of two new forts to guard the approaches to Port Royal harbor. He also sent a ship to Isla Vaca to recover the guns and shot from the wrecked *Jamaica Merchant*. The salvage operation succeeded in raising twenty-two guns, which were brought back to Port Royal and mounted in an emplacement which was called "Morgan's Lines."

When Hans Sloane came out to Jamaica in 1687 with the newly appointed Governor, the Duke of Albemarle, he found Morgan seriously ill and wrecked by years of dissolute living and the unpleasant effects of dropsy. He prescribed various medicines, which seemed to work well, but Morgan continued to indulge in gargantuan drinking bouts with his friends. "Falling after into his old course of life and not taking any advice to the contrary, his belly swelled so as not to be contained in his coat."[23] Morgan consulted a black doctor who plastered him all over with clay and water, and gave him clysters of urine, "but he languished and, his cough augmenting, died soon after."

WOMEN PIRATES AND PIRATES' WOMEN

T HE HARBOR AT Nassau is a long stretch of shimmering blue water which lies between the wharves lining the town's waterfront and a low offshore island of sandy beaches and palm trees. Today the harbor welcomes cruise ships and visiting yachts, but in the eighteenth century it provided a sheltered anchorage for small trading vessels and the occasional man-of-war. It was also a well-known refuge and meeting place for pirates. On August 22, 1720, a dozen pirates rowed out to a single-masted sailing vessel which was anchored in the middle of the channel. The vessel was a twelve-ton sloop called the *William,* which was owned by a local man, Captain John Ham. She had four guns on her broad, sun-bleached decks, and two swivel guns mounted on her rails. She was well equipped with ammunition and spare gear, and had a canoe lying alongside which was used as a tender.[1] The pirates climbed on board, heaved up the anchor, and set the sails. They were soon clear of the other vessels in the anchorage and heading out to sea in the stolen sloop. Thefts of this type were not uncommon in the Caribbean, but a keen-eyed observer might have noticed something about the pirate crew which was unusual. Although they were dressed in men's jackets and long seamen's trousers, two of the pirates were women.

The leader of the pirates was John Rackam, a bold and somewhat reckless character whose colorful clothes had earned him the nickname of Calico Jack.[2] He was fond of women, and it was said that he kept a harem of mistresses on the coast of Cuba. He had been quartermaster in Captain Vane's pirate company, but in November 1718 he had challenged his captain's decision not to attack a French frigate in the Windward Passage. The crew branded Vane a coward and elected Rackam as captain in his place. Taking command of Vane's ship, he proceeded to plunder a succession of small vessels in the seas around Jamaica. There is no record of Calico Jack using torture or murder, and he seems to have gone out of his way to treat his victims with restraint. When he had finished looting a Madeira ship, he returned the vessel to her master and arranged for Hosea Tisdale, a Jamaican tavern keeper, to be given a passage home. Compared to Bartholomew Roberts and Blackbeard, who commanded forty-gun warships and sailed into action with a flotilla of supporting vessels, Calico Jack was a small-time pirate. He preferred to operate with a modest sloop, and he restricted his attacks to small fishing boats and local trading ships. His chief claim to fame lay not in his exploits during his two years as a pirate captain but in his association with the female pirates Mary Read and Anne Bonny, whose lives were considerably more adventurous and interesting than his own.

Calico Jack met Anne Bonny in New Providence. He had sailed to the island in May 1719 to take advantage of the amnesty being offered by the Governor of the Bahamas. He accepted the royal pardon and for a while abandoned his life as a pirate. While frequenting the taverns on the waterfront at Nassau, he came across Anne Bonny and proceeded to court her in the same direct manner he used when attacking a ship: "no time wasted, straight up alongside, every gun brought to play, and the prize boarded."[3] He persuaded her to abandon her sailor husband and took her to sea with him. When she became pregnant, he took her to his friends in Cuba, and there she had their child. As soon as she was up and about, Calico Jack sent for her and she rejoined his crew, dressed as usual in men's clothes. He had taken up piracy again, and it was around this time that Mary Read joined his crew. She too was dressed as a man, and had been sailing on a merchant ship which he had captured. Anne Bonny found herself strongly attracted to the new member of the pirate crew, and in a quiet moment when they were alone she revealed herself as a woman. Mary Read, "knowing what she would be at, and being sensible of her own capacity in that way, was forced to come to a right understanding with her, and so to the great disappointment of Anne Bonny, she let her know that she was a woman also."[4] To avoid any further misunderstandings, Calico Jack was let into the secret.

By the summer of 1720 they were all back in New Providence, and were evidently well known to the authorities there. When they stole the sloop *William* from Nassau harbor, the Governor had no doubt about their identities. On September 5 he issued a proclamation which set out the details of the sloop and gave the names of Rackam and his associates. The list included "two women, by name, Ann Fulford alias Bonny and Mary Read." The proclamation declared that "the said John Rackum and his said Company are hereby proclaimed Pirates and Enemies to the Crown of Great Britain, and are to be so treated and Deem'd by all his Majesty's subjects."[5]

The Governor of the Bahamas at this time was Captain Woodes Rogers, a tough and resolute seaman who had commanded a successful privateering voyage around the world from 1708 to 1711. He had come out to the West Indies in 1718 with a commission from the British government to rid the Bahamas of the pirate colony which was based on New Providence. He sailed into Nassau harbor with three warships and had made strenuous efforts to reestablish law and order. He had authority from King George to issue pardons to pirates who agreed to abandon their trade, and Calico Jack was one of many who did so. The new Governor was prepared to use harsh measures if the pardons failed to produce results. When some of the pardoned pirates returned to their old ways, he had them rounded up and hanged on the waterfront at Nassau beneath the ramparts of the fort.

Woodes Rogers was equally decisive when he learned that the sloop *William* had been stolen from the harbor. As well as issuing the proclamation, he immediately dispatched a sloop with forty-five men to catch the pirates, and on September 2 he dispatched a second sloop armed with twelve guns and a crew of fifty-four men to join the chase.[6] Calico Jack must have learned that vessels were out looking for him. After attacking seven fishing boats off Harbour Island in the Bahamas, he headed south. He intercepted two merchant sloops off the coast of Hispaniola on October 1, and two weeks later he took a schooner near Port Maria on the north coast of Jamaica. During the next three weeks the *William* cruised slowly westward, past the coves and sandy beaches of Ocho Rios, Falmouth, and Montego Bay, until she came to Negril Point at the extreme western tip of the island. There Calico Jack's luck ran out.

Sailing in the vicinity was a heavily armed privateer sloop commanded by Captain Jonathan Barnet, "a brisk fellow," with a commission from the Governor of Jamaica to take pirates.[7] Hearing a gun fired from Rackam's anchored vessel, Barnet changed course to investigate. Alarmed by the appearance of Barnet's powerful-looking vessel, Rackam hurriedly got under way. Barnet gave chase and caught up with the pirates at ten o'clock at night. He hailed them and received the reply "John Rackam from Cuba." Barnet thereupon ordered him to surrender, but the pirates shouted defiance and fired a swivel gun at Barnet's ship. In the darkness it was difficult for either side to see its opponents clearly, but Barnet immediately retaliated with a broadside and a volley of small shot. The blast carried away the pirates' boom, effectively disabling their vessel,[8] and Barnet came alongside and boarded the pirate sloop. The only resistance came from Mary Read and Anne Bonny. They were armed with pistols and cutlasses and shouted and swore at everyone in sight, but they failed to rally their shipmates, who tamely surrendered. The next morning the pirates were put ashore at Davis's Cove, a tiny inlet halfway between Negril and Lucea. They were delivered to Major Richard James, a militia officer, who assembled a guard and escorted them across the island to Spanish Town jail.[9] On November 16, Calico Jack and the ten male members of his crew were tried for piracy; a few days later, on November 28, the Admiralty Court assembled again for the trial of the two female members of the pirate crew.

Mary Read and Anne Bonny never acquired the notoriety of Henry Morgan, Captain Kidd, or Blackbeard, but they have attracted more attention than many of the most successful and formidable pirate captains of history. This is partly due to the vivid description of their lives in Johnson's *General History of the Pirates,* and partly due to the fact that they were the only women pirates of the great age of piracy that we know anything about. This has given them a mythic quality which has inspired several books, plays, and films, and has led to their inclusion in the writings of feminist historians as well as in books on transvestism and cross-dressing.

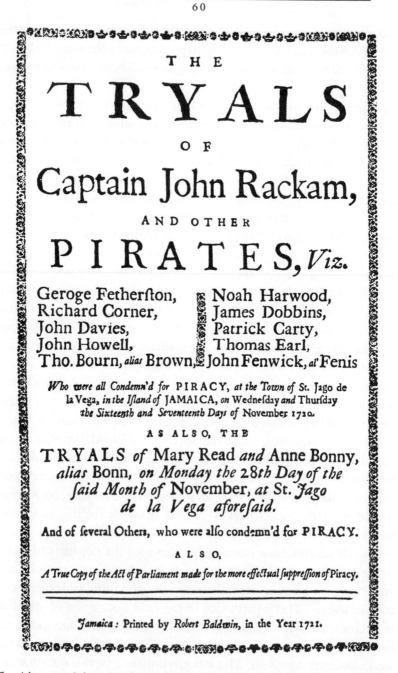

THE
TRYALS

OF

Captain John Rackam,

AND OTHER

PIRATES, *Viz.*

Geroge Fetherston,	Noah Harwood,
Richard Corner,	James Dobbins,
John Davies,	Patrick Carty,
John Howell,	Thomas Earl,
Tho. Bourn, *alias* Brown,	John Fenwick, *al'* Fenis

Who were all Condemn'd for PIRACY, *at the Town of* St. Jago de
la Vega, *in the Island of* JAMAICA, *on* Wednesday *and* Thursday
the Sixteenth and Seventeenth Days of November 1720.

AS ALSO, THE

TRYALS *of* Mary Read *and* Anne Bonny,
alias Bonn, *on Monday the* 28th *Day of the*
said Month of November, *at* St. Jago
de la Vega aforesaid.

And of several Others, who were also condemn'd for PIRACY.

ALSO,

A True Copy of the Act of Parliament made for the more effectual suppression of Piracy,

Jamaica : Printed by *Robert Baldwin*, in the Year 1721.

The title page of the printed transcript of the trial of Calico Jack (Captain John Rackam) and his crew in November 1720, and the trial of Mary Read and Anne Bonny a few days later. The trials were held in Spanish Town, Jamaica, which was then known as St. Jago de la Vega.

The problem with their story is the lack of documentation for their early lives. The printed record of their trial and brief references in the colonial documents and contemporary newspapers provide information about the last year or two of their lives, but for the rest we have to rely on Captain Johnson, who is usually accurate but rarely indicates the source of his information. And the story that he tells is almost too amazing to be true. As he himself says, their history is full of surprising turns and adventures, and "the odd incidents of their rambling lives are such, that some may be tempted to think the whole story no better than a novel or romance."[10]

According to Johnson, Mary Read was born in England, the second child of a young mother whose husband went away to sea and never returned. Following her husband's disappearance the young woman had an affair with another man and became pregnant, but she was so ashamed at the idea of giving birth to a bastard child that she went away into the country to stay with friends. Shortly before Mary was born, the elder child, who was a boy, died. The mother soon ran out of money and decided to approach her mother-in-law for help in providing for the child. She dressed Mary up as a boy so that she could pass her off as her son, and traveled up to London. The mother-in-law duly agreed to provide a crown a week for the child's maintenance.

Mary Read was brought up as a boy, and at the age of thirteen her mother secured her a post not as chambermaid but as a young footman to a French lady. She soon tired of this menial life, and "growing bold and strong, and having also a roving mind, she entered herself on board a man-of-war." She then went to Flanders and enlisted as a cadet in the army. She distinguished herself by her bravery in several military engagements, but fell in love with a Flemish soldier in her regiment. The soldier was delighted to find himself sharing a tent with a young woman, but Mary Read was not prepared to continue indefinitely as his mistress. When the campaign was over, the two lovers got married. They left the army and set up as proprietors of a public house near Breda called The Three Horse Shoes.

Unhappily, Mary's husband died not long after the marriage, and when the Peace of Ryswick was signed in 1697, the soldiers went elsewhere and The Three Horse Shoes lost most of its trade. Mary

Read had no option but to seek her fortune elsewhere. She dressed up as a man again, and after a spell in a foot regiment, she embarked on a ship bound for the West Indies. The ship was captured by pirates, and after further adventures she found herself on the ship commanded by Rackam with Anne Bonny among the crew.

Anne Bonny had also been brought up as a boy. She was born near Cork in Ireland, and was the illegitimate daughter of a lawyer. Her father separated from his wife following a quarrel: the wife was upset because she had discovered that her husband had been having an affair with the maid of the household; the husband was enraged when his wife accused the maid of stealing some silver spoons and had her sent to prison. The husband was so fond of the girl he had by the maid that he decided that she must come and live with him. To avoid a scandal, he dressed her up as a boy and pretended that he was training her up as a lawyer's clerk.

The lawyer's wife discovered what was going on and stopped the allowance she had been giving him. The scandal affected his practice and he decided to go abroad. Taking the maid and their daughter, Anne, he sailed to Carolina, where he made enough money as a merchant to be able to purchase a plantation. Anne disappointed her father by falling for a penniless young seaman called Bonny and marrying him. Turned out of the house by her father, she and Bonny sailed to the island of Providence, where, as we have seen, she met Calico Jack, became a pirate, and after two adventurous years ended up in the courthouse in Jamaica alongside Mary Read. The printed transcript of the trial at Spanish Town provides firsthand information about some of Calico Jack's exploits as well as descriptions of the appearance and behavior of Mary Read and Anne Bonny.[11] The Admiralty Court that assembled on November 16 was presided over by Sir Nicholas Lawes, the Governor of Jamaica. There were twelve commissioners, two of whom were Royal Navy captains. The men on trial were Rackam himself, described as "John Rackam, late of the island of Providence in America, mariner, late master and commander of a certain Pirate Sloop"; George Fetherston, also of Providence, "late Master of the said Sloop"; Richard Corner, the quartermaster; and John Davies, John Howell, Thomas Bourn, Noah Harwood, James Dobbins, Patrick Carty, Thomas Earl, and John Fenwick.[12]

There were four charges against the prisoners:

1. That they "did piratically, feloniously, and in an hostile manner, attack, engage and take, seven certain fishing boats" and that they assaulted the fishermen and stole their fish and fishing tackle.

2. That they did "upon the high sea, in a certain place, distance about three leagues from the island of Hispaniola . . . set upon, shoot at, and take, two certain merchant sloops," and did assault James Dobbin and other mariners.

3. That on the high sea about five leagues from Port Maria Bay in the island of Jamaica they did shoot at and take a schooner commanded by Thomas Spenlow and put Spenlow and other mariners "in corporeal fear of their lives."

4. That about one league from Dry Harbour Bay, Jamaica, they did board and enter a merchant sloop called *Mary*, commanded by Thomas Dillon, and did steal and carry away the sloop and her tackle.

There were two witnesses for the prosecution. Thomas Spenlow of Port Royal, Jamaica, described how his schooner was fired on by the sloop manned by the prisoners at the bar. He said they "boarded him, and took him; and took out of the said schooner, fifty rolls of tobacco, and nine bags of piemento and kept him in their custody about forty-eight hours, and then let him and his schooner depart." The second witness was James Spatchears, mariner of Port Royal, who gave a detailed description of the action between the pirate sloop and the trading sloop commanded by Jonathan Barnet.

The prisoners pleaded not guilty to the charges, but all were found guilty and sentenced to death. Five were hanged the next day at Gallows Point, a windswept and featureless promontory on the narrow spit of land which leads out to Port Royal; the other six were hanged the next day in Kingston. Calico Jack's body was put into an iron cage and hung from a gibbet on Deadman's Cay, a small island within sight of Port Royal which is today called Rackam's Cay.

The trial of Mary Read and Anne Bonny followed similar lines. The charges were exactly the same, but there were some additional witnesses for the prosecution, all of whom stressed that the female pirates were willing members of Rackam's crew and took an active part in the attacks on merchant vessels. The most graphic description of their appearance was provided by Dorothy Thomas, who was in a canoe on the north coast of Jamaica when she was attacked by the pirate sloop:

> . . . the two women, prisoners at the bar, were then on board the said sloop, and wore mens jackets, and long trousers, and handkerchiefs tied about their heads; and that each of them had a machet and pistol in their hands, and cursed and swore at the men, to murder the deponent; and that they should kill her, to prevent her coming against them; and the deponent further said, that the reason of her knowing and believing them to be women then was by the largeness of their breasts.[13]

Two Frenchmen who were present when Rackam attacked Spenlow's schooner explained with the aid of an interpreter how the women were very active on board, and that Anne Bonny handed gunpowder to the men; also, "that when they saw any vessel, gave chase, or attacked, they wore men's clothes; and at other times, they wore women's clothes."

Thomas Dillon, master of the sloop *Mary*, confirmed that both women were on board Rackam's sloop when they made their attack. He said that "Ann Bonny, one of the prisoners at the bar, had a gun in her hand, that they were both very profligate, cursing and swearing much, and very ready and willing to do any thing on board."

When the women were asked whether they had anything to say in their defense, they both said they had no witnesses, nor did they have any questions to ask. The prisoners and all the onlookers were ordered to withdraw from the courtroom while Sir Nicholas Lawes and the twelve commissioners considered the evidence. It was unanimously agreed that the two women were guilty of the piracies and robberies in the third and fourth charges brought against them. They were brought back to the bar and told that they had both been found guilty. They could offer no reason why sentence of death should not be passed upon them, and so Sir Nicholas, in his role as president of the court, sentenced them with the time-honored words:

> You Mary Read, and Anne Bonny, alias Bonn, are to go from hence to the place from whence you came, and from thence to the place of execution; where you shall be severally hanged by the neck till you

are severally dead. And God of his infinite mercy be merciful to both your souls.

For some reason the prisoners delayed their trump card until this moment; perhaps they did not believe they would be found guilty until they heard the president's doom-laden words. But immediately after the judgment was pronounced, they informed the court that they were both pregnant. Unfortunately we do not know how this news was received by those present, but it must have caused something of a sensation. All we do know from the printed transcript of the trial is that the court ordered that "the said Sentence should be respited, and then an inspection should be made."

An examination proved that both women were indeed pregnant and they were reprieved. Unhappily, Mary Read contracted fever soon after the trial and died in prison. The Parish Register for the district of St. Catherine in Jamaica records her burial on April 28, 1721.[14] It is not known for certain what happened to Anne Bonny or her child.

A separate trial was held on January 24, 1721, for nine unfortunate Englishmen who happened to be on board Rackam's ship when it was captured by Jonathan Barnet. A few hours earlier they had been in a canoe looking for turtles, and had been persuaded to join the pirates for a bowl of punch. On the basis that they were armed and apparently helped Rackam to row his sloop, the court convicted them of piracy. Six of them were hanged, "which everybody must allow proved somewhat unlucky to the poor fellows," as Captain Johnson noted.

THE STORY OF Mary Read and Anne Bonny raises a number of questions. Was it so unusual for women to go to sea, and if so, why? Were there other women pirates? Was it essential for a woman to dress as a man if she wanted to join the crew of a ship? How was it possible for a woman to pass herself off as a man in the cramped and primitive conditions on board an eighteenth-century ship?

During recent years an increasing number of women have taken up sailing and have proved themselves able to handle large and small yachts in all weathers. Several women have sailed single-handed across the Atlantic and around the world, and all-women crews have competed successfully in ocean races. But for hundreds of years seafaring was an almost exclusively male preserve. While the fishermen heaved in their nets and lines in the icy waters off Cape Cod or the Dogger Bank, their wives and daughters remained behind to look after the young children, to make and mend the nets, and to pray that the men survived the storms. All too often there were tragedies. In 1848 a gale blew up during the night of August 18 and swept across the seas off Scotland. The fishing fleets from the various harbors around the coast had put to sea that afternoon and were caught unawares. As the wind built up into a raging southeasterly gale, the men hauled up their nets and ran for shelter. At Wick the fishermen's families hurried down to the harbor and watched aghast as the boats battled against the foaming seas sweeping across the harbor entrance. Some boats were swamped and foundered on the harbor bar, some were smashed against the piers, and some were overwhelmed by the waves and sank offshore. Forty-one boats were lost, twenty-five men were drowned before the eyes of their relatives, and twelve were lost at sea. Seventeen widows and sixty children were left destitute. At Peterhead thirty-one men perished, and nineteen men from Stonehaven lost their lives in that summer gale.[15]

Life in the navy and the merchant service was equally dangerous. Their larger ships were better able to ride out storms than the open fishing boats, but they were at the mercy of uncharted shoals, poor navigation, and death from scurvy and tropical diseases. Apart from the dangers of life at sea, there were the long absences from home: it was not unusual for a seaman to say good-bye to his family and not see them again for months and sometimes years. When Edward Barlow sailed from England in the *Cadiz Merchant* in September 1678 on a routine trading voyage to the Mediterranean, it was fifteen months before he returned to London.[16] In the 1770s Nicholas Pocock made several voyages to the West Indies as captain of a small merchant ship; his trips from Bristol to the island of Dominica and back home took on average nine months. A seaman in the Royal Navy whose ship was sent to patrol the seas off Boston or the west coast of Africa might not see his home port for two years.

The dangers, the privations, and the absences from home did not discourage young men from going to sea, but in the days of sail it was unthinkable that women should be subjected to the physical demands of life on deck, and the wet, cramped, and foul-smelling conditions below. There was a widespread belief that a woman on board was likely to provoke jealousies and conflicts among the crew, and there was a tradition among seamen that a woman on a ship brought bad luck. In spite of all this, a surprising number of women did go to sea. Many traveled as passengers, of course, a few captains took their wives to sea with them,[17] and there were instances when captains and officers smuggled their mistresses aboard. But there are also well-documented cases of women going to sea as sailors. Indeed, the history of the Royal Navy and the merchant service is littered with examples of women who successfully dressed as men and worked alongside them for years on end without being discovered.[18] The life of Mary Anne Talbot has a number of parallels with that of Mary Read: she was illegitimate, she was dressed as a boy when she was young, and she spent part of her life as a soldier and part as a sailor. She was born on February 2, 1778, one of the sixteen bastard children of Lord William Talbot. She was seduced by her guardian, Captain Essex Bowen, who enlisted her as a young footman in his regiment. She sailed with him from Falmouth on the ship called *Crown* bound for Santo Domingo. She was present at the British capture of Valenciennes in July 1793, and some months later joined the crew of HMS *Brunswick,* where she served as cabin boy to her commander, Captain John Harvey. She was present at the Battle of the Glorious First of June in 1794, and was one of the few to survive the murderous action against the French ship *Vengeur.* She was, however, wounded by grapeshot and was sent to the naval hospital at Haslar. By 1800 she had left the navy and spent some time on the stage at Drury Lane before becoming a servant to a London publisher, R. S. Kirby, who wrote an account of her life which was published in 1804.[19]

Hannah Snell went to sea in 1745 to look for her husband, a Dutch sailor called James Summs who had abandoned her when she was six months pregnant. She served for a time on the British sloop HMS *Swallow,* commanded by Captain Rosier, and took part in the siege of Pondicherry in 1748. Marianne Rebecca Johnson served four years in a British collier *Mayflower* without her sex being detected, and her mother spent seven years in the Royal Navy before being mortally wounded at the Battle of Copenhagen.

These and other women were able to survive in a man's world by proving themselves as capable as the men in battle and in their duties as seamen. Mary Anne Arnold worked as an able seaman on the ship *Robert Small* until she was unmasked by Captain Scott, who became suspicious of her during the ritual shaving ceremony when crossing the line. He later declared that she was the best sailor on his ship and wrote, "I have seen Miss Arnold among the first aloft to reef the mizen-top-gallant sail during a heavy gale in the Bay of Biscay."[20] Whenever Hannah Snell was challenged for not being sufficiently masculine, she always retaliated by offering to beat her challenger at any shipboard task. Mary Anne Talbot adopted male habits and in later life was accused of having "masculine propensities more than became a female such as smoking, drinking grog, etc."[21]

But how did these women manage to disguise their physical appearance and prevent their shipmates' discovering their sex? Clearly the determination and ingenuity of the women who succeeded in fooling their shipmates was extraordinary. There was little privacy on board ship in the seventeenth and eighteenth centuries, though there were many dark corners in the badly lit areas belowdecks where a woman might have hidden her nakedness when necessary. Conditions on a ship in those days were very different from those on a modern vessel. Most people who travel on ships today expect them to be clean and shiny, with stainless steel fittings, running water in the taps, flush toilets, and comfortable bunk beds. An oceangoing merchantman in the eighteenth century was almost entirely constructed of wood, and was a confusing jumble of tarred rope, mildewed sails, spare masts and spars, muddy anchor cable, hen coops, hammocks, seamen's chests, wooden crates of various sizes, and numerous barrels containing water, beer, salt pork, and gunpowder. In order to provide fresh meat and milk during the voyage, an assorted collection of cows, goats, ducks, geese, and chickens were kept in pens belowdecks.[22] In fine weather the goats were often allowed to wander around on deck. Many of the seamen kept pets: dogs and cats were common, and so were parrots and monkeys.

In addition to the domestic animals and pets, merchant ships and naval ships often had a number of small boys on board who had been sent to sea to learn the ropes, and many of the most active members of the crew were boys in their teens. Dressed in the loose trousers, loose shirts, and jackets of the seamen, with a scarf or handkerchief around her neck, a strong young woman with a good head for heights would not have found it difficult to pass as a teenage boy when working on deck or up among the rigging. Belowdecks, amid the cargo and the animals and the smells of bilge water, manure, decaying wood, and tarred hemp, it would have been more difficult but not impossible for a woman to hide her sex, although she would have had to use some ingenuity to cope with the toilet facilities, which on most ships were extremely primitive.[23] The seamen either climbed onto the leeward channels (platforms along the ship's side for spreading the rigging) and urinated into the sea, or went forward to the beakhead or "heads." On the wooden structure overhanging the bows of the ship would be two or three boxes with holes in them. The seamen sat on the boxes, or "seats of easement" as they were called, and defecated through the hole into the water below. On smaller ships without a beakhead, the heads were inboard and the waste was discharged through a pipe in the ship's side.

Life on a pirate ship was similar to life on a merchantman, partly because most pirate ships were former merchant ships with a few more guns added, and partly because the majority of pirates were former merchant seamen. Pirate ships usually had bigger crews and the men adopted a more relaxed regime, but their habits and prejudices were similar, and most pirates had the seaman's traditional prejudice against taking women to sea. Article Three of the pirate code drawn up by Bartholomew Roberts and his crew stated that no boy or woman was to be allowed among them. "If any man were found seducing any of the latter sex, and carry'd her to sea, disguised, he was to suffer death."[24] Captain Johnson's explanation of this rule was that it was to prevent divisions and quarrels among the crew.

Many pirate captains preferred to take on men who were unmarried. It is difficult to obtain hard evidence on the numbers of pirates who were married, but one study of the Anglo-American pirates active in the years 1716 to 1726 shows that 23 pirates out of a sample of 521 are known to have married.[25] That is around 4 percent, a remarkably small proportion of the total until one remembers that most pirates were young men in their twenties and therefore had not reached an age when they wanted to settle down. When Sam Bellamy's pirate ship and her consorts were wrecked on the coast of Cape Cod, there were eight survivors. They were interrogated on the orders of the Governor of Massachusetts in May 1717, and their confessions indicate that married men were not welcome on Bellamy's ships. Thomas Baker said that when he and nine other men were taken by the pirates off Cape François, the other men "were sent away being married men." Peter Hoof stated that "No married men were forced," which means they were not compelled to sign the pirates' articles and join the crew. Thomas South confirmed that when his ship was captured, "The pirates forced such as were unmarried, being four in number."[26]

When Philip Ashton was captured by pirates in the harbor of Port Rossaway in June 1722, the first ordeal he had to face was an interrogation by Edward Low, the pirate captain. Brandishing a pistol, Low demanded to know whether Ashton, and the five men captured with him, were married men. None of them replied, which so enraged Low that he came up to Ashton, clapped a pistol to his head, and cried out, "You Dog! Why don't you answer me?" and swore vehemently that he would shoot Ashton through the head if he did not tell him immediately whether he was married or not.[27] When he learned that none of them were married, Low calmed down. Ashton subsequently learned that Low's wife had died shortly before he became a pirate. She had left a young child in Boston that Low was so fond of that he would sometimes sit down and weep at the thought of it. It was Ashton's conclusion that this was the reason why Low would only take unmarried men, "that he might have none with him under the influence of such powerful attractives as a wife and children, lest they should grow uneasy in his service, and have an inclination to desert him, and return home for the sake of their families."[28]

Some pirates did abandon their roving lives and settle down. When Howell Davis visited the Cape Verde Islands to carry out repairs to his ship, he left five of his crew behind when he sailed because they were so charmed with the women of the place: "one of them, whose name was Charles Franklin, a Monmouthshire man, married and settled himself, and lives there to this day."[29] In the Public Record Office in London is a petition which was sent to Queen Anne in 1709 from the wives and other relations "of the Pirates and Buccaneers of Madagascar and elsewhere in the East and West Indies."[30] It is signed by forty-seven women and is a plea for a royal pardon for all the offenses committed by the pirates. The petition was brought to the attention of the Council of Trade and Plantations. Lord Morton and others were in favor of a royal pardon as the only effective way of breaking up the pirate settlements in Madagascar, but it was not till 1717 that the pardon, or "Act of Grace," was issued, and by that time the pirate colony on Madagascar was in decline.

As far as can be gleaned from the meager information on the subject, very few of the pirate captains had wives and families. Henry Morgan was married but had no children. Captain Kidd had a wife and two daughters who lived in New York. Thomas Tew was married and also had two daughters. According to Captain Johnson, Blackbeard married a young girl of sixteen in North Carolina; she was reputed to be his fourteenth wife and apparently it was his custom after he had lain with her all night "to invite five or six of his brutal companions to come ashore, and he would force her to prostitute herself to them all, one after another, before his face."[31] While this seems entirely in character, it might equally well be a flight of fancy on the part of Johnson. Reporting one of Blackbeard's raids in January 1718, Governor Hamilton simply noted that "This Teach it's said has a wife and children in London."[32] None of the other pirate captains mentioned in Johnson's *History* are recorded as being married.

ALTHOUGH a surprising number of women seem to have gone to sea on merchant ships or joined the navy disguised as men, very few women became pirates. Apart from Mary Read and Anne Bonny, the only female pirates mentioned in any of the pirate histories are the Scandinavian pirate Alwilda, the Irishwoman Grace O'Malley, and the Chinese pirate leader Mrs. Cheng.

Very little is known about Alwilda.[33] She was the daughter of a Scandinavian king in the fifth century A.D. Her father had arranged for her to marry Prince Alf, the son of Sygarus, the King of Denmark, but she was so opposed to the marriage that she and some of her female companions dressed up as men, found a suitable vessel, and sailed away. The story goes that they came across a company of pirates who were bemoaning the recent loss of their captain. The pirates were so impressed by the regal air of Alwilda that they unanimously elected her as their leader. Under her command the pirates became such a formidable force in the Baltic that Prince Alf was dispatched to hunt them down. Their ships met in the Gulf of Finland, and a fierce battle took place during which Prince Alf and his men boarded the pirate vessel, killed most of the crew, and took Alwilda prisoner. Full of admiration for the Prince's fighting qualities, Alwilda changed her mind about him and was persuaded to accept his hand in marriage. They were married on board his ship, and she eventually became Queen of Denmark.

While the story of Alwilda has a legendary air about it, the history of Grace O'Malley is well documented. There are several references to her in the State Papers of Ireland, and recent research has uncovered the main events in her life and shown that behind the heroine of the Irish ballads was a commanding woman, "famous for her stoutness of courage and person, and for sundry exploits done by her at sea." [34] Grace O'Malley was born around 1530 in Connaught on the west coast of Ireland. Her father was a local chieftain and the descendant of an ancient Irish family which for centuries had ruled the area around Clew Bay. The O'Malleys had castles at Belclare and on Clare Island, and maintained a fleet of ships which were used for fishing, trading, and piratical raids on the surrounding territories. It seems likely that Grace went to sea as a girl, and it is said that she acquired her nickname "Granuaille" (which means "bald") because she cut her hair short like the boys she sailed with. [35] In 1546, when she was about sixteen, Grace was married to Donal O'Flaherty and moved to her husband's castle at Bunowen some thirty miles south along the coast. All that is known about this phase of her life is that Grace had three children and that after a few years of marriage her husband died, possibly murdered in a revenge attack. Grace returned to her father's domain and took command of the O'Malley fleet. She was by now beginning to build up a reputation as a bold and fearless sea captain. In 1566 she married Richard Burke, another local chieftain, and moved to Rockfleet Castle in County Mayo. This became the base for her seafaring operations and was her home for the remaining thirty-seven years of her life.

Rockfleet Castle still stands today on an inlet overlooking Clew Bay. It is a simple, square structure but is massively built of stone and stands four stories high above the surrounding moors. This wet and windswept stretch of the Irish coast makes a startling contrast with the pirate strongholds in the Bahamas. Both locations have beaches and bays and numerous offshore islands, but instead of palm trees rustling under the tropical sun, Rockfleet Castle stands among rolling hills covered with heather and bracken. While the heat of Nassau is cooled by fresh breezes in the evening, the gray waters of Galway and Connemara are swept by southwesterly gales blowing in from the Atlantic. But Clew Bay provided a secure anchorage for the O'Malley fleet, which in the time of Grace O'Malley consisted of around twenty vessels. All the documentary references indicate that several of these vessels were galleys, apparently the only vessels of this type on the Irish coast. Captain Plessington of HMS *Tremontaney* described an encounter with one of these vessels in 1601. "This galley comes out of Connaught, and belongs to Grany O'Malley," he wrote. He noted that the vessel "rowed with thirty oars, and had on board, ready to defend her, 100 good shot, which entertained skirmish with my boat at most an hour."[36] Some years earlier Sir Henry Sydney, the Lord Deputy of Ireland, reported to Walsingham, Queen Elizabeth's secretary: "There came to me also a most famous feminine sea captain called Grany Imallye, and offered her services unto me, wheresoever I would command her, with three galleys and 200 fighting men."[37] In theory an oared galley, a vessel developed to deal with the calms in the Mediterranean, was wholly unsuitable for the turbulent seas around the British Isles, and presumably the oars were only used in light winds or for raids in sheltered coastal waters. At other times the galleys, like the Viking longships, must have shipped their oars and relied on a single square sail for their motive power.

The nature of Grace O'Malley's piracy was determined by local circumstances. Although all Ireland was then part of the British kingdom ruled by Queen Elizabeth I, the government of each province was in the hands of a Governor appointed by the Queen. These Governors were usually English aristocrats or soldiers, and in Connaught they exerted an oppressive regime which led to constant rebellions from the local chieftains. Sometimes Grace led punitive raids against other chieftains, and sometimes she attacked and plundered passing merchant ships. In the 1570s her attacks provoked a storm of protest from the merchants of Galway and compelled Sir Edward Fitton, the Governor, to send an expedition against her. In March 1574 a fleet led by Captain William Martin sailed into Clew Bay and laid siege to Rockfleet Castle. Grace marshaled her forces and within a few days turned the tables on Martin and forced him to beat a retreat. But in

1577, during a plundering raid on the lands of the Earl of Desmond, she was captured and imprisoned in Limerick jail for eighteen months. She was described by Lord Justice Drury as "a woman that hath . . . been a great spoiler, and chief commander and director of thieves and murderers at sea to spoil this province." [38]

When Grace O'Malley's husband died in 1583, she found herself in a precarious position. She was vulnerable to raids from neighboring chieftains, and in financial hardship because, according to Irish custom, a widow had no right to her husband's lands. Believing that the best means of defense was attack, she launched a number of raids on the surrounding territories but incurred the hostility of Sir Richard Bingham, who had succeeded Fitton as Governor of the province. Bingham regarded her as a rebel and a traitor and sent a powerful force to Clew Bay which impounded her fleet. She felt her only recourse was to appeal to the Queen of England. In July 1593 a letter was received in London addressed to the Queen from "your loyal and faithful subject Grany Ne Mailly of Connaught in your Highness realm of Ireland." [39] Grace explained that she had been forced to conduct a warlike campaign on land and sea to defend her territory from aggressive neighbors. She asked the Queen "to grant her some reasonable maintenance for the little time she has to live" and promised that in return she would "invade with sword and fire all your highness enemies, wheresoever they are or shall be." While the Queen's advisers were looking into the matter, Grace O'Malley's son was arrested by Bingham on charges of inciting rebellion. Grace decided that she must go to London and make a personal appeal to the Queen.

The Irish ballads have made much of her voyage across the Irish Sea and her audience with Queen Elizabeth:

> 'Twas not her garb that caught the gazer's eye
> Tho' strange, 'twas rich, and after its fashion, good
> But the wild grandeur of her mien erect and high
> Before the English Queen she dauntless stood
> And none her bearing there could scorn as rude
> She seemed well used to power, as one that hath
> Dominion over men of savage mood
> And dared the tempest in its midnight wrath
> And thro' opposing billows cleft her fearless path. [40]

In fact no details exist of the voyage or what was said at their meeting. All we know is that they met at Greenwich Palace in September 1593, and a few days later the Queen sent a letter to Sir Richard Bingham ordering him to sort out "some maintenance for the rest of her living of her old years."[41] Bingham released her son from prison but continued to detain her ships and to harass her territories. However, in 1597 Bingham was succeeded by Sir Conyers Clifford and the O'Malley fleet was able to put to sea again. Grace was now nearly seventy years old and seems to have left it to her sons to run her fleet and defend the O'Malley lands. She died around 1603 at Rockfleet. Her son Tibbot proved a loyal subject and carried out Grace's promise to fight the Queen's enemies. In 1627 he was created Viscount Mayo.

Grace O'Malley stands out as an isolated example in her time of a woman who took command of ships and armed forces, and proved able to survive as a leader in a hostile environment ruled by warlike men. Aside from military commanders such as Boadicea and Joan of Arc, one of the few women to match her achievement was the Chinese pirate Mrs. Cheng, whose fleets of junks ruled the South China Sea in the early years of the nineteenth century. Her full name was Cheng I Sao, which means "wife of Cheng I," but she is often referred to as Ching Yih Saou, or Ching Shih.[42]

The customs, traditions, and way of life of the Chinese have for centuries been very different from those in the West. In the ports and along the rivers of southern China, entire communities lived and worked on the boats. In these floating villages the women played an active role in handling the sailing junks and small boats, and worked alongside the men when fishing and trading. The same conditions prevailed in the pirate communities. English observers such as Lieutenant Glasspoole noted that the pirates had no settled residences onshore but lived constantly on their vessels, which "are filled with their families, men, women and children."[43] It was not unusual for women to command the junks and to sail them into battle. The Chinese historian Yuan Yung-lun described a pirate action which took place in 1809: "There was a pirate's wife in one of the boats, holding so fast by the helm that she could scarcely be taken away. Having two cutlasses, she desperately defended herself, and wounded some soldiers; but on being wounded by a musket-ball, she fell back into the vessel and was taken prisoner."[44]

Against this background it was not so surprising that a woman should assume leadership of a pirate community, particularly as there was a long tradition in China of women rising to power through marriage. Mrs. Cheng was a former prostitute from Canton who married the pirate leader Cheng I in 1801. Between them they created a confederation which at its height included some fifty thousand pirates. By 1805 the pirates totally dominated the coastal waters of southern China. They attacked fishing craft and cargo vessels as well as the oceangoing junks returning from Batavia and Malaysia. They lived off the provisions and equipment which they plundered at sea, and when these supplies proved insufficient they went ashore and looted coastal villages. They frequently ransomed the ships which they captured, and they ran a protection racket in the area around Canton and the delta of the Pearl River.

When Cheng I died in 1807, his wife moved adroitly to take over command. She secured the support of the most influential of her husband's relatives, and she appointed Chang Pao as commander of the Red Flag Fleet, which was the most powerful of the various fleets in the confederation. This was a particularly shrewd move. Chang Pao was a fisherman's son who had been captured by her husband and proved himself a brilliant pirate leader. He commanded respect among the ranks of the pirates and had become the adopted son of Cheng I. Within weeks of her husband's death, Mrs. Cheng had also initiated a sexual relationship with Chang Pao, and several years later she married him. Henceforth Mrs. Cheng acted as commander in chief of the pirate confederation, with Chang Pao in charge of day-to-day operations. Between them they laid down a strict code of conduct, with punishments even harsher than the codes adopted by the pirates who operated in the West Indies in the 1720s. The punishment for disobeying an order or for stealing from the common treasure or public fund was death by beheading. For deserting or going absent without leave a man would have his ears cut off. For concealing or holding back plundered goods the offender would be whipped. If the offense was repeated, he would suffer death. The rules were equally strict over the treatment of women prisoners. The rape of a female captive was punishable by death. If it was found that the woman had agreed to have sex with her captor, the man was beheaded and the woman was thrown overboard with a weight attached to her legs.

For three years Mrs. Cheng and Chang Pao fought off all attempts by government forces to destroy the pirate fleets. In January 1808 General Li-Ch'ang-keng, the provincial commander in chief of Chekiang, led an attack on the pirates in Kwangtung waters. A fierce and bloody action took place during the night, and at one point Li sent in fire vessels. The result was an overwhelming victory for the pirates. Li was killed by pirate gunfire which tore out his throat. Fifteen of his junks were destroyed and most of the remainder were captured. Later that year Chang Pao advanced up the Pearl River and threatened the city of Canton. Attempts were made to starve out the pirates by cutting their supply lines, but this simply led to the pirates going ashore and looting the villages. Every naval force sent out to intercept the pirates was defeated, and by the end of 1808 the authorities had lost sixty-three vessels. Some of the local communities constructed barricades and formed militia units which managed to repel pirate raids: they would lure pirates into ambushes and pelt them with tiles and stones and buckets of lime. All too often the pirates swept aside the amateur forces and took a terrible revenge. At the village of Sanshan in August 1809 the pirates burned the place to the ground, beheaded eighty villagers, and hung their heads on a banyan tree near the shore. The women and children who had been hiding in the village temple were carried off by the pirates. When Chang Pao attacked the island of Tao-chiao in September 1809, his pirates killed a thousand of the islanders and abducted twenty of the women.

The sheer numbers involved in some of these pirate attacks make the activities of the pirates in the West Indies pale into insignificance. Sometimes Mrs. Cheng's forces went into action with several hundred vessels and up to two thousand pirates. At the height of its power in 1809 the confederation's fleet was larger than the navy of many countries. There were some two hundred oceangoing junks, each armed with twenty to thirty cannon and able to carry up to four hundred pirates. There were between six and eight hundred coastal vessels armed with twelve to twenty-five guns and carrying two hundred men. And there were dozens of small river junks which were manned by crews of twenty to thirty men. These vessels had sails and up to twenty oars, and were used for going up shallow rivers to plunder villages or to destroy farms when local communities had failed to pay protection money.[45]

Mrs. Cheng's reign as a pirate leader came to an end in 1810. Chinese officials had enlisted the assistance of Portuguese and British warships, and increasingly large forces were being assembled to counter the pirates. When the Chinese government offered an amnesty to the pirates, Mrs. Cheng resolved to take the initiative and secure the best possible terms. She decided to go unarmed to the Governor-General in Canton, and on April 18, 1810, she arrived at his residence with a delegation of seventeen women and children. It was a bold move and proved entirely successful. She was negotiating from a position of strength because the Governor-General and his advisers were only too aware of the terrible damage and casualties which her pirate squadrons were capable of inflicting. It was agreed that the pirates would surrender their junks and their weapons, but in return they would be able to keep their plunder and those who were willing were allowed to join the army. Mrs. Cheng also negotiated that her lieutenant and lover, Chang Pao, be given the rank of lieutenant and allowed to keep a private fleet of twenty junks. On April 20 no less than 17,318 pirates formally surrendered and 226 junks were handed over to the authorities. Not all the pirates got off scot-free: 60 were banished for two years, 151 were permanently exiled, and 126 were executed.[46]

Mrs. Cheng and Chang Pao settled in Canton but later moved to Fukien, where they had a son. Chang Pao eventually rose to the rank of colonel and died in 1822 at the age of thirty-six. Mrs. Cheng, who was a wealthy woman, returned to Canton. She kept a gambling house but led a peaceful life and died in 1844 at the age of sixty-nine. It is a pity that there are no authentic descriptions of Mrs. Cheng's appearance or character. The exploits and battles of the pirate confederation are recorded in detail in Chinese documents, but she herself remains a shadowy figure. She was evidently a resourceful and powerful woman. Whether she justifies the claim of one historian[47] that she was "the greatest pirate, male or female, in all history" is questionable, but for three years she controlled and masterminded the activities of one of the largest pirate communities there has ever been.

STORMS, SHiPWRECKS, AnD LiFE AT SEA

T HE MOST FAMOUS pirate shipwreck took place on the shores of Cape Cod on April 26, 1717. Sam Bellamy had captured the slave ship *Whydah* a few weeks before in the Windward Passage as she headed for London. He took command of her, and in company with a captured sloop commanded by his quartermaster Paul Williams, he headed north. After plundering a number of merchant ships off the coast of Virginia, they agreed to make for Block Island in order to careen and refit the two pirate ships. As he approached the treacherous shoals off Cape Cod, Bellamy was leading a small fleet of four vessels, which included the *Mary Anne,* a small merchant vessel of the type known as a pink. She had been captured earlier in the day, and her captain taken off. Three members of her crew had been left on board, and seven armed pirates placed in charge of her.

During the evening of April 26 the weather turned nasty. Driving rain reduced visibility so that the ships lost touch with each other, but more serious than the rain was the strong easterly wind which sprang up, sweeping in from the Atlantic and building up to gale force. Bellamy and his prizes were now sailing off a lee shore on a stretch of coast which has claimed hundreds of ships over the years. At some time between ten and eleven at night the *Mary Anne* found herself among breaking waves and ran aground. The crew cut down her masts to reduce the strain on the hull, but the wind and the waves simply drove the vessel further up the beach. The men decided to stay on board, and they spent an unpleasant night battened down in the hold. In the morning they found the pink was high and dry on a barren island. They were rescued by two men in a canoe, who raised the alarm. Within hours the seven pirates were in the hands of a deputy sheriff and his men. On October 18 they were tried before an Admiralty Court at Boston, and six of them were hanged a month later.[1]

The *Whydah* did not survive the storm. Ten miles further up the coast she was swept toward the breakers. The anchors were dropped, but they dragged and Bellamy ordered his men to cut the anchor cables. A large square-rigged ship had no hope of sailing off a lee shore once she was among the breakers. The *Whydah* struck on a shoal a few hundred yards off the beach. Her mainmast went by the board and the ship began to break up. Only two men reached the shore alive: Thomas Davis, a young Welsh shipwright, and John Julian, an Indian who had been born on Cape Cod. One hundred and forty-four men, including Bellamy, died in the storm, and during the next few days many of the bodies were washed up on the beach.

Every pirate ship had to be prepared to ride out gales and storms at sea. The Caribbean and the Gulf of Mexico had the advantage of warm and sunny winters, but they were (and of course still are) subject to hurricanes which built up in the Atlantic and swept across the region with devastating results. Jamaica was a regular target. In 1712 Governor Hamilton reported that a hurricane had destroyed thirty-eight ships in the harbor at Port Royal and nine ships at Kingston. Ten years later, on August 28, 1722, a hurricane hit the island at half past eight in the morning. According to Captain Chaloner Ogle of HMS *Swallow,* who was at anchor off Port Royal, there was "as much wind in my opinion as could possibly blow out of the heavens . . . all the merchantmen in the harbour foundered or drove ashore excepting one sloop."[2] The seas threw up rocks and stones and flooded the town to a depth of five feet.

The pirate Edward Low was heading for the Leeward Islands in a brigantine when the same hurricane swept across his path. Mountainous waves threatened to overcome them, and the crew were forced to throw overboard six of their guns, their provisions, and all their heavy goods to lighten the vessel. For hours they worked the pumps and

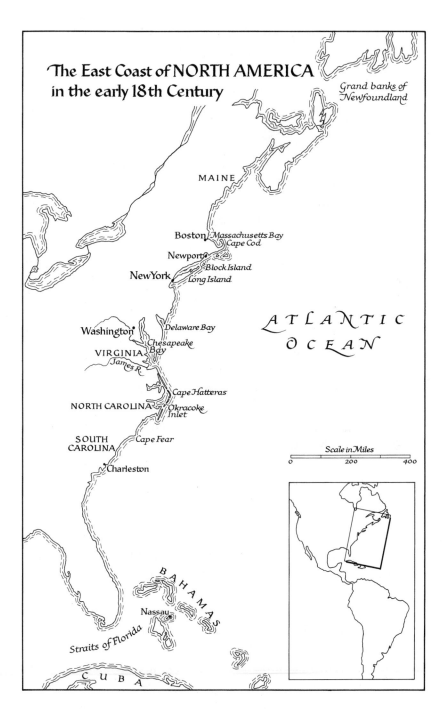

The East Coast of NORTH AMERICA
in the early 18th Century

Grand banks of
Newfoundland

MAINE

Boston   Massachusetts Bay
          Cape Cod
Newport
          Block Island
NewYork   Long Island

ATLANTIC
OCEAN

Washington   Delaware Bay
          Chesapeake
          Bay
VIRGINIA
    James R.

          Cape Hatteras
NORTH CAROLINA   Okracoke
                 Inlet

SOUTH   Cape Fear
CAROLINA

Charleston

Scale in Miles
0   200   400

BAHAMAS

Nassau

Straits of Florida

CUBA

used buckets to bail out the water. They debated whether to cut away the masts but decided against this and instead rigged preventer shrouds to secure the mainmast "and lay to upon the other tack, till the storm was over."[3] The schooner which was sailing in company with the brigantine had her mainsail split by the force of the wind and her crew had to cut away the anchors at her bows, but otherwise she came through the storm unscathed.

Charles Vane was not so fortunate. In February 1719 he was cruising in the seas to the south of Jamaica when his pirate sloop was overtaken by a violent hurricane. He was swept by the storm toward a small, uninhabited island in the Bay of Honduras. Here his sloop was driven ashore and smashed to pieces. Most of her crew were drowned. Vane survived the shipwreck but spent several weeks on the island in a miserable state. The local fishermen who visited the island to catch turtles helped him to survive, and eventually he was taken off by a ship from Jamaica commanded by Captain Holford, a former buccaneer. He was taken to Jamaica and hanged.

It was a shipwreck which ended the travels of Robert Dangerfield, a thirty-two-year-old seaman from Jamaica who was captured by pirates and forced to join them. After an eventful voyage which took them from the West Indies to Boston, across the Atlantic to the west coast of Africa, and back to North America, they found themselves off the coast of Carolina. Violent onshore winds forced them to anchor some miles to the south of the Ashley River in the hope of riding out the gale. The anchors dragged and the ship was swept ashore; "she struck and as the tide fell away and the sea growing very high was forced on a reef of sand and was forced to cut away our mainmast and seeing our condition desperate we made floats to save our lives and so got ashore having 8 white men drowned out of 44 and 7 negroes drowned. . . ."[4]

Considering the primitive state of navigation and charts in the early part of the eighteenth century it is surprising that more pirate ships were not wrecked. Any competent ship's master could determine latitude by measuring the altitude of the sun at midday with a quadrant or backstaff and making some simple calculations, but until the introduction of lunar distance tables in the 1760s, and John Harrison's invention of the marine chronometer around the same time, there was no accurate method of finding longitude at sea. This meant that a mariner could find out to within five or ten miles where he was in a north-south direction, but could not be certain where he was in an east-west direction.

There were charts, of course, but although these were beautifully drawn and gave the general shape of coastlines and the position of islands, they were often inaccurate. William Dampier, the buccaneer and explorer, reckoned that most of the charts overestimated the width of the Atlantic by as much as ten degrees: "Mr Canby particularly, who hath sailed as a Mate in a great many voyages from Cape Lopez, on the Coast of Guinea, to Barbadoes, and is much esteemed as a very sensible man, hath often told me that he constantly found the distance to be between 60 and 62 degrees; whereas 'tis laid down in 68, 69, 70 and 72 degrees, in the common draughts."[5] Ten degrees was the equivalent of six hundred nautical miles, a dangerously large error for a ship at the end of an ocean crossing.

Dampier is one of the most interesting of all the people who were involved with piracy, and his published journals are a valuable source of information about the navigational problems which faced the ocean-going seamen of his day. He was born in 1652 and was the son of a Somerset farmer. He went to sea at the age of seventeen and sailed on a merchant ship to Newfoundland, and then joined the crew of an East Indiaman bound for Java. In 1673 he joined the Royal Navy, which at this period was engaged in a long-running campaign against the Dutch. He was present at the two battles of Schooneveld on board the *Royal Prince,* the flagship of Sir Edward Spragge, but he fell ill and was invalided out of the navy. He went home to his brother in Somerset to recover his health. There he received an offer from Colonel Hellier, one of his neighbors, to go out to Jamaica to manage his plantation.

Dampier sailed from the Thames early in 1674, working his passage as a seaman on a ship commanded by Captain Kent. After a year in Jamaica, he headed for the Bay of Campeche, where he spent ten months working among the logwood cutters, an experience which is vividly described in his journals. Tiring of this heavy work in one of the most unhealthy regions of the world, he headed back to England. Before setting off on his travels again, he married Judith, a woman on the household staff of the Duchess of Arlington. His wife saw little of him during the next ten years because he was almost continuously at sea. From 1679 to 1681 he was with the buccaneers led by Captain Bartholomew Sharp, being present at the attack on Portobello and several of the other raids described in the journal of Basil Ringrose, a member of Sharp's crew. In 1683 he joined a buccaneer expedition led by Captain John Cook: they sailed from Virginia to the Guinea coast of Africa, back across the Atlantic to South America, around Cape Horn and up the coast of Chile to the Juan Fernández Islands, and then out into the Pacific to the Galápagos Islands.

By 1685 Dampier was back in the region of Panama, where he joined a group of buccaneers led by Captain Swan, who commanded a ship appropriately named the *Cygnet*. In March 1686 they set sail for the East Indies. During the course of the next two years they voyaged among the Philippines, they explored the coast of China near Macau, and they threaded their way among the Spice Islands of Indonesia to Australia, then known as New Holland. They anchored in a bay on a barren stretch of the north coast, careened their ship, and observed the native aborigines, who Dampier considered to be "the miserablest people in the world." After a stay of two months on the Australian coast, they sailed northwest, past Sumatra, to the island of Nicobar in the Indian Ocean. There Dampier and several other members of the ship's company left the buccaneers and set off on their own. He spent an eventful period making trading voyages among the Indonesian islands before heading for home. He returned to England in September 1691.

Dampier kept notes of everything he saw during his travels, and in 1697 he published a book entitled *A New Voyage Around the World*. This is remarkable not simply as a record of the exploits of some particularly enterprising buccaneers, but also for its wonderful descriptions of new lands, native peoples, and strange birds and animals. His second book, *A Voyage to New Holland,* was published in 1709, and described his ill-fated expedition to the northwest coast of Australia in command of HMS *Roebuck,* a small naval vessel of 290 tons and twelve guns. On the return passage the ship sprang a leak off Ascension Island in the Atlantic. They managed to anchor in seven fathoms, but were forced to abandon ship. Dampier and his men went ashore in a raft, leaving the ship to sink to the bottom. They were picked up several weeks later by a squadron of British warships. Dampier had to face a court-martial on his return and was declared unfit to command a King's ship. This was not the end of his travels, however. His knowledge of the South Seas was invaluable, and he was taken on as pilot by

Captain Woodes Rogers for his privateering expedition of 1708–1711. This took them around the world and, unlike any of Dampier's previous trips, resulted in the capture of some rich prizes and a handsome profit for the investors.

Dampier's writings do not have the lurid accounts of torture and murder which ensured the popularity of Exquemelin's *Buccaneers of America*, but they do provide an extraordinary insight into the perils and hardships which faced the buccaneers who ventured beyond the Caribbean. Dampier combined the curiosity of a scientist and naturalist with the keen observations of a seaman. It is little wonder that his work has been admired and consulted by generations of explorers and navigators. James Burney, who traveled with Captain Cook and rose to the rank of admiral, wrote of Dampier: "It is not easy to name another voyager or traveller who has given more useful information to the world; to whom the merchant and mariner are so much indebted; or who has communicated his information in a more unembarrassed and intelligible manner."[6]

Dampier reproduces in his books several pages from his logbooks (see Appendix IV). These show the calculations which were made to plot the daily course of his ship. A rough estimate of longitude was obtained by "dead reckoning"; this involved keeping a record of the distance sailed each day and the compass course being steered. When heading for a particular island or harbor during a lengthy sea passage, it was usual for the captain to put his ship in the correct latitude and to sail along that line until his lookout spotted the destination. In this way Dampier located the Galápagos Islands: "We steered away NW by N intending to run into the latitude of the Isles Gallapagos, and steer off West, because we did not know the certain distance, and therefore could not shape a direct course to them. When we came within 40 minutes of the Equator, we steered west. . . ."[7] The method worked well, and on May 31, 1684, they saw the islands ahead of them, "some of them appeared on our weather bow, some on our lee bow, others right ahead."

Ships' captains frequently made use of pilots with local knowledge to guide them through dangerous channels or into harbors or estuaries. This was fine in theory, but all too often the pilots proved to be useless. On the first leg of his privateering voyage around the world, Captain Woodes Rogers used a Kinsale pilot when approaching the

Irish port of Cork. It was dark and foggy, and the pilot was so incompetent that he nearly wrecked the ship. If Rogers had not prevented him, he would have guided them into the wrong bay, "which provoked me to chastise him for undertaking to pilot a ship, since he understood his business no better."[8] Dampier had a similar problem on the Gulf of Panama, where the pilots were found to be "at a loss on these less frequented coasts."[9] Fortunately there were some Spanish pilot books on board which had been taken from one of their prizes, and these proved to be reliable guides to that stretch of coast.

It was not unusual for ships' officers to make their own charts of anchorages and to draw coastal profiles to assist them in recognizing landmarks on future voyages. These were sometimes published later or were incorporated into "waggoners" or volumes of sea charts. At a period when the maritime nations of Europe were competing for overseas colonies and were challenging Spain's rule in the New World, good charts were highly valued. In July 1681 a group of buccaneers led by Captain Bartholomew Sharp seized a volume of charts from the Spanish ship *El Santo Rosario*. It proved to be of major strategic importance. An account of the capture of this volume was given by William Dick:

> In this ship, the *Rosario,* we took also a great book full of sea-charts and maps, containing a very accurate and exact description of all the ports, soundings, creeks, rivers, capes, and coasts belonging to the South Sea, and all the navigations usually performed by the Spaniards in that ocean. This, it seemeth, serveth them for an entire and completed *Wagenaer,* in those parts, and for its novelty and curiosity was presented unto His Majesty after our return to England. It has been since translated into English, as I hear, by His Majesty's order, and the copy of the translation, made by a Jew, I have seen at Wapping; but withal the printing thereof is severely prohibited, lest other nations should get into those seas and make use thereof, which is wished may be reserved only for England against its due time.[10]

William Dick was with Basil Ringrose and the buccaneers who traveled around the coast of South America from March 1679 to February 1682. The voyage was made at a time when Spain was at peace with England, so that the buccaneers' capture or destruction of twenty-five Spanish ships and their plundering of Spanish towns along the South

American coast were outright acts of piracy. When Sharp and his men returned to England, the Spanish authorities expected them to be tried and punished, but the capture of the charts was such a coup that King Charles II and his advisers refused to listen to the protests of England's traditional enemy and the pirates were given a free pardon. The copies of the Spanish charts were made by William Hack, a London chartmaker. Several of these handsome charts survive today. The copy of the chart dedicated to the King by Sharp himself is in the British Library, and there is another copy in the National Maritime Museum in London.

The journals of Dampier, Woodes Rogers, and Ringrose provide much information about the navigational methods employed by the buccaneers and privateers of the late seventeenth and early eighteenth centuries, but less is known about the navigational skills of the Anglo-American pirates who were operating in the 1720s. Presumably these pirates used similar methods, and it must be assumed that on every pirate ship there was at least one man capable of taking noonday sights and working out the latitude. The pirate captain or one of his crew must also have kept a logbook with dead-reckoning calculations. Local knowledge would have been sufficient to navigate familiar coasts, but the long sea passages which were such a feature of pirate life and the location of islands to careen and recuperate would have required accurate calculations and access to charts. Presumably charts, navigational tables, and instruments were taken from plundered ships. Henry Bostock, master of the sloop *Margaret,* which was taken by Blackbeard in December 1717, reported that as well as stealing cutlasses, and thirty-five hogs, the pirates took his books and instruments.[11] Among the archaeological finds recovered from the pirate ship *Whydah* are four brass dividers, three navigational rulers, three sounding leads, a sounding lead rope, and a ring dial which would have been used with a compass to work out the altitude of the sun when calculating latitude.

Lack of expertise in navigation could have unfortunate results. When a group of pirates led by Walter Kennedy broke away from Bartholomew Roberts' squadron and set off on their own, they discovered that they had a serious problem: "In this company there was but one that pretended to any skill in navigation, (for Kennedy could neither write nor read, he being preferred to the command merely for his courage . . .) and he proved to be a pretender only."[12] They headed for

Ireland but found themselves off the northwest coast of Scotland, tossed about by storms and with no idea where they were. They were lucky to avoid being shipwrecked and eventually found shelter in a small creek, where they abandoned their vessel and went ashore. Some of the pirates rampaged through the countryside, "drinking and roaring at such a rate that the people shut themselves up in their houses, not daring to venture out among so many mad fellows."[13] Two were murdered on the roadside and had their money stolen. Seventeen were arrested near Edinburgh and tried for piracy; nine of them were convicted and hanged. Kennedy, a former pickpocket and housebreaker, ended up in London, where he kept a brothel in Deptford Road until one of his whores accused him of robbery. He was committed to Bridewell Prison, where he was identified as a pirate by the mate of a ship he had once attacked. He was transferred to Marshalsea Prison, tried, convicted, and hanged at Execution Dock on July 19, 1721.

The cruising grounds of the pirates were largely determined by the shipping lanes in the Atlantic, the Caribbean, and the Indian Ocean. The Bahamas were much frequented by the pirates because they could intercept Spanish ships en route from Central America to Spain as they passed through the Florida Straits. The Windward Passage between Cuba and Hispaniola (now Haiti) was a favorite cruising ground because there the pirates could intercept merchant ships bound from Europe and Africa to Jamaica. Madagascar became a pirate haven because it lay in the path of ships trading with India.

But while the movement of merchant ships determined the cruising grounds, it was the weather which dictated the pace and pattern of daily life. As east coast Americans know well, the shores and harbors of New England are inhospitable places in winter. In the eighteenth century the worst winters prevented any ships from moving, sometimes for weeks on end: "Our rivers are all frozen up, so that we have no vessels arrived, nor entered and cleared this last week," reported the *Boston News Letter* in January 1712. A report from New York in the same paper noted that HMS *Lowestoft* could not sail until the ice had gone, "which may perhaps be the middle of next month."[14] In 1720 the Charles River at Boston froze so deep that men and horses could cross on the ice. This had its dangers: "On Wednesday night last we had here a flurry of snow with a gust of wind at south-east, wherein two men on horseback going over our Neck, missed their path, their horses were froze to death, the men also much froze. . . ."[15]

There was therefore a seasonal pattern to the pirates' voyages. Most of the winter months were spent in the warm waters of the Caribbean, and not till April or May did they head north. Bartholomew Roberts, for instance, attacked shipping on the Newfoundland Banks in June and July 1720, but was back in the West Indies by the winter. Blackbeard was on the coast of Virginia in October 1717 and blockading Charleston, South Carolina, in June 1718, but in the intervening winter he went south and plundered ships off St. Kitts and in the Bay of Honduras. Edward Low was cruising off Rhode Island and Newfoundland in July 1723, but by September he had headed across the Atlantic to the Azores.

There were some exceptions to this seasonal movement of pirate ships. In the summer of 1722 George Lowther attacked the ship *Amy* off the coast of South Carolina. Her captain retaliated with a broadside which killed and wounded so many of Lowther's crew that he was forced to put into a nearby inlet to recuperate. They laid up the ship and spent all winter among the woods of North Carolina. They "hunted generally in the day times, killing of black cattle, hogs, &c, for their substance, and in the night retired to their tents and huts, which they made for lodging; and sometimes when the weather grew very cold, they would stay aboard their sloop."[16]

In addition to the north-south movement there was an east-west movement of pirate ships. The west coast of Africa attracted a number of pirate crews, particularly the regions which were known as the Guinea Coast, the Gold Coast, the Ivory Coast, and the Slave Coast. As their names suggest, these places supplied ships with gold, ivory, and black African slaves. Some pirates made the additional journey around the Cape of Good Hope to the Indian Ocean and attacked ships loaded with the exotic products of India. For a short period around 1700, regular commerce was established between trading posts in Madagascar and merchants and corrupt officials in New York and other North American ports. Thomas Tew was a leading figure in this illegal trade, which came to be known as the Pirate Round. However, the practice was not typical of pirate life. Apart from the obvious desire to avoid North America in winter, and a sensible use of the trade winds when crossing the Atlantic, there was no consistency in the planning and execution of most voyages. Indeed, there was very little forward planning by any of the pirate crews. The democratic nature of the pirate community meant that a vote must be taken by the entire crew before the destination of the next voyage could be agreed on, and this inevitably led to many decisions being made on the spur of the moment. A study of the tracks of the pirate ships shows many of them zigzagging all over the place without apparent reason.

Historians in recent years have been able to provide a remarkably detailed picture of life in the Royal Navy and the merchant service by drawing on the extensive records in the Public Record Office and elsewhere. Hundreds of the logbooks of the ships of the Royal Navy have been preserved, and so have the letters of captains and admirals. The records of the Navy Board and the Lords of the Admiralty may be studied in the Public Record Office, and numerous biographies have been written about the more famous naval officers. Port records, the journals and logs of merchant sea captains, and the records of the East India Company, the Royal African Company, and organizations like the Merchant Venturers Company of Bristol have enabled historians to build up a similar picture of life in the merchant service.

There are no such archives for the pirates. We are dependent on the depositions of captured pirates and their victims, on the surviving records of pirate trials, on the reports of the colonial governors, on newspaper reports, and on a few valuable journals written by seamen who encountered pirates or were themselves buccaneers or privateers. This means that our picture of the pirates is inevitably fragmentary, and no more so than in the matter of their daily lives. The accounts of pirate life given by Exquemelin and Captain Johnson suggest an anarchic round of drinking and gambling and womanizing, interspersed with fierce raids on helpless victims. There was much of this, of course, but a closer look suggests that pirate life at sea was well organized, and similar in many respects to life on a merchant ship. This is not surprising, partly because the majority of pirates were former merchant seamen and would have adopted similar routines, and partly because ocean voyaging demanded a certain level of discipline if the crew were to survive the perils of the sea. There was the same need to establish watches, to post lookouts, to take soundings in shallow waters, and to navigate as accurately as possible. In heavy weather life would have been as wet, as cold, as physically demanding, and as dangerous as on a merchant ship. In calm weather there would have been days and sometimes weeks with little to do but mend sails and gear, carry out minor repairs, and eat and drink.

There were, however, considerable differences too. Apart from the inevitable dangers involved when attacking a ship which might fight back, the daily routine on a pirate ship was considerably easier than life on a merchantman because the crew were not driven by owners and captains to make the fastest possible passage with the biggest possible cargo, and because the pirates operated with very much larger crews. The typical crew of a merchantman of 100 tons was around twelve men.[17] A pirate ship of similar size would frequently have a crew of eighty or more. The pirates therefore had many more hands to haul on ropes, heave up the anchor, set the sails, work the pumps, load and unload provisions, man the boats, and go ashore for firewood and water.

In 1726 a book published in London and entitled *The Four Years Voyages of Capt. George Roberts* included a lengthy account of Roberts' experiences while a prisoner of the pirate Edward Low.[18] It is believed to have been written by Daniel Defoe and may be entirely fictitious, but the nautical detail is so authentic that it seems likely that it was based on interviews with former pirates or, like *Robinson Crusoe,* was based on real events. What is particularly convincing is the picture it creates of life on board a pirate ship in the early eighteenth century. It tells how Captain Roberts was taken by Edward Low and his squadron of pirate ships off the Cape Verde Islands in September 1721. Low, who could be savagely cruel to his victims, was remarkably courteous to Captain Roberts. He invited him to join him in his great cabin, where he ordered a large silver bowl of punch, some wine, and two bottles of claret. After they had drunk each other's health and talked awhile, Low ordered a hammock and bedding to be fixed up and told Roberts that he might come and go as wished and to help himself to food and drink. The weather was calm, and with the ship hove to, "no body had any thing to do, but the lookers-out, at the topmast-head; the mate of the watch, quarter-master of the watch, helmsman, &c being gone down to drink a dram, I suppose, or to smoke a pipe of tobacco, or the like."[19]

Low was on deck early in the morning and ordered the consultation signal to be made. A green silk flag with a yellow figure of a man blowing a trumpet was hoisted at the mizzen peak, and as the flag was raised, the pirates in the other ships came across in their boats. As many as could find space joined Low for breakfast in the great cabin; the rest found places in the steerage. After breakfast Low asked Roberts to remain in the cabin while the pirates went on deck to discuss what to do about Roberts and his ship. The crew were divided, and the arguments went back and forth. Low ordered the punch bowl to be filled and passed around, and the conversation turned to reminiscences of past adventures.

> In this manner they passed the time away, drinking and carousing merrily, both before and after dinner, which they eat in a very disorderly manner, more like a kennel of hounds, than like men, snatching and catching the victuals from one another; which, though it was very odious to me, it seemed one their chief diversions, and, they said, looked martial-like.[20]

After dinner the pirates returned to their ships, while Roberts sat up with Low and three or four of the crew. They drank a couple of bottles of wine and somewhat improbably talked at some length about the affairs of church and state, "as also about trade." When he had gone to bed, Roberts heard Low give the orders for the night. The ship was to lie to with her head to the northwest; they must mind the top light, and be sure to keep a good lookout, and call him if they saw anything or if any of the other ships made signals.

Captain Roberts' observations suggest a regime that was relaxed and easygoing, with an underlying sense of order provided by the need to keep watch and work the ship. If there is any truth in the account, it is little wonder that many captured seamen, accustomed to the hard labor of sailing a merchant ship with a tiny crew under a demanding captain, were willing to join the pirates.

But pirate life was not always as pleasant as Roberts' account might suggest. Roberts was able to have a civilized discussion in the captain's cabin, but his description of the uncouth behavior of the pirates at meal times is a more accurate pointer to the mood of the average pirate ship. In the tough, all-male regime of the pirate community, many of the men cultivated a macho image which was expressed in hard drinking, coarse language, threatening behavior, and casual cruelty. Philip

Ashton, who was captured by pirates in 1722, was appalled by the experience:

> I soon found that any death was preferable to being linked with such a vile crew of miscreants, to whom it was a sport to do mischief, where prodigious drinking, monstrous cursing and swearing, hideous blasphemies, and open defiance of Heaven, and contempt of hell itself, was the constant employment, unless when sleep something abated the noise and revellings.[21]

The trial of Bartholomew Roberts' crew at Cape Coast Castle reveals that many men spent most of their days incapacitated by drink.[22] According to one witness, Robert Devins was never sober or fit for any duty, and Robert Johnson was so helplessly drunk that he had to be hoisted out of the ship with the aid of a block and tackle. It was common for pirates on trial to blame their problems on drink. Before his execution in May 1724, John Archer confessed that "one wickedness that has led me as much as any, to all the rest, has been my brutish drunkenness. By strong drink I have been heated and hardened into the crimes that are now more bitter than death unto me."[23]

The problem was not confined to pirate ships; all seamen were notorious for their drinking habits. Marcus Rediker has pointed out that seamen drank for a variety of reasons: because good drink was easier to find on a ship than good victuals and fortified them against the cold and wet; because drink enabled them to forget the rigors of shipboard life for a while; and because drinking performed a valuable social function.[24] Seamen drank together to relax, to celebrate, to gossip and get to know each other. During meals they drank toasts to their wives and mistresses, to the King, to a successful voyage. The pirates were more irreverent in their toasts and drank to the devil, or to the Pretender to the British throne. Edward North, captured by Charles Vane in 1718, said that "during his continuance on board the said sloop the expressions following, viz. Curse the King and all the Higher Powers, Damn the Governor, were generally made use of by them, and other expressions at drinking was Damnation to King George."[25]

Among the hundreds of artifacts recovered from the pirate ship *Whydah* are twenty-eight lead gaming pieces. They are a reminder that gambling was almost as popular as drinking among seamen. Backgammon was a favorite occupation of officers in the Royal Navy, but all ranks of seamen, whether they were in the navy, in the merchant service, or operating as privateers or pirates, spent much of their spare time playing cards or dice, and it was common to place bets on the results. Captain Woodes Rogers found that some of his crew had gambled away most of their clothes and personal possessions during the voyage, and had to take drastic action to prevent trouble. While cruising off California in November 1703, he drew up a formal agreement which was designed "to prevent the growing evil now arising amongst us, occasioned by frequent gaming, wagering, and abetting at others gaming, so that some by chance might thus too slightly get possession of what his fellow-adventurers have dangerously and painfully earned."[26] The agreement was signed by the entire ship's company of the *Duke* and put an end to all forms of gambling and the associated notes of hand, contracts, and bills.

Exquemelin describes how the pirates led by L'Ollonais shared out 260,000 pieces of eight after raids on the coast of South America and then squandered the lot in three weeks, "having spent it all in things of little value, or at play either of cards or dice."[27] The journal of Basil Ringrose records that when the buccaneers went ashore at Antigua in 1682 at the end of their voyage, it was mutually agreed to leave the ship to those of the company who had no money left from their share of the plunder, "having lost it all at play."[28]

Music was another feature of life at sea. Singing, dancing, playing the fiddle, and even small bands and orchestras were common aboard naval vessels and merchantmen. To what extent the pirates employed music is hard to tell from the fragmentary records. The pirates' code of conduct drawn up by Bartholomew Roberts includes the following rule: "The musicians to have rest on the Sabbath Day, but the other six days and nights, none have special favour." When the *Royal Fortune,* the flagship of Bartholomew Roberts' squadron, was captured by HMS *Swallow,* there were two musicians on board. Nicholas Brattler was a fiddler who had been taken out of the *Cornwall Galley* at Calabar and compelled to join the pirates and sign their articles. In his defense at trial it was said that "the prisoner was only made use of, as music, which he dared not refuse."[29] He was acquitted by the court, as was James White, "whose business as music was upon the poop in time of action." Presumably he played the fiddle as well, although this is not made clear in the trial documents. During the cross-examination of James Barrow at the same trial it emerged that some of the pirates had killed all Barrow's chickens and then fell to drinking hard, so that by supper time they were singing "Spanish and French songs out of a Dutch Prayer Book."

As they sailed among the West Indian islands or along the coast of South America, the pirates would drop anchor in a sheltered bay or river estuary and send men ashore for wood and water. The wood was needed for the galley stove, and the water was for cooking, or for drinking if there was a shortage of beer or wine on board. Finding wood and chopping it up was usually no problem, but collecting water was not so easy. A boat or boats full of empty barrels had to be rowed ashore, and a search made for a freshwater spring or stream. The barrels were filled and then carried or rolled back to the boats, lifted aboard, and rowed out through the surf to the anchored ship. The whole exercise could take several hours or days, and in tropical climates was hot work. Often it was hard to locate sources of freshwater, particularly in the dry season in the tropics. Sometimes they found water, but it tasted bitter or was too muddy and cloudy to risk drinking.

During these trips ashore the men would catch turtles, which could be found in great numbers among the West Indian islands: "the choice of all for fine eating is the turtle or sea tortoise," wrote Francis Rogers when he visited Jamaica in 1704. "The flesh looks and eats much like choice veal, but the fat is of a green colour, very luscious and sweet; the liver is likewise green, very wholesome, searching and purging."[30] The pirates would shoot birds for the cooking pot and hunt cattle, goats, or pigs if they could be found. Sometimes they had to resort to more unusual provisions. On the coast of South America the buccaneers led by Captain Sharp were eating "Indian conies, monkeys, snakes, oysters, conchs, periwinkles, and a few small turtle, with some other sorts of good fish."[31] When no ships could be found to plunder and food was in short supply, the pirates raided coastal towns and villages.

Every few months the pirate ship had to be beached in some secluded estuary or bay so that she could be careened. This was a major operation which involved running the ship ashore, heaving her over with the aid of blocks and tackle made fast to the masts, scraping and burning off the seaweed and barnacles, caulking and replacing rotten planks, and then applying a mixture of tallow, oil, and brimstone as a form of antifouling. In the warm waters of the Caribbean and the Indian Ocean, seaweed built up rapidly on the bottom of a ship and could drastically affect her speed, and since speed was essential for the pirates to catch their victims and evade the navy, regular careening was essential. The ship's carpenter usually took charge of the whole operation. Captain Howell Davis took his pirate sloop to Coxon's Hole at the east end of Cuba: "Here they cleaned with much difficulty, for they had no carpenter in their company, a person of great use upon such exigencies."[32] In addition to careening and routine repairs to masts and spars, there could be damage from storms or encounters with uncharted reefs. The pirates faced the same problems as explorers like Captain James Cook who aimed to be entirely self-sufficient for months on end, and carried spare gear and spars as well as a team of craftsmen.

The most significant difference between pirate and other ships was the manner in which the pirate company was organized, and the code by which the pirates operated. Unlike the Royal Navy, the merchant navy, or indeed any other institutions in the seventeenth and eighteenth centuries, the pirate communities were, as already noted, democracies. A hundred years before the French Revolution, the pirate companies were run on lines in which liberty, equality, and brotherhood were the rule rather than the exception. In a pirate ship, the captain was elected by the votes of the majority of the crew and he could be deposed if the crew were not happy with his performance. The crew, and not the captain, decided the destination of each voyage and whether to attack a particular ship or to raid a coastal village. At the start of a voyage, or on the election of a new captain, a set of written articles was drawn up which every member of the ship's company was expected to sign. These articles regulated the distribution of plunder, the scale of compensation for injuries received in battle, and set out the basic rules for shipboard life and the punishments for those who broke the rules. The articles differed from ship to ship, but they all followed similar lines.

One of the earliest descriptions of the pirates' code of conduct appears in Exquemelin's *Buccaneers of America,* which was first published in 1678. Exquemelin tells how the pirates called a council on

board ship before embarking on a voyage of plunder. At this preliminary gathering it was decided where to get hold of provisions for the
voyage. When this was agreed, the pirates went out and raided some
Spanish settlement and returned to the ship with a supply of pigs
augmented by turtles and other supplies. A daily food allowance was
then worked out for the voyage; Exquemelin notes that the allowance
for the captain was no more than that for the humblest mariner.

A second council was then held to draw up the code of conduct for
the forthcoming voyage. These articles, which everyone was bound to
observe, were put in writing. Every pirate expedition, in common with
most privateering expeditions, worked on the principle of "No prey,
no pay." The first requirement of the articles was to determine exactly
how the plunder should be divided when the pirates had captured
their prey. The captain received an agreed amount for the ship, plus a
proportion of the share of the cargo, usually five or six shares. The
salary of the carpenter or shipwright who had mended and rigged
the ship was agreed at 100 or 150 pieces of eight, and the salary of the
surgeon was 200 or 250 pieces of eight. Sums were then set aside to
recompense for injuries. It is interesting to observe how this early form
of medical insurance determined the value of the different parts of a
pirate's body. The highest payment of 600 pieces of eight was awarded
for the loss of a right arm; next came the loss of a left arm at 500 pieces
of eight; the right leg was worth 500 pieces of eight, but the left leg
was only valued at 400 pieces of eight; the loss of an eye or a finger
was rewarded with a payment of 100 pieces of eight. Once these sums
had been agreed, the remainder of the plunder was divided out. The
master's mate received two shares, and the rest of the crew received
one share each. Any boys in the crew received half a share. The buccaneers were insistent that no man should receive more than his fair due,
and everyone had to make a solemn oath that he would not conceal
and steal for himself anything in a captured ship. Anyone breaking this
rule would be turned out of the company.

The application of this code of conduct can be observed in the
journal of Basil Ringrose. In July 1681 they captured the Spanish ship
San Pedro off the coast of Chile. She was laden with wine, gunpowder,
and 37,000 pieces of eight in chests and bags. "We shared our plunder
among ourselves," Ringrose noted in his journal. "Our dividend
amounted to the sum of 234 pieces-of-eight to each man."[33]

For most of the voyage the buccaneers were led by Captain Bartholomew Sharp, "a man of undaunted courage and of an excellent conduct." He was a natural leader, and was skillful at the practical and
theoretical aspects of navigation, but in January 1681, following weeks
of storms and hardships, the men become mutinous. By a majority
decision they deposed Captain Sharp and elected John Watling, a
tough seaman and a former privateer. Sharp was compelled to relin-
quish his command, and the crew signed a new set of articles with
Watling. Three weeks later Watling was killed during an attack on a
coastal fort, and Sharp was persuaded to resume his command of the
expedition.

Johnson's *General History of the Pirates* describes the similar role of
the pirate captains in the early years of the eighteenth century. As with
the earlier buccaneers, the captain had absolute power in battle and
when "fighting, chasing, or being chased," but in all other matters he
was governed by the majority wishes of the crew.[34] Although he was
given the use of the great cabin, he did not have it exclusively to
himself, but must expect other members of the company to come in
and out, to use his crockery, and to share his food and drink.

The captain's authority was further limited by the powers which
were given to the quartermaster. He too was elected by the crew, and
is described as being "a sort of civil magistrate on board a pirate
ship."[35] He was the crew's representative and "trustee for the whole."
His job was to settle minor disputes, and he had the authority to
punish with whipping or drubbing. He was expected to lead the attack
when boarding a ship, and he usually took command of captured
prizes.

The pirates had no use for the ranks of lieutenant and midshipman,
but they did elect men to do the jobs carried out by warrant officers
and petty officers on merchant ships and naval vessels. In addition to
the quartermaster, most pirate ships had a boatswain, a gunner, a
carpenter, and a cook; there was usually also a first mate and a second
mate.

Several examples of the articles drawn up by the crews of different
pirate captains have been preserved. Those adopted by the men led by
Bartholomew Roberts are the most comprehensive, and are worth
quoting in full because they provide a revealing slant on the pirate's

way of life. These are taken from Captain Johnson's *General History of the Pirates*,[36] and the passages in italics are Johnson's comments:

I. Every man has a vote in affairs of moment; has equal title to the fresh provisions, or strong liquors, at any time seized, and may use them at pleasure, unless a scarcity *(no uncommon thing among them)* makes it necessary, for the good of all, to vote a retrenchment.

II. Every man to be called fairly in turn, by list, on board of prizes because, (over and above their proper share) they were on these occasions allowed a shift of clothes: but if they defrauded the company to the value of a dollar in plate, jewels, or money, marooning was their punishment. *This was a barbarous custom of putting the offender on shore, on some desolate or uninhabited cape or island, with a gun, a few shot, a bottle of water, and a bottle of powder, to subsist with or starve.* If the robbery was only betwixt one another, they contented themselves with slitting the ears and nose of him that was guilty, and set him on shore, not in an uninhabited place, but somewhere, where he was sure to encounter hardships.

III. No person to game at cards or dice for money.

IV. The lights and candles to be put out at eight o'clock at night: if any of the crew, after that hour still remained inclined for drinking, they were to do it on the open deck; *which Roberts believed would give a check to their debauches, for he was a sober man himself, but found at length, that all his endeavours to put an end to this debauch proved ineffectual.*

V. To keep their piece, pistols, and cutlass clean and fit for service. *In this they were extravagantly nice, endeavouring to outdo one another in the beauty and richness of their arms, giving sometimes at an auction (at the mast) £30 or £40 a pair for pistols. These were slung in time of service, with different coloured ribbands over their shoulders in a way peculiar to these fellows, in which they took great delight.*

VI. No boy or woman to be allowed amongst them. If any man were to be found seducing any of the latter sex, and carried her to sea, disguised, he was to suffer death; *so that when any fell into their hands, as it chanced in the Onslow, they put a sentinel immediately over her to prevent ill consequences from so dangerous an instrument of division and quarrel; but then here lies the roguery; they contend who shall be sentinel, which happens generally to one of the greatest bullies, who, to secure the lady's virtue, will let none lie with her but himself.*

VII. To desert the ship or their quarters in battle, was punished with death or marooning.

VIII. No striking one another on board, but every man's quarrels to be ended on shore, at sword and pistol. *The quarter-master of the ship, when the parties will not come to any reconciliation, accompanies them on shore with what assistance he thinks proper, and turns the disputant back to back, at so many paces distance; at the word of command, they turn and fire immediately, (or else the piece is knocked out of their hands). If both miss, they come to their cutlasses, and then he is declared victor who draws the first blood.*

IX. No man to talk of breaking up their way of living, till each had shared £1,000. If in order to this, any man should lose a limb, or become a cripple in their service, he was to have 800 dollars, out of the public stock, and for lesser hurts, proportionately.

X. The captain and quartermaster to receive two shares of a prize: the master, boatswain, and gunner, one share and a half, and other officers one and a quarter.

XI. The musicians to have rest on the Sabbath Day, but the other six days and nights, none without special favour.

There is no mention in this code, or indeed in the codes drawn up by other pirate companies, of homosexuality. Since it is hard to believe that the pirates were ever prudish about such matters, we must assume either that homosexuality was never an issue among them, or that it was so widely practiced and tolerated that it was not necessary to include it in any code of conduct.

Until recently the image of the pirate as a lusty womanizer was so powerful that any suggestion that pirates might be gay was unthinkable. However, the macho image was seriously dented by a book published in 1983 with the arresting title *Sodomy and the Pirate Tradition,* and the subtitle *English Sea Rovers in the Seventeenth-Century Carib-*

bean. However, it covers a considerably wider canvas, being a sweeping survey of attitudes to homosexuality in the sixteenth and seventeenth centuries in Britain and her overseas colonies. Written by B. R. Burg, professor of history at Arizona State University, the book examines court cases, county records, newspaper reports, Restoration plays, Pepys' diaries, accounts of voyages, and an impressive array of works on social history, the West Indies, and piracy. The resulting picture of sexual activity in England and the West Indies among all classes from aristocrats to beggars and vagabonds is remarkable for its graphic detail and illuminating examples.

Less convincing are Professor Burg's examination of homosexual activity among seamen and the parallels he draws with recent studies of homosexuality among all-male prison populations. He draws attention to the unequal proportion of men and women on the Caribbean islands: in 1661 the ratio of white men to white women on Jamaica was six to one; on Barbados in 1673 there were 9,274 white men to 3,800 white women; there was a similar ratio of two white men to every white woman on Nevis, Antigua, and Montserrat during the same decade. Burg suggests that this led to men resorting to homosexual practices. He comes to the same conclusions regarding the communities of hunters and buccaneers on the island of Hispaniola, and the all-male crews of pirate ships:

> If freedom from social and behavioral constraints increased sexual activity for buccaneers as it apparently does for convicts, then the West Indian sea rovers surely made the most of their liberty. . . . They gloried in the freedom or licence they enjoyed as buccaneers, and, if research on modern convicts does in fact provide clues to pirate behaviour, it seems likely enough that their joy in exercising their wills was not confined only to the non-sexual phases of their lives. Life experiences of buccaneers before they sailed under the pirate flag may also have acted to increase incidence and frequency of homosexual acts.[37]

It is an interesting theory and there may be some truth in it, but there is little evidence to prove things one way or the other. Exquemelin's *Buccaneers of America* has numerous examples of the buccaneers "giving themselves to all manner of debauchery with strumpets and wine," but nothing to back up Burg's thesis. The journal of Basil

Ringrose is equally devoid of information on the subject, and so is
Captain Johnson's *General History of the Pirates*. Where Burg is on
firmer ground is in the possibility of sexual relations between the
captains of ships and their young servants and cabin boys. The nature
of command inevitably isolated the captain from his men and from the
easy fraternization with whores which most sailors indulged in whenever their vessel was in port, and there is evidence to show that some
captains attempted sexual relations with young members of their crew.
Among the papers of the High Court of Admiralty there is a case that
was heard before a judge in chambers involving a fourteen-year-old
boy, Richard Mandervell. While his ship was at anchor in Oporto in
1722 the captain, Samuel Norman, ordered the boy to bring a pail of
water and to wash him. The captain then "had the carnal use of him &
was then guilty of the crime commonly called buggery or sodomy &
he twice afterwards used the Informant in the same way whilst the said
ship lay in the river of Oporto." [38]

Homosexuality was a frequent practice among the thousands of
Chinese pirates who cruised the South China coast in the early years
of the nineteenth century. Professor Dian Murray, who has made a
detailed study of the Chinese pirates based on research in the archives
in Taiwan and Beijing, has found fifty documented cases among the
testimonials of men tried for piracy between 1796 and 1800 [39] When
pirate gangs needed new recruits, it was not unusual to take captives
and force them to join the pirate community by means of sexual assaults. The pirate leader Ya-tsung initiated three male captives into
piracy by sodomizing them, and several other pirate leaders made
catamites of handsome boys. As Murray points out, it is difficult to
know to what extent homosexuality was willingly practiced between
the participants, and to what extent it was forced on captives by pirate
leaders.

Life in an all-male community did not necessarily lead to widespread
homosexual activity. In *The Wooden World,* his masterly study of the
Georgian Navy, Nicholas Rodger concludes that the vast majority of
the young seamen were "of vigorously heterosexual inclination." [40]
Senior officers make no mention in their correspondence of homosexuality being a problem, and everything suggests that it was not a major
issue. During the course of the Seven Years War (1756–63) there
were only eleven courts-martial for sodomy. Four of the cases led to

acquittals, and the remaining seven convictions were on the lesser charges of indecency. Professor Burg's arguments concerning gay pirates are ingenious, but it seems likely that the percentage of pirates who were actively homosexual was similar to that in the Royal Navy, and reflected the proportion of homosexuals in the population at large.

6

into Action
Under the
Pirate Flag

THE *Princes Galley* was nearing the end of a voyage which had taken her from London to the west coast of Africa. There she had picked up black slaves and set her course across the Atlantic to the southeastern corner of the Caribbean. On September 14, 1723, she was approaching the island of Barbados when her crew were alarmed to discover that a vessel was heading their way with a black flag flying at her masthead. As she drew closer, they saw that she was a sloop armed with eight guns on her main deck and ten swivel guns mounted along the rails. There were between thirty and forty pirates on board.[1]

John Wickstead, the forty-five-year-old captain of the *Princes Galley*, decided that his ship was no match for the pirates. He set more sail and endeavored to escape, but the heavily laden merchant ship was unable to throw off the pirate sloop, which gained on her steadily and began firing her guns. At eight o'clock in the evening the pirates came alongside and the chase was over. Captain Wickstead was ordered to send a boat across. The merchant ship's longboat was hoisted over the side and rowed across to the pirate ship. Several pirates jumped into the boat and were ferried back to the *Princes Galley*.

The next twenty-four hours were a nightmare for Wickstead and his crew. John Crawford, the ship's surgeon, who was twenty-five, and the second mate, Goldsmith Blowers, twenty-four, were held down while lighted fuses were put between their fingers to force them to reveal the whereabouts of the gold. The pirates were soon in possession of more than fifty-four ounces of gold, and proceeded to ransack the ship. They seized the gunpowder, pistols, the gunner's stores and bosun's stores. They removed two quarterdeck guns and two swivel guns and sent them across to the pirate sloop. Eleven black slaves valued at £500 were brought up from the hold and taken by the pirates.

Two seamen with specialist skills were forced to join the pirate crew: they were William Gibbons, the surgeon's mate, and James Sedgwick, the carpenter's mate. Two other members of the merchant ship's crew, Robert Corp and Henry Wynn, decided to join the pirates of their own accord. When they were later tried for piracy, a witness told the Admiralty Court that he "saw the said Henry Wynn voluntarily sign a paper which the said pirates called their Articles of Regulation."[2]

Having stripped the *Princes Galley* of everything of value, the pirates, who were led by George Lowther, sailed away. Captain Wickstead was left to make his way to Barbados with the remnants of his crew.

A similar attack had taken place three years earlier in the cold, gray waters of the North Atlantic. The merchant ship *Samuel* had left the port of London on May 29, 1720, bound for Boston with a cargo of ironware, forty-five barrels of gunpowder, and an assortment of English goods in bales and trunks. She had a crew of ten men to work the ship, and carried several passengers. She was commanded by Captain Samuel Cary, who was later able to provide a detailed account of the incident.[3]

On July 13 the *Samuel* was forty miles east of the banks of Newfoundland when two ships hove in sight. Captain Cary watched their approach with increasing concern, and his worst fears were confirmed when the two ships fired their guns and hoisted pirate flags. The larger vessel was a three-masted ship of about 220 tons and was armed with twenty-six guns. From her main topmast head she flew a black flag on which a skull and a cutlass were clearly visible. The smaller vessel was an 80-ton sloop of ten guns flying a Union flag emblazoned with four blazing balls. Captain Cary reckoned that there were about one hundred men on board each of the vessels, which meant that he and his crew were outnumbered by twenty to one. The *Samuel* had only six guns mounted on carriages, so she was completely outgunned as well.

The pirates hailed the *Samuel* and ordered her captain to hoist out his boat and come on board the pirate ship. Captain Cary did as he was told and learned that the pirates were commanded by the formidable Welshman Bartholomew Roberts. For the past month Roberts had been cruising the coast of North America, leaving behind him a trail of destruction. In one harbor alone he had plundered and burned no less than seventeen vessels.

The pirates swarmed on board the *Samuel* and began taking the ship apart. They tore open the hatches and attacked the cargo like madmen, cutting open bales, trunks, and boxes with their boarding axes and cutlasses. Some of the goods they carried off to their ship, but much of the cargo they hacked to pieces and threw overboard. They took two of the mounted guns and all the spare rigging and stores, but they threw the anchor cables over the side. They carried off forty barrels of gunpowder and commandeered the ship's boat. All this was done "with incessant cursing and swearing, more like fiends than men."[4] Captain Cary was told that the pirates had no intention of accepting the King's Pardon, and if they should ever be overpowered, they would set fire to the gunpowder with a pistol, "and go all merrily to Hell together."

When they had finished looting the *Samuel*, the pirates turned their attention to the crew. All except one Irishman and the captain were forced at pistol point to leave the ship and join the pirates. The pirates were debating whether to sink or burn the merchant ship when they spotted another ship on the horizon and abandoned the *Samuel* in order to give chase. Captain Cary was left with one seaman and three passengers. With their assistance he sailed to Boston and reported the attack to Joseph Hiller, the public notary.

These two attacks are typical of dozens of raids which took place in the Caribbean and North American waters in the early eighteenth century. The two incidents have a number of features in common: in the first place, the victims did not attempt to resist the pirates; in the second place, the pirates did not disguise their hostile intentions during their approach. It was not uncommon for pirates to catch their victims off guard by using the flags of a friendly nation, but in the majority of cases the pirates flew a version of the piratical black flag

This fearsome image of pirates raising the black flag
was painted by N. C. Wyeth, who was commissioned to illustrate
the 1911 edition of Stevenson's *Treasure Island*. Wyeth was a pupil
of Howard Pyle, and the pirate illustrations of both artists
are notable for their realism and attention to detail.

A map created by Stevenson for the frontispiece of *Treasure Island*.
It has been the main inspiration for the popular myth of the treasure map
with "X" marking the spot where pirates buried their loot.

Portrait of Robert Louis Stevenson at the age of thirty-seven.
It was painted by W. B. Richmond in 1887, when the author had
already established his reputation through books such as *Treasure Island,*
Dr. Jekyll and Mr. Hyde, and *Kidnapped.*

The Sea Cook, one of a series of pictures
of British seamen painted by Thomas
Rowlandson in 1780. It was common
practice in the Royal Navy for cooks to
be disabled seamen, and no doubt
Stevenson was aware of this when
he created the character of Long
John Silver, a former cook who lost
a leg during a battle at sea.

Henry Morgan and his men after the raid on Portobello in 1668.
Illustration by Howard Pyle for *Harper's Monthly Magazine*, 1888.

Portrait of Henry Morgan
from an early edition of
Exquemelin's *The Buccaneers
of America*.

Mary Read, pirate, former soldier, and adventurer, was saved from the gallows by her pregnancy, but she later died of fever in a Jamaican prison shortly after her trial. Engraving from an edition of Johnson's *General History of the Pirates*.

Anne Bonny became the lover of Calico Jack and was tried for piracy in Spanish Town, Jamaica. A witness at the trial said that Anne had a gun in her hand during an attack on his ship, and that she and Mary Read "were both profligate, cursing and swearing much, and very ready and willing to do anything on board." Engraving from an edition of Johnson's *General History of the Pirates*.

Captain Woodes Rogers and his family,
painted by William Hogarth in 1729. After an eventful career
as a privateer, Rogers was appointed Governor of the Bahamas.
He was responsible for driving the pirates out of Nassau and
restoring order to the colony.

Portrait by Thomas Murray of the privateer and
explorer William Dampier, who worked among the notorious
logwood cutters of Campeche and sailed with buccaneers on
several plundering expeditions. During one of his voyages he was
on the ship that called at the Juan Fernández islands and
picked up Alexander Selkirk, the castaway on whom
Defoe's Robinson Crusoe was modeled.

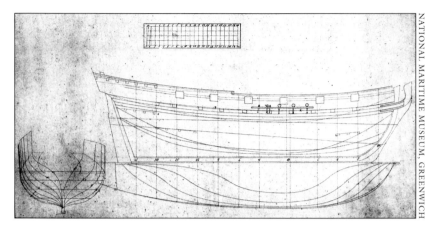

Plans of the British sloop HMS *Ferret*, built at Deptford in 1711.
She had a crew of one hundred, and was armed with ten or twelve mounted
guns and four swivel guns. Many of the pirate sloops operating in the
West Indies and off the east coast of America in the early eighteenth century
would have been similar in size and appearance.

A British naval sloop of twelve guns anchored off Boston lighthouse,
from an engraving by William Burgis dated 1729. This shows the rig of the
sloops operating in American waters in the early eighteenth century.

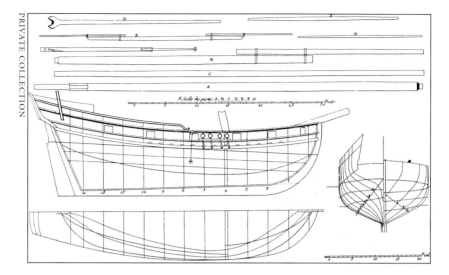

Plans of a Bermuda sloop, from *Architectura Navalis Mercatoria,*
the treatise on ships and shipbuilding published by the great naval
architect F. H. Chapman in 1768. The vessel shown here was 65 feet long
and 21 feet wide and carried ten four-pounder guns on deck and twelve
swivel guns. Sloops built in Bermuda and Jamaica were renowned for their
speed and were much in demand by traders, privateers, and pirates.

The English ship *Charles Galley,* from a painting by Willem van der Velde
the Younger dated 1677. The *Charles Galley* (thirty-two guns) was built
in 1676 and underwent a rebuild at Deptford in 1693. Captain Kidd's ship,
the *Adventure Galley* (thirty-two guns), was built at Deptford in 1695
and was very similar in appearance. Both vessels had oarports so they
could be rowed in calms.

Walking the plank, from an engraving by Howard Pyle.
Examples of pirates making people walk the plank are rare, and it is
probable that Barrie's play *Peter Pan* and powerful images such as this
book illustration have been responsible for the popular association of
pirates with this particular method of victim disposal.

Errol Flynn in the 1940 production of *The Sea Hawk*. Flynn played the part of Captain Thorpe, a dashing privateer commander whose adventures in the service of Queen Elizabeth I were loosely based on those of Drake and Hawkins. The film was directed by Michael Curtiz, who also directed Errol Flynn in several other swashbuckling epics such as *Captain Blood* and *The Adventures of Robin Hood*.

Douglas Fairbanks, Sr., in the title role of *The Black Pirate*, a silent film made by United Artists in 1926. In this action-packed yarn, Fairbanks swings through the rigging, captures a vast Spanish galleon single-handedly, fights several duels, and walks the plank.

Blackbeard's Last Fight, by Howard Pyle, 1895. This small oil painting gives a vivid impression of the scene on the deck of Lieutenant Maynard's sloop as British sailors close in on the embattled figure of Blackbeard, who can be glimpsed beneath the raised cutlass in the center of the picture. Again, the almost photographic realism is typical of Pyle's work.

LEFT: Captain Teach, alias Blackbeard, in theatrical pose. Engraving from one of the many editions of Johnson's *General History of the Pirates*. RIGHT: Blackbeard the Pirate Chief. The celebrated pirate captain is again shown with lighted fuses under his hat, "which appearing on each side of his face, his eyes naturally looking fierce and wild, made him altogether such a figure that imagination cannot form an idea of a fury, from Hell, to look more frightful."

LEFT: Mr. Helme playing the part of the pirate captain in the popular melodrama *Blackbeard, or The Captive Princess*, first performed on the London stage in 1798. RIGHT: Robert Newton as Blackbeard and Linda Darnell as his adopted daughter in the 1952 film *Blackbeard the Pirate*, directed by Raoul Walsh.

A pirate on the scaffold at Execution Dock on the banks of the Thames in London, from an engraving by Robert Dodd. On the left, on horseback, is the marshall holding the silver Admiralty oar. The prison chaplain stands beside the condemned man on the scaffold. The church of St. Mary, Rotherhithe, can be seen in the background.

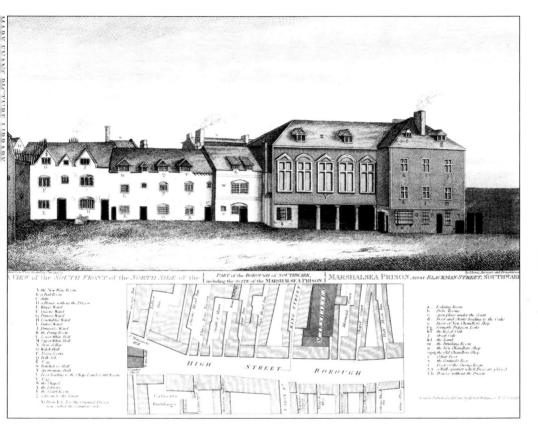

A view of the Marshalsea Prison in Southwark, 1773.
Apart from Captain Kidd, who was imprisoned in Newgate gaol,
all pirates brought to trial in London were confined here.

Captain Kidd in chains. After being hanged at Execution Dock, the body of Kidd was fitted into iron hoops and chains and suspended from a gibbet at Tilbury Point on the lower reaches of the Thames estuary. The artist has taken some liberties with the scene and includes the masthouse at Blackwall in the background: this was a prominent Thames landmark but would not have been visible from Tilbury.

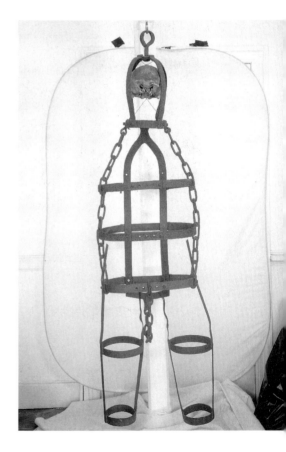

An early-eighteenth-century set of chains from the town of Rye in Sussex. It was usual practice in Britain and her overseas colonies to display the bodies of notorious pirates near the entrance to a port, as a warning to seamen.

from the masthead and bore down on the victim with their guns firing. Having forced the victim to heave to, the pirates would not immediately come alongside and board the merchant ship; it was common practice to demand that the captain of the merchant ship launch a boat and come across to the pirate ship. No doubt the purpose of this was to find out what the ship was carrying, and then to hold the captain hostage while the pirates looted his ship.

Another common feature of the attacks was that the pirates took their time over looting the ships. It is often said that the essence of a pirate attack was to hit and run. This was certainly a feature of attacks by the Barbary pirates in the Mediterranean, and it is a characteristic of most of today's pirate attacks in Indonesian waters, when the pirates may be on board the victim's ship for no more than nine or ten minutes. However, this was not the case in the West Indies during the great age of piracy. According to Captain Cary, the pirates spent forty-eight hours plundering the *Samuel*, and the pirates who attacked the *Princes Galley* were also in no hurry.

The pirates had every reason to take their time. Most attacks took place out of sight of land, and in the days before the invention of radio there was no way the victims could call for help. Even when the attack took place in or near a harbor and the alarm was raised, the chances of getting help were remote. In the year 1715, for instance, there were only four naval warships and two naval sloops to patrol the entire Caribbean Sea—an area which extended more than two thousand miles from east to west and fifteen hundred miles from north to south, and included several hundred islands.[5] Consequently the pirates had a field day. There is a note of despair in the report sent to London from the Governor of Jamaica, Sir Nicholas Lawes, in June 1718: "It is with great concern that I must still acquaint your Lordships of the daily complaints I receive of piracies and robberies committed in these parts, insomuch that there is hardly one ship or vessel, coming in or going out of this island that is not plundered."[6] The Governor and Council of South Carolina echoed his views and requested "that a ship of war be sent to our assistance and protection, without which our trade must be inevitably ruined."[7]

Another common feature of pirate attacks was that much of the loot which was stolen consisted of ship's gear and what might be termed "household goods." This is a point which does not come across in pirate stories of fiction. The single objective of Long John Silver and his cronies was treasure. Real pirates were certainly interested in treasure, which was the motivating force behind most pirate raids, but they also needed food and drink as well as ropes and sails for their ships. Unlike the merchant ships on which they preyed, they were not able to go into harbor and overhaul their ships in a dockyard; nor did they have ready access to ships' chandlers and sailmakers. Repairs had to be carried out at sea or in a secluded bay or river estuary far from civilization, and they were therefore ruthless in stripping their prizes of essential equipment. When the snow *Restoration* was attacked in August 1717, the pirates took all the goods and provisions on board as well as "sails, pump-bolts, log-lines, needles, twine, kettle, frying pan."[8] The sloop *Content,* which was taken near Barbados in October 1723, was looted of "fourteen boxes of candles, and two boxes of soap, together with a flying-jib, flying-jib-boom, flying-jib-halliards, main halliards, anchor and cable and several carpenters tools."[9]

The two attacks described at the beginning of this chapter do differ in one important respect, and that is in the size of the force brought to bear on the victims. In the case of the *Samuel,* the pirates attacked in two heavily armed ships manned by a total of two hundred men, while the *Princes Galley* was taken by a single pirate ship with a crew estimated at between thirty and forty men. A study of seventy-six attacks which took place between 1715 and 1720 in American and West Indian waters shows that fifty-three of the incidents involved a single pirate ship; in nineteen incidents there were two pirate vessels involved; and in four cases there were three or more vessels involved.[10] In other words, in the great majority of attacks (72 percent) a single pirate ship was a sufficient threat to persuade the captain of a merchant ship to surrender.

It is perhaps not surprising to find that pirate captains who restricted their attacking force to a single ship rarely captured merchant ships of any great size. In 1719 Edward England rampaged down the west African coast in the *Royal James* and took more than a dozen ships; the largest of these was the *Bentworth* of Bristol, with twelve guns and thirty men. Most of them were small four- to six-gun merchant ships with crews of fourteen to eighteen men. John Rackam (Calico Jack) caused considerable alarm at one time in the West Indies, but his targets were relatively small vessels. In 1720, for instance, he entered

Providence Roads and took a twelve-ton sloop armed with four mounted guns on deck and two swivel guns. A year later he was plundering shipping along the coast of Jamaica, where he took three merchant sloops, a schooner, and seven fishing boats (these would have been open canoes of the type still used by Jamaican fishermen).[11]

While most victims of attacks by single pirate ships were small merchantmen, there was one conspicuous exception. In March 1717 Sam Bellamy was cruising the Windward Passage between Cuba and Hispaniola (Haiti) in the sloop *Sultana,* of fourteen guns, when a large merchant ship hove in sight. She was the slave ship *Whydah,* heading back to England after a voyage which had taken her from London to Africa for slaves and ivory, and then across the Atlantic to Jamaica.[12] Bellamy chased her for three days and finally caught up with her near Long Island in the Bahamas. Apart from firing two chase guns, the *Whydah* offered no resistance and was soon in the hands of the pirates. Bellamy and his men found themselves in possession of one of the richest hauls ever made by pirates: her cargo included ivory, indigo, sugar, Jesuits' bark (*cinchona,* used for making quinine), and gold and silver later valued at between £20,000 and £30,000. Bellamy had no hesitation in taking over the *Whydah* for his own use. With the addition of ten guns from the *Sultana,* he became the captain of a twenty-eight-gun ship which could have taken on any merchant ship trading in the Caribbean.

The most successful pirate captains in the early eighteenth century were those who carried out their attacks with two or more vessels; they acquired the largest ships for their own use and they notched up the highest score of victims. Bartholomew Roberts heads the list. He is reputed to have taken four hundred vessels during his piratical career, and this figure seems to be borne out by reports from colonial governors, by newspaper accounts, and by the depositions of his victims. Roberts, also known as Black Bart, was a remarkable pirate captain. He comes across as a stern, disciplined man with a natural flair for leadership and the ability to make bold decisions. His most successful raid took place on the coast of Brazil, and for sheer audacity can be compared with Drake's attack on Cádiz and Morgan's raid on Portobello.

Roberts was cruising along the South American coast when his ship caught up with a fleet of forty-two Portuguese merchantmen off the Bay of Los Todos Santos. The merchantmen were waiting to be joined by two warships before setting off in convoy to Lisbon. Roberts coolly came alongside one of the ships and threatened to kill her crew if they made any signal of distress. Her captain was ordered to come aboard the pirate ship, where he was interrogated by Roberts.

Having discovered that the richest ship in the fleet was a powerful vessel of forty guns and a crew of 150 men, Roberts immediately headed toward her. He took with him as his prisoner the Portuguese captain, and forced him to hail the intended victim and to invite her captain on board Roberts' ship. The captain of the big merchant ship became suspicious and began clearing his ship for action. Roberts immediately fired a broadside at her, came alongside, flung out grappling hooks, and boarded her. After a brisk fight she surrendered. Meanwhile the other ships were desperately firing warning guns to attract the attention of the anchored warships. By the time they had set sail, though, Roberts had made off with his prize, which proved to be a major haul: 90,000 gold moidores, a cross set with diamonds which was intended for the King of Portugal, chains and jewels of considerable value, and a cargo of sugar, skins, and tobacco.

It is curious that Bartholomew Roberts has never acquired the fame of Blackbeard or Captain Kidd, because he was infinitely more successful than either of them, and was a considerably more attractive figure. He was tall and dark, "of good natural parts and personal bravery," and adopted a magisterial air.[13] He dressed in some style, and was apparently fond of music. Unlike the vast majority of his fellow pirates, he abstained from heavy drinking, and he discouraged gambling on his ships. He was born near Haverfordwest in the southwest corner of Wales around 1682. He joined the merchant navy and eventually became second mate of the ship *Princess of London*. In November 1719 the *Princess*, under the command of Captain Plumb, set sail for the west coast of Africa to collect a cargo of slaves for the West Indies. On her arrival at Anaboe on the Guinea coast, the *Princess* was captured by pirates led by another Welshman, Howell Davis. A few weeks later Davis was killed and Roberts was elected as pirate captain in his place; in a remarkably short time he had impressed an unruly bunch of men with his abilities as a seaman and navigator, and was chosen above several other candidates for the post. Captain Johnson tells us that Roberts accepted the post, "saying that since he had dipped his hands in muddy water, and must be a pirate, it was better being a commander than a common man."

Not only was Robert a natural leader, but he also proved to be absolutely ruthless. His attacks were swift and savage, and he had no qualms about resorting to torture and murder to achieve his ends. During the course of the next three years he caused havoc among the merchant shipping on both sides of the Atlantic. In 1721, at the height of his career, Roberts commanded a squadron of four vessels. His flagship was the *Royal Fortune* of forty-two guns, a former French warship. His consorts were the thirty-gun brigantine *Sea King*, the French ship *Ranger*, and a small ship of sixteen guns which was used "as a store ship, to clean by." The total number of men under his command at this time was 508.[14]

Blackbeard was another pirate captain who operated with a squadron of three and sometimes four ships. In May 1718 the Governor of Bermuda reported that the pirates at sea in the area of New Providence included "one Tatch [Blackbeard] with whom is Major Bonnett of Barbados in a ship of 36 guns and 300 men, also in company with them a sloop of 12 guns and 115 men and two other ships."[15] Blackbeard's flagship at this period was nearly as formidable as that of Bartholomew Roberts: she was a French Guineaman of thirty-six guns which Blackbeard had converted to a forty-gun warship, the equivalent of one of the Royal Navy's fifth-rates (see page 165).

The most successful season in the career of Captain Vane was in 1718, when he was operating with two ships under his command: a brigantine of twelve guns and a large sloop of eight guns commanded by Captain Yeats. In October of that year, he captured eight ships on the coast of South Carolina, including a Guineaman from which he took ninety blacks.

During the same period William Moody was cruising the Caribbean in the ship *Rising Sun* accompanied by a brigantine of eight guns commanded by Captain Frowd, and a sloop of eight guns. Writing from St. Christophers, where he had gone on a tour of inspection, Governor Hamilton reported that "they have taken, stranded, and burnt several vessels between this island and Santa Cruix."[16] It was Moody's attacks which prompted Hamilton to demand that the authorities in England send out a forty-gun warship to protect the islands.

There are many other examples of pirates cruising together: Kentish and Edwards, Pyme and Sprigg, Napin and Nichols. In his analysis of the Anglo-American pirates, Marcus Rediker has traced the numerous connections among the pirate crews. He has calculated that more than 70 percent of the pirates active between 1716 and 1726 fitted into two groups, with interconnections within each group: one group stemmed from Captain Hornigold and the much-frequented pirate rendezvous in the Bahamas; a second group developed from the chance meeting of the crews of George Lowther and Edward Low in 1722. Rediker makes the point that these connections ensured a social uniformity and a consciousness of kind among the pirates.[17]

The exchanges of information at these meetings of pirates helps to explain the similarity in their rules of conduct and articles of association. It accounts for the comparatively rapid adoption of the piratical black flag among a group of men operating across thousands of miles of ocean, and it led to a form of teamwork which, however fragile and liable to fragmentation, could produce squadrons of pirates which were considerably more formidable than pirate crews operating on their own.

While the majority of attacks were made by pirates in sailing ships, there was another method which was sometimes used, and that was to attack in open boats. When the Royal Navy made a boat attack, they invariably used the launches and longboats which they carried on deck, but the pirates and buccaneers operating in the West Indies preferred to use canoes stolen from local fishermen. These canoes were dugouts carved from tree trunks and fell into two categories. The larger and heavier canoe, called in Spanish *piragua,* which was variously corrupted to "perigua" and "perianger," could carry up to twenty-five men and was either rowed or fitted with a single sail. The smaller version of the dugout was simply referred to as a canoe and could carry five or six people. There is a precise description of one of these in Basil Ringrose's journal: "Here in the gulf it went very hard with us whensoever any wave dashed against the sides of our canoe, for it was nearly twenty-three feet in length and yet not quite one-foot-and-a-half in breadth where it was the broadest, so that we had only just room to sit down in her."[18]

The attack in open boats was a favorite tactic of the buccaneers of the late seventeenth century. Sir Henry Morgan used canoes in his devastating raids on Spanish coastal settlements, of which his attack on Portobello (see pages 44 to 48) was the most spectacular example.[19] Morgan selected canoes for the final approach along the coast because they were much harder to detect from the shore than a fleet of sailing ships. But in the journal of Basil Ringrose there is a remarkable incident when the buccaneers used canoes not simply as ferries but as fighting machines with which to attack a squadron of three Spanish warships within sight of Panama. The buccaneers approached the anchorage from the sea on April 23, 1680. There were sixty-eight of them spread between five canoes and two heavy *piraguas*. The warships had been warned of their presence in the area, and as soon as they spotted them, they weighed anchor and got under way. The buccaneers were exhausted by hours of paddling, but they succeeded in getting to windward of the ships.

From their vulnerable and unstable canoes, the buccaneers began firing their long-barreled muskets with devastating accuracy. With the first volley they killed several men on the decks of the nearest ship as she swept past them. The flagship of the admiral of the squadron was the next to suffer the buccaneers' onslaught. They succeeded in killing the man at the helm, which resulted in the ship swinging into the wind with her sails aback. The buccaneers came up under the stern of the vessel, keeping up a continuous fire with lethal effect as they did so. Every seaman who attempted to take over the helm was killed, and the mainsheet and brace (the ropes controlling the mainsail) were shot away.

The third ship hastened to the admiral's aid but was intercepted by one of the canoes and hotly engaged. When the first ship came about and attempted to assist, the buccaneers killed so many of her crew that there were hardly enough men left alive to work the ship. The buccaneers further disabled the flagship by wedging her rudder. With the admiral, the chief pilot, and two thirds of the crew killed, the survivors on the flagship surrendered. Two explosions on one of the other ships enabled the buccaneers to take her also. The third ship fled.

Ringrose went on board the two captured ships to see what condition they were in. The combined effect of the explosions and the shooting on the first ship was appalling: ". . . such a miserable sight I never saw in my life, for not one man there was found but was either killed, desperately wounded, or horribly burnt with powder, insomuch that their black skins were turned white in several places, the powder having torn it from their flesh and bones."[20] On the admiral's ship there were only twenty-five men alive out of a complement of eighty-six: "Their blood ran down the decks in whole streams, scarce one place in the ship was found that was free from blood."[21]

Boat attacks were rarely used by the early-eighteenth-century pirates, but they were occasionally reported. In April 1713 Lieutenant Governor Pulleine of Bermuda wrote that the islands had become "a retreat for three sets of pirates, who committed their depredations in open boats, with about five and twenty men in a boat."[22] Twelve years later the sloop *Snapper* of New Providence, commanded by Thomas Petty, was sailing in the same waters. The weather was calm, and as he was approaching Ragged Island in the Bahamas, he was attacked by Spanish pirates who rowed alongside his vessel in a *piragua*. They were led by Captain Augustin Blanco, who captured the sloop and took it to a nearby island, where they landed and robbed a local family. A similar incident was reported in the *Boston Gazette* of November 1, 1725, which noted that the sloop *Dove* of Boston was attacked by a "pirate periangar of 22 men of several nations commanded by St. Jago Dedwanies."

The pirates always had the advantage when approaching a victim. They could follow a ship for hours or days at a safe distance while they worked out her potential strength in terms of guns and crew. If she proved to be a powerful Indiaman or a man-of-war, the pirates would veer away and seek a weaker victim. If the vessel appeared vulnerable, the pirates had a choice: they could take her by surprise, or they could make a frontal attack.

The simplest method of catching a victim off guard was to use false flags, a *ruse de guerre* which naval ships frequently adopted in time of war. Before the advent of radio or Morse code signaling, the only way that a sailing ship out at sea could identify the nationality of another vessel was by her flags. By 1700 the design of national flags was well established, and an experienced seaman was able to identify the ships of all the seafaring nations by the colors flying at their mastheads or ensign staffs.

Pirates had flags of their own, which were red or black and emblazoned with skulls and other symbols, but they also collected a variety of other flags. When they wished to hide their identity, they simply flew an appropriate national flag. It is interesting to note that British pirates had no qualms about flying the Union flag or the St. George's flag, and frequently did so. In October 1723 Walter Moor, commander of the sloop *Eagle*, discovered Lowther's pirate ship on the beach of the deserted island of Blanco, where he had gone to careen after attacking the *Princes Galley*. Moor had to hoist his own colors and fire a gun at the pirate sloop "to oblige her to show her colours, and she answered with hoisting a Saint George's flag at the topmast head."[23] Sam Bellamy flew the King's ensign and pennant from the masts of the *Whydah* when attacking the Irish pink *Mary Anne*. When Bartholomew Roberts was hunted down by HMS *Swallow* in 1721, he was ready for all comers with "an English ensign jack and Dutch pennant and ye black flag hoisted at the mizen peak."[24]

On a previous occasion Roberts deliberately deceived the shipping off Martinique by flying Dutch flags and making the signals normally used by Dutch ships arriving from the Guinea coast with black slaves. The ruse enabled him to capture fourteen French sloops which came out to meet him with large sums of money on board for trading slaves. In March 1723 Captain Low performed the classic procedure with false flags when he encountered a Spanish merchant ship in the Bay of Honduras: the pirates "hoisted up Spanish colours, and continued them till they drew near the sloop, then they hauled them down, hoisted their black flag, fired a broadside and boarded her."[25]

For more than two centuries a black flag with a white skull and crossbones emblazoned on it has been the symbol for pirates throughout the Western world. In this form it appears in all the pirate stories from Walter Scott to Robert Louis Stevenson, and the artists took their lead from the writers. The masterful pictures in Howard Pyle's *Book of Pirates* and N. C. Wyeth's illustrations to the 1911 edition of *Treasure Island* no doubt helped to fix the image in people's minds, and it was constantly reinforced by its use on the stage and screen. W. S. Gilbert's stage directions in *The Pirates of Penzance* instruct the pirate king to unfold a black flag with the skull and crossbones as he sings the verse which begins, "Oh better far to live and die/Under the brave black flag I fly." The 1926 silent film *The Black Pirate* with Douglas Fairbanks, Sr., begins and ends with a shot of the traditional pirate flag billowing in the wind. Almost every pirate film has used the same motif to a greater or lesser extent.

It is therefore surprising to discover that the skull and crossbones device was only one of many symbols originally associated with piracy. In the great age of piracy in the early eighteenth century a variety of images appear on pirate flags, including bleeding hearts, blazing balls, hourglasses, spears, cutlasses, and whole skeletons. Red or "bloody" flags are mentioned as often as black flags until the middle of the eighteenth century.

What all the pirate flags had in common (and this applied to the Barbary pirates as much as the Anglo-American pirates) was their need to strike terror in the minds of the merchant seamen who were their victims. Often the devices on the flags formed what Marcus Rediker has described as a "triad of interlocking symbols—death, violence, limited time," to underline the message that the pirates expected immediate surrender or the consequences would be fatal.

There has been some debate about the earliest use of recognizable flags by pirates. A skull, or what was more commonly referred to as a "death's-head," with crossed bones underneath it, has been an accepted symbol for death since medieval times. It frequently appears on tombs in churches and cathedrals, and on gravestones in country churchyards, sometimes giving rise to the mistaken belief that the occupant of the grave must have been a pirate. Ship's captains sometimes used the symbol in their logbooks when recording the deaths of members of the crew. At some time between 1700 and 1720 it was adopted by a number of pirates as a menacing symbol, often in conjunction with an hourglass or weapons. During the height of the pirate era individual pirate captains created their own versions of the flag. Bartholomew Roberts ordered his men to produce a flag showing his own figure standing on two skulls representing a Barbadian's head and a Martinican's head; this was to indicate his rage at the attempts of the authorities in those islands to capture him. Calico Jack had a death's-head above crossed cutlasses.

By 1730 the skull and crossbones on a black flag seem to have edged out the other symbols and been adopted by English, French, and Spanish pirates operating in the West Indies. Before that date, however, there are examples of plain red or plain black flags being used according to a generally understood color symbolism: black for death and red for battle. Although Francis Drake usually flew the English flag of St. George on his ships, it is recorded that when he raided

Cartagena in 1585 he was "flying black banners and streamers, menacing war to the death." Basil Ringrose's account of his voyage with the buccaneers led by Captain Bartholomew Sharp includes an incident in January 1681. The buccaneers, in their captured prize the *Trinidad,* encountered three Spanish warships off the islands of Juan Fernández. "As soon as they saw us, they instantly put out their bloody flags, and we, to show them that we were not as yet daunted, did the same with ours."

There was an alternative meaning to the plain red and black flags. A French flag book of 1721 includes hand-colored engravings of pirate flags, including a black flag with various insignia, and a plain red flag alongside a red pennant. Under the red flags is written *"Pavillon nomme Sansquartier"* ("Flag called No Quarter"). The idea that a red flag could mean no quarter is confirmed by Captain Richard Hawkins, who was captured by pirates in 1724. He later described how "they all came on deck and hoisted Jolly Roger (for so they call their black ensign, in the middle of which is a large white skeleton with a dart in one hand, striking a bleeding heart, and in the other an hourglass). When they fight under Jolly Roger, they give quarter, which they do not when they fight under the red or bloody flag."

There is no mention of black pirate flags or death's-heads in Exquemelin's classic work *The Buccaneers of America.* On the few occasions when any mention is made of flags at sea, the English buccaneers are recorded as sailing under English colors, and this includes Sir Henry Morgan, who, in spite of his reputation as a pirate, always regarded himself as an English privateer. There is, however, an interesting passage in Basil Ringrose's journal which describes the flags used by the crews of the various ships when they marched on the town of Santa María in April 1680. There were some three hundred buccaneers, and they must have made a colorful sight as they headed inland:

> First, Captain Bartholomew Sharp with his company had a red flag, with a bunch of white and green ribbons. The second division, led by Captain Richard Sawkins with his men, had a red flag striped with yellow. The third and fourth, led by Captain Peter Harris, had two green flags, his company being divided into several divisions. The fifth and sixth, led by Captain John Coxon . . . made two divisions and had each of them a red flag. The seventh was led by Captain

Edmund Cook, with red colours striped with yellow, with a hand and sword for his device. All or most of them were armed with fuzee, pistol, and hangar.

It is notable that most of the flags were red or red with stripes. The hand and sword device used by Edmund Cook later appears on the pirate flags of Thomas Tew and Christopher Moody, and is among several symbols shown on an eighteenth-century illustration of the Barbary corsairs' flag.

The Anglo-American pirates followed in the wake of the buccaneers of the West Indies, and it is among them that the black flag with its symbols of death became established. One of the earliest accounts is a reference in the trial of Captain John Quelch, who was executed with his pirate crew at Boston in 1702: "Three months later the pirates were off the coast of Brazil flying as a flag the Old Roger which was ornamented by an anatomy with an hourglass in one hand, and a dart in the heart with three drops of blood proceeding from it in the other." This is one of the earliest mentions of the term "Old Roger," which later became the Jolly Roger. There are differing theories about the origins of the term. One theory is that it was an anglicized version of *"Jolie rouge,"* used to describe the red or bloody flag. Another theory suggests that it came from Ali Raja, the name of a Tamil pirate captain who operated in the Indian Ocean. A third and perhaps more convincing theory is that it was derived from the nickname for the devil, which was "Old Roger."

In the year 1717 there are a number of detailed references to the flags flown by pirates operating in the West Indies and along the American coast. A report in the *Boston News Letter* of August 12, 1717, describes how Captain Nathaniel Brooker in the snow *Restoration* was attacked by two pirate sloops while en route from London to Boston. One of the sloops was commanded by Captain Napin, "who had in his flag a Deaths Head and an hour glass"; the other vessel was commanded by Captain Nichols, "who had in his flag a dart and a bleeding heart." During the trial of the pirates from Sam Bellamy's crew, reference is made to the confession of Thomas Baker, who was examined on May 6, 1717. Baker said that Bellamy's men "spread a large black flag, with a death's head and bones across and gave chase to Captain Prince under the same colours." A description of a similar image but in black on a white ground appears on the flyleaf of a well-worn edition of Jeremy Taylor's *Holy Living and Holy Dying*. The handwritten inscription reads: "Septr. 28th: 1717 at 8 in the morning in ye Lat. of 32'8' about 160 Leag: west from Madaira we were attacked by a French Pyratt with Death's head in black in ye middle of a white ensign, and by the Providence of God were delivered."

From this date onward we find constant references to piratical flags. Most of them are black with white symbols, but red flags continue. When Blackbeard's squadron attacked the *Protestant Caesar* in the Bay of Honduras in 1718, two of the pirate ships flew black flags with death's-heads and three ships flew red flags. Since fiction has so often proved more effective than fact in establishing pirate images, it is worth noting that Defoe included two descriptions of pirate flags in *Captain Singleton,* published in 1720, the year after *Robinson Crusoe.* Before going into action in the Indian Ocean, the pirates hoist a black flag with two cross daggers, and on another occasion they fly "the black flag or ancient at the poop and the bloody flag at the topmasthead."

So confident were they of overcoming their victims that pirates usually had no need to use false flags or other deceptions when they made their attacks. Their confidence was based on the knowledge that they were superior in firepower and in numbers of men, and on the terrifying reputation which they had acquired, and indeed cultivated. Few merchant seamen had any experience of battle, and being attacked by a pirate ship was like being attacked by a naval warship—with the added threat of torture and death for any survivors. Some pirates added to the terror of their first approach by hurling lethal missiles at their victim. In December 1718 Governor Lawes of Jamaica sent out two sloops to capture a pirate ship commanded by Captain Thompson, who had had the nerve to take a merchant ship within sight of Port Royal harbor. The first sloop to reach the pirates was shocked into submission when the pirates "threw vast numbers of powder flasks, granado shells, and stinkpots into her which killed and wounded several and made others jump overboard."[26] The second sloop was so demoralized by the attack that she fled back to harbor.

"Granado shells" (also called grenadoes) were an early form of hand grenade and were in common use by 1700. The name was derived from the Spanish word *granada,* meaning "pomegranate." They were also called "powder flasks." The grenades used by the pirates were hollow balls weighing about two ounces. They were made of iron or wood and filled with gunpowder. They had a touch hole and a fuse which was lit before the grenade was thrown among the seamen on the deck of the merchant ship. The resulting explosion was designed to cause death and injury, and could totally demoralize a crew with no experience of battle. It is interesting to note that fifteen grenades have been excavated from the wreck of the pirate ship *Whydah*.

Equally frightening but more devastating in its effect was the broadside. This was rarely used by pirates because they did not want to damage a potential prize, but they had no hesitation in firing a broadside if they needed to blast a victim into submission. Captain John Frost was chased for twelve hours by a pirate ship in July 1717. It was nine o'clock in the evening when the pirates drew alongside. The pirate ship, which was commanded by the Frenchman Captain La Bouse, had twenty guns and a crew of 170. She fired a broadside of "double round and partridges, and a volley of small shot,"[27] which meant that each of the ten guns on one side of the ship was loaded with two round cannonballs and a bag of partridge shot. This would have been a lethal combination at close range, and it was accompanied by a volley of fire from the muskets and pistols. The bombardment beat the men off the deck and so shattered the hull, rigging, and sails of Frost's ship that he surrendered without a fight.

Pirates did not appreciate a brave resistance from a merchant ship, but expected and demanded instant surrender. On February 15, 1718, Captain Robert Leonard was in latitude 23° in the vicinity of the Bahamas and heading northwest when a ship approached and fired two shots over his vessel. Captain Leonard hove to and was commanded to come on board the pirate ship at once, or they would fire a broadside into his vessel. When he reached the deck of the pirate ship, Captain Leonard was beaten with a cutlass by Edward England, the pirate captain, "for not bringing to at the first shot."[28]

If a merchant ship surrendered without a fight, the pirates usually refrained from inflicting violence on the crew. Indeed, some pirates were almost gentlemanly in their behavior. Captain Stone, who was taken by a pirate called Jennings, reported that he was treated civilly and told that the pirates did not hurt Englishmen. They restricted their looting to twenty gallons of rum, for which they paid him handsomely.

Thomas Knight was a member of the ship *Mountserrat Merchant,*
which encountered three ships off the island of Nevis on November
29, 1717. Not realizing that they were pirates, Knight and three other
seamen rowed across in the ship's longboat to inquire whether they
had any letters (it was common practice in the days of sail for ships in
foreign waters to pass on letters and news of events back home). As
they came alongside, they saw that one of the ships had a flag at her
stern with the death's-head on it. The pirates commanded them to
come aboard, and when they reluctantly did so, the first words of the
pirates were "You are welcome on board." They were then invited to
eat, but refused. The pirates did not take kindly to this, however, and
before they would let them go, they interrogated them on the number
of guns in the forts in the area.[29]

In the great majority of cases merchant ships surrendered without a
fight when attacked by pirates. However, there were a few occasions
when a courageous captain with a loyal crew fought back. In 1710 a
small galley from Liverpool was attacked by a French privateer when
she was a day out from Antigua. The captain of the galley covered his
decks with broken bottles, and when the privateer came up, he fired
his chase guns at him in such a way that "he made a lane fore and aft
on the Frenchman's decks."[30] The privateer kept going and managed
to board the galley, but the combined effect of the broken bottles and
the volley of fire from the defenders forced the pirates to flee the deck
of the galley and abandon the attack.

A particularly violent episode was described by John Philmore of
Ipswich, who was captured by a pirate schooner at Newfoundland in
August 1723.[31] The pirate schooner was under the command of John
Phillips with a small crew which included John Nut, the master, and
James Sparks, the gunner. After taking and looting several ships in
Newfoundland, the pirates sailed south to the West Indies. Some miles
north of Tobago they captured the sloop of Andrew Harradine. The
captured men decided to overcome the pirates and agreed to make
their move at midday. The carpenter brought up his tools and laid
them out on deck on pretense of working with them. At the given
moment the carpenter got hold of Nut, master of the pirates, who was
walking on deck, and threw him overboard. Harradine took up the
carpenter's adze and struck down another pirate with a blow to his

head. John Philmore struck a further victim "with the broad axe as he was cleaning his arms and killed him at the first stroke." Sparks, the gunner, was killed and thrown overboard, and the fight was over.

In the attack on the *Princes Galley* described at the beginning of this chapter, it was noted that the pirates forced two men, a carpenter's mate and a surgeon's mate, to join them. The capture and forcible detention of skilled men was a regular feature of pirate attacks. The pirates had no difficulty in recruiting ordinary seamen to their ranks, but they also needed men with specialist skills. Of these the most in demand were the carpenters and coopers. In a naval warship the carpenter was one of the most valued men on board. He had usually served as an apprentice in a shipyard and was a qualified shipwright. He was responsible for the maintenance of all the wooden parts of the ship, which included most of the structure from the keel to the masts and spars. Since the strains on a ship in heavy weather were considerable, the carpenter was constantly busy, but he really came into his own during and after a battle, when he and his mate would be called on to patch up holes in the hull, repair damaged gear, and replace broken spars. On a pirate ship in the Caribbean with no access to shipyards, the carpenter was even more crucial. The intense heat, alternating with tropical downpours, caused seams to open and wood to rot. As well as the growth of seaweed and barnacles, the warm water encouraged attacks from the teredo worm, making regular careening vital to the security of the ship.

The cooper was less essential for the safety of the ship but was a key figure in the provision of victuals for the crew. Apart from the live animals and chickens, virtually all the food and drink in a sailing ship in the seventeenth and eighteenth centuries was stored in barrels. A cross section through a merchant ship or a warship would show most of the lower part of the vessel filled with barrels of various sizes; there were barrels for beef, biscuit, water, beer, wine, and spirits. The cooper made the barrels and repaired them and played an important part in provisioning the ship.

So when the pirates took a ship, they were on the lookout for these skilled craftsmen. When the snow *Barbados Merchant* was taken by the pirate Farrington Spriggs in October 1724, "they forced John Bibby the mate, John Jones the carpenter, and Richard Fleet the cooper."[32] James Blois, the carpenter of the ship *Wade Frigate,* was inevitably picked out by the French pirates who attacked his ship in February 1718. When interviewed later, he reported that "the said pirates forced and detained him this deponent on board their vessel as carpenter for about six months."[33] When Blackbeard took the sloop *Margaret* in December 1717, only two men were forced to join the pirates; one of them was Edward Latter, a cooper.

The most dramatic account of the pirates' need for such skilled men appears in the *Boston Gazette* for November 29, 1725. The sloop *Fancy* was en route from Boston to the West Indies when she was approached by a pirate sloop called the *Sea Nymph* commanded by Philip Lyne. On seeing her black flag and realizing she was a pirate, Ebenezer Mower "shewed more concern than any of us, crying and saying he was sure they would force him because he was a cooper." Mower was a Boston man, thirty years of age, "of short stature, thin favoured, and dark complexion," and he had good reason to be worried. No sooner had the pirates taken the ship than they decided to force Mower to join them. The methods which they used left him with little choice:

> One of the pirates struck Mower many blows on his head with the helve of an axe, whereby his head was much bruised and bloodied, after which the same pirate forced him said Mower to lay his head down on the coamings of the hatch, and lifting the axe over his head swore that if he did not sign their Articles immediately, he would chop his head off, the said Mower begging hard for his life. After this the same pirate carried said Mower into the Round House where they continued a short time, and said Mower coming out told the declarant and other prisoners that he was ruined and undone, for they forced him to sign their Articles.

There is no record of what happened to Mower. One hopes he did not meet the same fate as Richard Luntly, a carpenter who was captured by the pirate Howell Davis when his ship was on the Guinea coast of Africa. After many adventures, Luntly found himself among the crew of pirates led by Bartholomew Roberts, "and we that were forced men were compelled by the force of arms to do things that our conscience thought to be unlawful."[34] One night he and the other forced men were planning to take the ship and head for the West Indies when they were overheard by one of the pirates. They were reported to Roberts and his quartermaster, "and immediately all hands were called up to know what they should do with us, some of them was for shooting us, others not, and so they consented to put us away upon a desolate island." Rescued from the island by a ship bound for Britain, poor Luntly was hauled before an Admiralty Court in Scotland and condemned to death for piracy. He was hanged on the shore at Leith on January 11, 1721.

7

TORTURE, VIOLENCE, AND MAROONING

O N NOVEMBER 3, 1724, a savage act of mutiny took place on board a ship called the *George Galley* while she was en route from Santa Cruz in the Canary Islands to the Strait of Gibraltar. At ten o'clock at night, seven members of the crew launched a bloodthirsty attack. The surgeon, the chief mate, and the clerk were set upon while they slept and had their throats cut. Captain Oliver Ferneau, an elderly man with a reputation for being mean and peevish, was up on deck. Two of the mutineers seized him and attempted to throw him overboard, but he put up a fight and escaped from their clutches. He found himself confronted by another mutineer holding a knife which was red with blood from the butchery carried out below. The captain was slashed in the throat, recaptured, and as he struggled, he was shot at close range with a pistol. While he lay dying, the other three victims managed to crawl up onto the deck, bleeding profusely from their wounds. Daniel McCawley, the clerk, asked the mutineers to let him live long enough to say his prayers. "Damn you," he was told, "this is no time to pray." He was shot dead along with the other wounded men. The four bodies were heaved over the side.

The leader of the mutiny was John Gow, alias John Smith, a thirty-five-year-old Scotsman.[1] He was an experienced seaman and had served on men-of-war as well as merchant ships. He had joined the

George Galley at Rotterdam a few months before and been appointed second mate and gunner. He had selected the twenty-gun merchant ship with the deliberate intention of inciting a mutiny and taking over command of the vessel.

Following the murder of Captain Ferneau and his officers, Gow and his accomplices forced the rest of the crew to turn pirate. The ship was renamed the *Revenge,* and they set off on a voyage of plunder. They took several merchantmen off the coasts of Spain and Portugal, and then held a council to decide whether to head for the West Indies, the Guinea coast, or Scotland. Gow had been born near Thurso on the northeast coast of Scotland, but had moved with his father to Stromness on the mainland of Orkney. He knew that the great natural harbor of Scapa Flow in the Orkneys would provide shelter during the winter gales, as well as deserted beaches where they could safely careen their ship. He therefore persuaded the crew to head for Scotland, and told them that they would pretend to be honest merchantmen driven north by the weather.

They arrived in the Orkney Islands toward the end of January 1725 and anchored "under the lee of a small island at some distance from Cariston." Gow went ashore to visit a young woman he had been courting before he had gone to sea. She was evidently impressed that he was now the captain of a ship, and agreed to marry him. But then everything began to go wrong. A young member of Gow's crew gave the pirate ringleaders the slip, hired a horse, and rode to Kirkwall, the capital town of the Orkneys, where he warned the magistrates that there was a pirate ship in the vicinity. Twelve other members of the crew escaped in the ship's longboat and made their way to the Scottish mainland, where they too alerted the authorities. Although he knew the alarm had been raised, Gow sent his men to plunder the house of the local sheriff before weighing anchor and sailing to the small island of Cava. There they abducted three women. According to one account, the women were "kept on board some time, and used so inhumanly, that when they set them on shore again, they were not able to go or to stand; and we hear that one of them died on the beach where they left them."[2]

Gow then headed for another island where he intended to plunder the house of Mr. Fea, a wealthy landowner he had known as a boy.

However, his ship got into difficulties in the swift current which swept through Calf Sound and the pirates were forced to appeal to Fea for assistance. On February 14 the wind got up and the pirate ship was blown ashore on Calf Island. Gow tried to bargain with Fea but was outwitted, and he and all the remaining pirates were arrested. The Admiralty ordered a warship to be sent to Scotland to pick up the pirates and bring them to London for trial. The ship selected was HMS *Greyhound,* commanded by Captain Solgard, which three years before had captured Low's pirates off Long Island. Solgard described his voyage north as a cold and troublesome cruise, but by March 25 he was back in the Thames with thirty prisoners on board and the pirate ship anchored alongside.

The prisoners were transferred to Marshalsea Prison to await trial. Gow refused to plead and was therefore subjected to having his thumbs bound together and squeezed with whipcord. Although the executioner and another officer pulled the cord until it broke, Gow still refused to cooperate. He was taken to Newgate Prison to await torture and death in the Press Yard. The thought of the slow, agonizing death by the gradual buildup of weights on his prone body was too much for Gow, and he agreed to plead not guilty. The trial was held at the Old Bailey before Sir Henry Penrice, Judge of the Admiralty. Gow was charged with murder and piracy. Together with nine members of his crew he was found guilty and sentenced to death. After the execution, the bodies of Gow and Williams, his lieutenant, were ordered to be hanged in chains, "the one over-against Greenwich, the other over-against Deptford."[3]

Apart from his decision to head for Scotland rather than the Caribbean or the African coast, John Gow was typical of many of the pirates of the great age of piracy. He was a former seaman, he was a relatively young man, and his career as a pirate was short and involved extreme violence both on his part and on the part of the authorities. His story was reported in some detail in the English newspapers of the day, and attracted the attention of two of Britain's greatest writers. In 1725 Daniel Defoe wrote a pamphlet which was published by John Applebee under the title *An Account of the Conduct and Proceedings of the late John Gow, alias Smith, Captain of the late Pirates, executed for Murther and Piracy committed on board the George Galley.* This was a racy description which closely followed the facts reported in the newspapers and at the trial, and included additional material which Defoe had gathered about Gow and his accomplices.

A century later Sir Walter Scott used Gow's story as the basis for a full-length historical novel which he entitled *The Pirate*.[4] In 1814 Scott had visited some of the relevant locations in the Orkneys with Robert Stevenson, lighthouse engineer and grandfather of Robert Louis Stevenson. Scott traveled as a guest of the Lighthouse Commissioners and was able to put his observations to good use in his book, which has extended descriptions of wild and mysterious Orkney landscapes and seascapes. Gow's part is played in the book by Captain Cleveland, a considerably more attractive character than Gow himself appears to have been. The novel is full of local legends of mermaids and monsters and has an unusually rich cast of eccentric characters. Scott seized on Gow's reported courtship of a local girl to create a complex plot which centers on the two beautiful daughters of Magnus Troil, a rich Zetlander of noble ancestry. It is the high-minded and imaginative Minna who falls in love with Captain Cleveland, the pirate, while her cheerful and more down-to-earth sister ends up with Mordaunt, the gallant hero of the story.

Scott created an adventure story full of drama and romance which no doubt pleased his thousands of devoted readers, but like so many writers before and since, he played down the atrocities committed by the pirates. Captain Cleveland is a tragic figure who, like Byron's corsair, is attractive to women and admired by his crew—a far cry from the brutal men who terrorized the seamen and passengers of merchant ships in their quest for plunder. The real world of the pirates was often closer to some of today's horror movies than anything which appeared in contemporary books or plays. The depositions of two seamen who were attacked by pirates led by Charles Vane provide a vivid glimpse of the type of violence which was common among the pirates of the Caribbean.

In May 1718 Nathaniel Catling came ashore in Bermuda and went to see Governor Bennett. He told the Governor that he was one of the crew of the Bermuda sloop *Diamond*. On April 14 they were sailing off Rum Key in the Bahamas when they were intercepted by the pirate ship *Ranger* commanded by Captain Vane. The pirates beat up the captain and all the crew of the *Diamond*, and looted the vessel of a black man and 300 pieces of eight. Nathaniel Catling was singled out and hanged by the neck until they thought he was dead. When they let him down on the deck, he was seen to revive, whereupon one of the pirates hacked him across the collarbone with his cutlass and would have continued until he had murdered him had not one of the other pirates persuaded him it "was too great a cruelty."[5] The pirates' final act was to set fire to the *Diamond*.

Five days after Catling had made his report, Edward North, the commander of the Bermuda sloop *William and Martha*, came to see Governor Bennett with a similar story.[6] He said that his ship had been attacked by Vane off Rum Key within three hours of the attack on the *Diamond*. The pirates had boarded his vessel, violently beaten him and his crew, then dragged one of the seamen to the bows, bound him hand and foot, and tied him to the bowsprit. As he lay there helpless on his back, the pirates put burning matches to his eyes and the muzzle of a loaded pistol in his mouth, "thereby to oblige him to confess what money was on board." In this instance they did not set fire to the ship, but Captain North reported that while they were on board, the pirates were continually cursing the King and the higher powers, and swearing damnation on the Governor.

Although some of the pirate violence reported by colonial governors was the work of sadists and men looking for kicks to relieve the boredom of their existence, this was not always the case. Many pirate crews only resorted to torture and murder to achieve specific ends. Violence was most commonly used to enable the pirates to find out as quickly as possible where the captain, the crew, and any passengers on board had hidden their valuables; it was also used deliberately to create a terrifying image. As word spread of pirate atrocities, it was hoped that future victims would surrender without a fight. Another motive behind many of the reported cruelties was revenge. Pirates were quick to avenge any attempt to curb their activities, and many atrocities were revenge attacks on islands or the ships of nations which had imprisoned or hanged pirates in the recent past. According to the account of Edward North, the violence used by Charles Vane in the two attacks in the Bahamas described above was because a certain Thomas Brown had been detained for some time in the Bahamas on suspicion of piracy. Bartholomew Roberts was merciless in his treatment of seamen from Martinique or Barbados because the governors of those islands had made various attempts to capture him. In 1721 he raided shipping off Martinique and captured their crews. According to the report sent to London on February 18, 1721, "Some they almost whipped to death, others had their ears cut off, others they fixed to the yard arms and fired at them as a mark."[7] In 1721 Roberts endeavored to board a Dutch ship anchored at St. Lucia. The crew tried to prevent the attack by running out booms and fenders, and then opened fire. For nearly four hours they fought off the pirates and killed a great number of them. When the Dutch ship was at length overpowered, the pirates were ruthless in revenging the death of their comrades, and slaughtered any men they found alive.[8]

Ships' captains who hid or refused to reveal the whereabouts of valuables could expect no mercy. One captain was told by the crew of Edward England that if he concealed his money, they would immediately sink his vessel and throw him overboard with a double-headed shot about his neck. The captain decided not to risk the consequences.[9] Another captain made the mistake of upsetting Edward Low, a sadist whose cruelties became a byword in the Caribbean. Here is Governor Hart writing to the Council of Trade and Plantations in London from St. Kitts on March 25, 1724. He describes how Low "took a Portuguese ship bound home from Brazil; the Master of which had hung eleven thousand moydores of gold in a bag out of the cabin window, and as soon as he was taken by the said Low, cut the rope and let them drop into the sea; for which Low cut off the said Master's lips and broiled them before his face, and afterwards murdered the whole crew being thirty two persons."[10] Governor Hart obtained this information and other details of Low's atrocities from Nicholas Lewis, who was quartermaster to Low and was one of sixteen pirates captured and brought before an Admiralty Court presided over by Hart. Fourteen of the pirates were condemned to death and hanged.

There is no mention of walking the plank in any of the accounts covering the great age of piracy in the seventeenth and early eighteenth centuries, and most writers on piracy have dismissed the practice as a myth created and made popular by works of fiction. However, one example of walking the plank has come to light. *The Times* of July 23, 1829, contains a report of a pirate attack in the Caribbean.[11] The Dutch brig *Vhan Fredericka*, of 200 tons, sailed from Jamaica on April 12 bound for Haarlem in the Netherlands. She was in the Leeward

Passage, two days from Cuba, when she was intercepted by a schooner. She endeavored to escape but was overtaken by the schooner, which hoisted Buenos Aires colors, fired a gun, and forced her to heave to. Thirty pirates boarded the *Vhan Fredericka* and proceeded to loot her. The Dutchmen protested, "but were laughed at by the ruffians, who proceeded deliberately to compel the wretched men to what is termed 'walk the plank.' " The men were pinioned and blindfolded and had shot fastened to their feet before being forced into the sea. One passenger escaped because he revealed the whereabouts of the gold, and was later put ashore at Cuba by the pirates. It is possible that other examples of walking the plank may be found, but the fact remains that it was never the common pirate punishment suggested by so many books, films, and comic strips.

Most of the Anglo-American pirates used forms of torture which were in common use among the buccaneers of the late seventeenth century. Some of these were described by Exquemelin:

> Among other tortures then used, one was to stretch their limbs with cords, and at the same time beat them with sticks and other instruments. Others had burning matches placed betwixt their fingers, which were thus burnt alive. Others had slender cords or matches twisted about their heads, till their eyes burst out of the skull.[12]

The latter method was called "woolding," after the word used to describe the binding of cords around a mast. It was a favorite pirate torture because it was fast and effective and only required the use of a short length of rope or cord. Some buccaneer tortures were more elaborate. Although Henry Morgan always maintained that he treated prisoners, and especially ladies, with respect, the reports from the Spanish side suggest otherwise. The citizens of Portobello suffered numerous cruelties after the capture of the town in 1668. Don Pedro Ladrón de Guevara maintained that the female prisoners were maltreated and oppressed and some were "burned in parts that for decency he will not refer to."[13] Another report describes the horrible fate of one of these prisoners: "A woman there was by some set bare upon a baking stove and roasted, because she did not confess of money which she had only in their conceit. This he heard some declare boasting, and one that was sick confess with sorrow."[14] A shipowner from Cartagena described how the buccaneers tortured Doña Agustín de Rojas, the leading lady of Portobello. She was stripped naked and forced to stand in an empty wine barrel. The barrel was then filled with gunpowder, and one of the buccaneers held a lighted fuse to her face and demanded to know where she had hidden her treasure.[15]

One of the most ingenious and revolting displays of cruelty was that devised by Montbars of Languedoc. He would cut open the stomach of his victim, extract one end of his guts, nail it to a post and then force the wretched man to dance to his death by beating his backside with a burning log. Exquemelin describes the prolonged torture of a Portuguese by Morgan's men after the taking of Gibraltar. Four stakes were set into the ground, and the man was suspended between them by cords attached to his thumbs and big toes:

> Then they thrashed upon the cords with great sticks and all their strength, so that the body of this miserable man was ready to perish at every stroke, under the severity of those horrible pains. Not satisfied as yet with this cruel torture, they took a stone which weighed above 200 pound, and laid it upon his belly, as if they intended to press him to death. At which time they also kindled palm leaves, and applied the flame unto the face of this unfortunate Portuguese, burning with them the whole skin, beard and hair.[16]

The buccaneers then untied the cords binding him to the stakes and took him into a nearby church, where they lashed him to a pillar and let him starve for a few days. Eventually the man, who protested that he was only a poor tavern keeper, managed to raise the sum of 1,000 pieces of eight and was set free, "although so horribly maimed in his body that 'tis scarce to be believed he could survive many weeks after."

While the catalog of pirate cruelties is endless, it needs to be put into perspective. Pirates were not the only people guilty of violence and atrocities. Life for the common sailor in the merchant navy could be a living hell if he found himself on board a ship run by a captain who took a delight in bullying his men. In his book *Between the Devil and the Deep Blue Sea*, Marcus Rediker has set down a devastating list of cruelties perpetrated by merchant sea captains during the early years of the eighteenth century. There was the case of Captain Haskins, commander of the *Laventon Galley*, who attacked John Phillips while he was asleep. He punched him several times and then gave him a dozen blows with a marlinspike. Phillips began to have convulsions, but he was forced up on deck and told to go aloft. In cold, driving rain and dressed only in his shirt and breeches, he was ordered to loose the fore topgallant sail. This was the highest of the three sails on the foremast, and was about 120 feet above the swaying deck. Handling the heavy, sodden canvas alone was a dangerous enough operation for a man in good condition, but Phillips was dazed and bleeding heavily from his wounds. He had another fit while he was clinging to the sail. Several members of the crew wanted to go to his assistance, but Captain Haskins swore that he would shoot anyone who attempted to help him. Phillips managed to complete the task and survived.[17]

Richard Baker, a seaman on the ship *Europa,* did not survive. He had fallen sick during a voyage from St. Kitts to London in 1734 and was too weak to come on deck when ordered to do so. Deliberately and maliciously, the captain made him take two turns at the helm; after four hours of this, he whipped him and then tied him to the mizzenmast, where he hung for an hour and a half. Baker died four days later.[18]

It is usual nowadays to regard a sailing ship as a thing of beauty, but it could be turned into a torture chamber by a sadistic captain. There were boat hooks and brooms and iron bars to beat men with. There were axes and hammers and cutlasses to cause grievous wounds. There were ropes of all sizes which could be used to whip, strangle, and stretch bodies and limbs. The shrouds and rigging were ideal places for hanging up a stubborn man by his arms for a few hours. And after a man had been flogged till his skin was flayed off, there were barrels of brine to throw over the wounds and plenty of salt to add to the brine to increase the pain. The records of the High Court of Admiralty are filled with horror stories of the brutality inflicted on seamen.

The savagery of some of the punishments they were forced to endure is astonishing. John Cressey was ordered to place his middle finger in the hole of a block of wood. Captain Thomas Brown drove wedges into the hole with such violence that the finger was crushed and the arm swollen up. The block weighed nearly fifty pounds, and Cressey was forced to carry it around for the next half an hour.[19] For stealing a chicken Anthony Comerford was lashed to the shrouds and condemned to receive two lashes from every member of the crew. Before he died, Comerford forgave all the ship's company except the captain and the mate.[20] Edward Hamlin was flogged, clamped into irons, and for eight days and nights was exposed to wind, rain, and sun on the deck of his ship in Cádiz harbor.[21]

It is not known how many merchant seamen were murdered or injured for life while at sea, but the barbaric behavior of the more tyrannical captains was certainly responsible for some men turning to piracy. Before his execution in 1724 the pirate John Archer declared, "I could wish that Masters of vessels would not use their men with so much severity, as many of them do, which exposes us to great temptations."[22] And at the trial of the crew of Bartholomew Roberts' pirates in 1722, John Philps accused one of his former officers of starving the men: "it was such dogs as he that put men on pyrating."[23]

Life for the common seaman in the Royal Navy was nothing like so hard as life in the merchant service. The much larger crews meant that there were more men to share the heavy jobs, and a sadistic captain was likely to find himself court-martialed. The maximum punishment a captain could order on his own authority was twelve lashes. Nevertheless, life in the navy could be hard and dangerous, and serious offenses were dealt with ruthlessly. A single court-martial in 1758 sentenced a deserter to two hundred lashes, a mutineer to three hundred lashes, and a thief to five hundred lashes.[24] Sodomy often meant a death penalty, and in one case the sentence was one thousand lashes.[25]

In many respects life in the seventeenth and eighteenth centuries was as harsh and violent as life in medieval times, and some of the punishments employed by the authorities in England and the colonies were as barbaric as anything dreamed up by the pirates and buccaneers. The usual treatment for men or women who refused to plead innocent or guilty was to be sent to the Press Yard at Newgate Prison or the Marshalsea. There they were stretched out on the ground, and as they lay there on their backs, weights were put on their chests. More and more weights were piled on until the prisoner agreed to plead. If he refused to plead, he was slowly crushed to death. The whole process could take several days, and the prisoner would be kept alive by being fed sparingly with coarse bread and water.

Women were given the same treatment. When Mary Andrews refused to plead in 1721, she "by ancient law was liable to be pressed to death; but first having her thumbs drawn by the common executioner with a strong whipcord, she submitted to plead."[26] She was acquitted for lack of evidence. Not so Katharine Hayes, who was sentenced to death for the murder of one of her sons and for incestuously sleeping with her other son. She was ordered to be burned at Tyburn. Nine other people were executed the same day: three for sodomy, one for murder, two for burglary, one for felony, and two for highway robbery. It was usual for crowds of two or three thousand spectators to attend executions at Tyburn, but on this occasion so many people thronged the specially erected stands that the scaffolding broke and five or six people were crushed and many others suffered broken arms and legs.

Katharine Hayes was drawn to Tyburn on a hurdle, and "to strike a proper terror in the spectators of so horrid a crime," it was ordered that she was to be burned alive and not strangled first as was customary. There is a harrowing description of her last moments in the pages of the *London Journal:* "She was fastened to the stake by an iron collar round her neck, and an iron chain round her body, having an halter also about her neck, (running through the stake) which the executioner pulled when she began to shriek. In about an hour's time she was reduced to ashes."[27]

The hanging of men for sodomy alongside murderers and highwaymen was unusual. Although the punishment for sodomy in the Royal Navy and in civilian life at this period was death, those convicted were more likely to be imprisoned or sentenced to stand in the pillory.

OF THE MANY WICKED deeds attributed to pirates, there is one which has a secure foundation, and that is the marooning of victims on desert islands. It was particularly common among the pirates in the West Indies. In 1718 ten pirates were put on trial at Nassau, accused of combining together at an island called Green Cay, robbing a number of vessels, "and by force caused to be put ashore upon the said desolate island one James Kerr, merchant, and sundry others with him."[28] Roger Stevens of Bristol was attacked by pirates while en route to Jamaica in 1724. The pirates burned his ship and put the commander and boatswain ashore on the island of Rattan.[29]

Marooning was also used among the pirates themselves as a punishment for certain offenses, such as deserting the ship or quarters in battle, or for stealing from other pirates. In the pirate code recorded in Captain Johnson's *General History of the Pirates* (see pages 98 to 100), the second of the eleven articles decreed that if any pirates defrauded the crew of money, jewels, or plate, they were to be punished with marooning. On one occasion Blackbeard made use of marooning as a means of ridding himself of some of his crew. Following a successful raid on Charleston, South Carolina, he decided to disband his fleet and keep the plunder for himself. He ran two of his ships aground and escaped in the sloop used as a tender to his warship *Queen Anne's Revenge*. He then took seventeen of his crew and marooned them "upon a small sandy island, about a league from the main, where there was neither bird, beast or herb for their subsistence. . . ."[30]

A description of privateers using marooning as a method of settling differences can be found in the deposition of Robert Dangerfield, which was recorded at Carolina in 1684. Dangerfield joined the crew of a barque commanded by Jeremy Rendell which set sail from Jamaica on a privateering voyage. They made for the Bay of Honduras, where a dispute arose among the crew. Rendell and three men were for going to the Bay of Campeche, but the rest of the crew, headed by John Graham, the ship's doctor, were determined to head across the Atlantic to the coast of Guinea. The majority rule prevailed, and the unfortunate Rendell and his supporters were put ashore "upon an island, giving them a turtle net and a canoe with their arms to shift for themselves, the said island not being inhabited and about 10 leagues from the main or any other inhabited place."[31]

Although marooning could and sometimes did mean a slow death from starvation or exposure, it has acquired a romantic image which is far removed from the reality of the experience. Part of the reason for this is no doubt the association with islands, because islands have always had a powerful hold on people's imagination. Most of us have memories of particular islands we have visited, but there are also the islands of legends and romance: the island of Crete, home of the Minotaur; those other Greek islands where Odysseus encountered the Sirens, the Cyclops, and Circe, the enchantress; the isle "full of noises, sounds, and sweet airs" created by Shakespeare in *The Tempest*; the island of Lilliput, where Gulliver found himself stranded and tied down on the beach; Coral Island; Treasure Island; and the island of Never Never Land, to which Peter Pan took Wendy, John, and Michael.

In particular, there is the image conjured up by desert islands. What is curious about this image is that, far from being an island with nothing but desert sand, for most of us a desert island is a tropical island with sheltered bays and wooded hills; it is uninhabited, but it has palm trees and wild berries and parrots and goats. It would be lonely to be cast away on such an island, but it would be possible with some ingenuity to survive. This widely shared image is almost entirely due to a book which was first published in 1719 when its author was sixty years old. The full inscription on the title page of the first edition is as follows:

> The Life and Strange Surprising Adventures of Robinson Crusoe, of York, Mariner: Who lived Eight and Twenty Years all alone in an un-inhabited Island on the Coast of America, near the Mouth of the Great River of Oroonoque; Having been cast on shore by Shipwreck, where-in all the Men perished but himself. With An Account how he was at last strangely deliver'd by Pyrates. Written by Himself.

Daniel Defoe's most celebrated work is not about pirates, but about the physical and mental challenges faced by a young man who has run away to sea and after many adventures finds himself washed up on the beach of an uninhabited island. It is a complex work which addresses moral and spiritual dilemmas as well as the more basic problems of finding food and creating a shelter. Considered by many to be the first English novel, the book has been the subject of exhaustive study by scholars, but at a simple level it is an absorbing study of survival written with such conviction and attention to detail that we identify with the hero and find it hard to believe that it is a work of fiction.

Robinson Crusoe was first published in an edition of one thousand copies, and proved an immediate success. A second edition of a thousand was published within a fortnight of the first, and two further editions followed in rapid succession. Within a year it had been translated into French, German, and Dutch. In spite of some sniping by jealous critics, the book proved popular with the man and woman in the street, as well as in literary circles.[32] It was highly praised by Dr. Johnson and Alexander Pope, and was a formative influence on

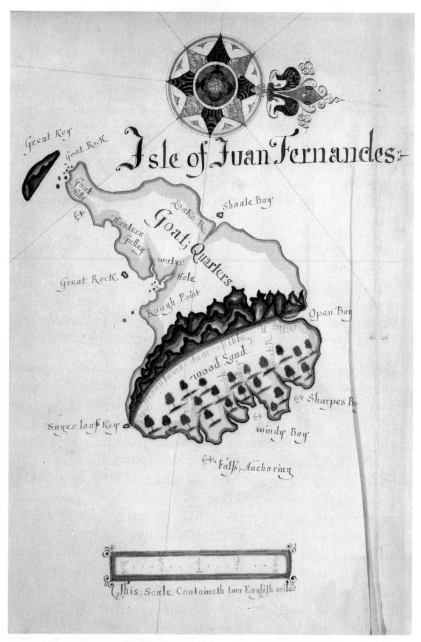

The island of Juan Fernández in the Pacific Ocean, some 350 miles west of the coast of South America. It was here that Alexander Selkirk, the model for Robinson Crusoe, was marooned between 1704 and 1709. The map comes from William Hack's Waggoner of the South Seas of 1684 and was based on information supplied by the buccaneer Basil Ringrose.

Gulliver's Travels and, a century later, on Coleridge's *Rime of the Ancient Mariner*. In 1806 a clergyman wrote: "I have never known but one person of sense who disliked it. Rousseau, and after him all France, applauded it."[33]

While piracy does not feature prominently in the story, there are a number of other connections. Defoe himself was fascinated by pirates. He had once encountered Algerian pirates on a voyage from Harwich to Holland, and he made pirates the subject of several publications, notably *The Life, Adventures, and Pyracies of the famous Captain Singleton,* which was published in 1720. This was a work of fiction, but it was partly inspired by the career of Captain Avery, who appears in the story and was also the subject of *The King of the Pirates,* a popular biography which is considered by many scholars to be the work of Defoe. A further link between *Robinson Crusoe* and piracy is provided by the story of Alexander Selkirk, the Scottish seaman who spent four years marooned on one of the islands of Juan Fernández off the coast of Chile. There is no doubt that Alexander Selkirk was the prototype for Robinson Crusoe; what is not certain is the extent to which Defoe was influenced by the Scottish seaman's story. It is generally agreed that Defoe never met Selkirk, but it is relevant that a second edition of Captain Woodes Rogers' account of rescuing the castaway sailor appeared in 1718, the year before *Robinson Crusoe* was published.

Selkirk sailed with the buccaneer William Dampier on a privateering expedition to the South Seas. The two ships *St. George* and *Cinque Ports* left England in September 1703, and by February of the following year they had rounded Cape Horn and were sailing off the coast of Chile. After various unsatisfactory operations, the two ships parted company. The *Cinque Ports,* under the command of Captain Stradling and with Selkirk as sailing master, headed for the Juan Fernández Islands to careen and refit. They dropped anchor off Mas-a-Tierra, the largest of the islands, an occasional refuge for buccaneers and pirates, and the scene of a number of accidental and intentional maroonings over the years.

Captain Stradling was an unpopular commander and had quarreled with Selkirk. When the order was given to set sail, Selkirk protested that the ship was unseaworthy, and demanded to be left on the island. Stradling took him at his word and sailed away without him. It was the beginning of October 1704.

Selkirk was alone on the island until February 2, 1709, when a privateering expedition under the command of Captain Woodes Rogers dropped anchor in the bay. The seamen who went ashore in the ship's pinnace encountered "a man clothed in goat'skins, who looked wilder than the first owners of them." [34] William Dampier, who was acting as pilot, recognized Selkirk and recommended him as an excellent seaman. Woodes Rogers agreed to appoint the castaway as mate of his ship the *Duke*. They set sail on February 12 and, after taking a number of prizes, headed for home. When Selkirk eventually landed in London on October 14, 1711, he had been away from England for more than eight years.

The story of Selkirk's solitary existence on the Juan Fernández Islands was told in Woodes Rogers' book *A Cruising Voyage Round the World,* which came out in 1712. People were fascinated by the description of the island and Selkirk's struggle to overcome the melancholy and fear of being alone in such a desolate place. In particular they admired his ingenuity. When he was put ashore, "He had with him his clothes and bedding, with a fire-lock, some powder, bullets, and tobacco, a hatchet, a knife, a kettle, a Bible, some practical pieces, and his mathematical instruments and books." [35] When his seaman's clothes fell to pieces he stitched together a cap and coat from goatskins, using a nail in place of a needle. When rats chewed his feet at night, he tamed the wild cats of the island; they kept him company and solved the rat problem. He built two huts from branches covered with long grasses. He made fire by rubbing two sticks of pimento wood together upon his knee. Apart from the practical details, the story was also a moral tale, because Selkirk overcame his fears and his boredom by reading, and praying and singing psalms, "so that he said he was a better Christian while in this solitude than ever he was before." [36]

PIRATE ISLANDS
AND
OTHER HAUNTS

D URING THE LATE SUMMER OF 1692 news began to reach
England of a catastrophe on the island of Jamaica. It was reported that the town of Port Royal had been hit by an earthquake so
violent that whole houses had been swallowed by the earth, and much
of the town had sunk beneath the sea. It was said that two thirds of
the inhabitants had been drowned or buried under timber and ma-
sonry, and that the graves in the submerged churchyard had opened
up so that long-dead corpses were floating to and fro in the harbor.
There were accounts of sailors using their boats to loot houses and
strip the rings and valuables from the floating bodies. A local minister
reported that "a company of lewd rogues whom they call privateers,
fell to breaking open warehouses and houses deserted, to rob and rifle
their neighbours whilst the earth trembled under them, and some of
the houses fell on them in the act; and those audacious whores that
remain still upon the place, are as impudent and as drunken as ever."[1]
The opinion of many was that the catastrophe was the judgment of
God on an evil and impenitent town, the home of pirates and prostitutes, and the wickedest port in Christendom.

As the letters and reports from eyewitnesses reached England, it
became clear that all the stories were true. A massive earthquake had
hit Jamaica between eleven and twelve noon on June 7, 1692, and

shaken the whole town of Port Royal. Two further tremors followed, and the ground moved in a series of undulations which caused the sand in the unpaved streets to rise and fall like waves. Brick and stone buildings, including the church, collapsed, and the wharf next to the harbor and two entire streets with all their houses and shops slid beneath the sea. A tidal wave followed in the wake of the earthquake and swept through the town. "Nothing else was seen but the dead and dying, and heard but shrieks and cries."[2] More than two thousand people died that day, and a further two thousand died later from the wounds they received or from disease and fever. There were so few people left alive that for a long time the bodies drifted in the tide or lay unburied on the rocks and beaches where they were thrown by the waves. John Pike, a joiner, wrote to his brother and told him that his house had sunk beneath the sea. "I lost my wife, my son, a 'prentice, a white-maid and 6 slaves and all that ever I had in the world. My land where I was ready to raise five houses, and had room to raise ten more, is all sunk, a good sloop may sail over it as well as over the Point."[3]

The town which was so devastated by the earthquake had been one of the richest and busiest ports in the Americas. The English, who had captured Jamaica from the Spanish in 1655, built a fort at the end of the narrow strip of land which curves out into the blue waters of the Caribbean on the southern shores of the island. The spit of land formed a great natural harbor, and the fort was well placed to protect it from attack. Within four years there were two hundred houses clustered around the fort, as well as workshops and storehouses. Port Royal, as the town was named on the Restoration of Charles II, became a thriving center for trade from England and the American colonies. It also became one of the major slave ports in the West Indies, and in the period between 1671 and 1679 nearly 12,000 black Africans were landed from slave ships anchored in the harbor. By 1680 there were 2,850 people, white and black, living in the town.[4] These included carpenters, goldsmiths, pewterers, sailmakers, shipwrights, and seamen. Above all there were the merchants, who lived "to the height of splendour, in full ease and plenty, being sumptuously arrayed, and attended on and served by their negro slaves."[5]

Much of the town looked very like Bristol or Boston or any busy English or American port of the period. The houses of brick and timber were huddled close together along roads and alleys with familiar

English names: Thames Street, Lime Street, Queen Street, Smith's Alley, and Fishers Row. There was an Anglican church, a Roman Catholic chapel, a Quaker meetinghouse, and two prisons. There were also a large number of taverns and brothels, and "a crew of vile strumpets and common prostitutes."[6] The largest whorehouse was run by John Starr and had twenty-one white and two black women. The most celebrated of Port Royal's whores was Mary Carleton. She was born in Canterbury around 1634 and was a teenage criminal before she went on the London stage, where she had a play called *The German Princess* written specially for her. She was arrested for theft and bigamy in 1671, and transported for life to Jamaica. She set herself up as a prostitute in Port Royal, where she lived a scandalous life for two years. She was described as being "as common as a barber's chair: no sooner was one out, but another was in. Cunning, crafty, subtle, and hot in the pursuit of her intended designs."[7]

Where Port Royal differed from Bristol or London was, of course, in the climate, and also in the number of buccaneers and pirates who frequented the bars and taverns. The tropical conditions which were so pleasant on the slopes of the Blue Mountains above Kingston could be roasting on calm days, and the occasional storms and hurricanes caused much damage to houses and shipping alike. But it was the buccaneers who gave the town its wicked reputation and who brought it so much wealth. The governors of the island actively encouraged them to use Port Royal as a base, hoping that the presence of heavily armed ships would discourage the Spanish and French from attempting to capture the island. The policy proved remarkably successful. There were no serious attempts to attack Jamaica, and the merchants and shopkeepers of Port Royal grew rich on the plunder brought in from the raids on Spanish ships and towns.

The arrangement also suited the pirates. Jamaica was well placed as a base from which to launch attacks on the Spanish settlements in Central America or on the ships passing to and fro among the West Indian islands. Port Royal provided them with a fine harbor where they could moor their vessels, and the facilities to careen and repair them. During the 1660s the pirates had a field day. This was the period when Henry Morgan based himself at Port Royal and launched his attacks on Portobello, Maracaibo, and Panama. His raid on Portobello alone yielded treasure on a fabulous scale, most of which was squan-

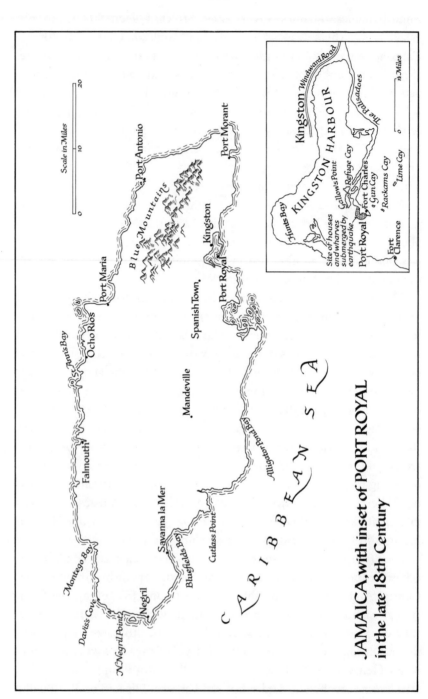

JAMAICA, with inset of PORT ROYAL
in the late 18th Century

dered in the taverns and whorehouses of Port Royal. The prodigality of the buccaneers became legendary and was described vividly by Charles Leslie in the history of Jamaica which he published in 1740:

> Wine and women drained their wealth to such a degree that, in a little time, some of them became reduced to beggary. They have been known to spend 2 or 3,000 pieces of eight in one night; and one gave a strumpet 500 to see her naked. They used to buy a pipe of wine, place it in the street, and oblige everyone that passed to drink.

This riotous life was brought to an end when Morgan and the Governor, Sir Thomas Modyford, were recalled to England in 1671 following the sacking of Panama, and piracy against the Spanish could no longer be supported by the English court. After the earthquake twenty years later, many of the surviving inhabitants moved across the harbor to the town of Kingston and took their businesses with them. A section of the spit of land leading out to Port Royal had sunk beneath the sea, and for the next seventy years what remained of the town was an island. However, ferryboats from Kingston continued to ply to and fro across the harbor, and ships continued to anchor in the lee of the island. The Royal Navy used the town as a base, and slowly Port Royal recovered, though never to its former state. Pirates were no longer welcomed, and Governor Hamilton even issued commissions to privateers authorizing them "to seize, take and apprehend all Pyratical Ships and Vessels with their Commander, Officers and Crew."[8]

Port Royal became notorious not as a pirate haven but as a place where pirates were hanged. Charles Vane, whose men had viciously tortured the crews of two sloops off the Bahamas in 1718 and had attacked shipping up and down the Caribbean, was shipwrecked on a small island in the Bay of Honduras. He was eventually rescued by a ship bound for Jamaica, but was recognized by a former buccaneer and delivered up to the authorities. Vane was tried at a Vice-Admiralty Court held at Spanish Town on March 22, 1720. He was found guilty of piracy and hanged at Gallows Point, a bleak stretch of shore adjoining Port Royal where Calico Jack was also hanged in November of the same year.

Further pirate executions continued to take place at Gallows Point. In May 1722 forty-one men of a crew of fifty-eight pirates were hanged there. John Eles, a carpenter at Port Royal, sent the council a bill for £25 for building five scaffolds for the execution of pirates between September 1724 and May 1725.[9] Port Royal was still the scene of executions a century later. Captain Boteler of HMS *Gloucester* witnessed the hanging of twenty Spanish pirates in 1823:

> Early in the morning the *Gloucester*'s boats, manned and armed with a guard of marine drums and fifes, went up to Kingston, returning in procession towing the launch with the captain and nine pirates, the drums and fifes giving out the "Dead March in Saul," "Adeste Fideles," etc. The following morning the other ten were also executed—a fearful sight. No men could go to their death with less apparent concern. Before the captain first went up the ladder he called upon his men to remember they were before foreigners and to die like Spaniards.[10]

Madagascar, in the Indian Ocean, was another island which acquired a legendary status as a haunt of pirates. Seamen returning from the East told stories of a tropical kingdom called Libertalia, where a community of pirates had devised their own laws, and lived like lords in unimaginable luxury. "They married the most beautiful of the negro women, not one or two, but as many as they liked; so that every one of them had as great a seraglio as the Grand Seignior at Constantinople: their slaves they employed in planting rice, in fishing, hunting, etc., besides which, they had abundance of others, who lived, as it were, under their protection."[11] As with many pirate legends, some of the stories were true, but the real picture was not as idyllic as it was painted.

The huge island of Madagascar, larger than California and twice as big as Great Britain, had been put on the map by Portuguese explorers in 1506. Ships voyaging to and from India would sometimes anchor in its bays, and during the course of the seventeenth century it became a base for privateers and buccaneers who made use of the natural harbor at St. Mary's Island (Ile Sainte Marie) on the northeast coast. In 1691 Adam Baldridge, a former buccaneer, arrived at the island and set up a trading post. He carried on a lucrative business for six years, supplying pirates and privateers with food and drink in exchange for looted gold, silver, silks, and slaves which were dispatched to merchants in New York. When Captain Kidd arrived at St. Mary's Island in April 1698, Edward Welsh had taken the place of Baldridge as the resident trader.[12]

At the southern end of Madagascar another pirate colony had been established at Fort Dauphin by Abraham Samuel around 1696. He had been quartermaster of a pirate ship and had put in to St. Mary's Island with one of his prizes. Attacked by local natives, he fled to the abandoned French settlement at Fort Dauphin. Here he was welcomed by the natives, who hailed him as heir to the throne of their kingdom. Styling himself King Samuel, he set up in business as a trader and kept an armed bodyguard and a harem of wives. Another petty kingdom was ruled over by James Plantain, who called himself King of Ranter Bay, which was a few miles north of St. Mary's Island. Like Samuel, Plantain lived "with many wives whom he kept in great subjection. . . . They were dressed in richest silks and some of them had diamond necklaces."[13]

It was from Madagascar that Henry Avery sailed in 1695 with a fleet of six ships and captured the Mogul's great treasure ship the *Ganj-i-Sawai*. And it was to Madagascar that Thomas Tew sailed from Rhode Island and established a lucrative trade between the pirates and the merchants of New York and Boston. A visitor to the island in 1700 reported seeing seventeen pirate ships and reckoned there were fifteen hundred men living there.

But just as Fletcher Christian and the mutineers of HMS *Bounty* found that life on Pitcairn Island with their Tahitian girls deteriorated into a grim struggle for survival, so the pirate kingdoms on Madagascar fell apart. There were internal rivalries and disputes with the native peoples, and tropical diseases took their toll. When Captain Woodes Rogers visited Cape Town in 1711, he spoke to an Englishman and an Irishman who had spent several years with the Madagascar pirates. "They told me that those miserable wretches, who had made such a noise in the world, were now dwindled to between 60 or 70, most of them very poor and despicable, even to the natives, among whom they had married."[14]

Another part of the world which was much frequented by buccaneers and pirates was along the shores of Central America. In the Bay of Campeche and the Bay of Honduras were communities of logwood cutters. Many pirates found a temporary refuge among these men, and the logwood cutters themselves often joined the crews of the privateers

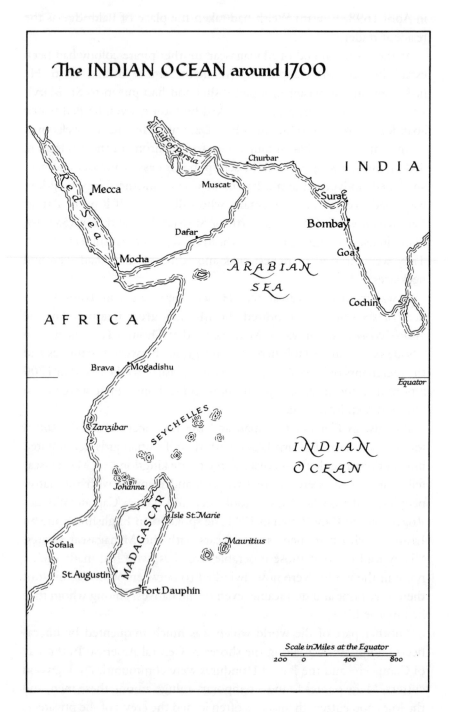

The INDIAN OCEAN around 1700

Gulf of Persia

Churbar

INDIA

Red Sea

Mecca

Muscat

Surat

Bombay

Dafar

Goa

Mocha

ARABIAN SEA

Cochin

AFRICA

Brava / Mogadishu

Equator

Zanzibar

SEYCHELLES

INDIAN OCEAN

Johanna

MADAGASCAR

Isle St. Marie

Mauritius

Sofala

St. Augustin

Fort Dauphin

Scale in Miles at the Equator

200   0   400   800

and pirates who waged intermittent war on the Spanish settlers of the region.

Captain Nathaniel Uring spent four or five months among the logwood cutters who lived and worked on the banks of the River Belize in the Bay of Honduras. He did not enjoy the experience. He described the log cutters as "a rude, drunken crew, some of which have been pirates, and most of them sailors; their chief delight is in drinking."[15] They drank rum punch, wine, ale, or cider by the barrel until they were senseless; then, when they woke up, they would start drinking again. Sometimes they spent a week in this fashion, scarcely moving from the spot. It was the same with the logwood cutters of the Bay of Campeche, except that they were more active and noisier. According to Dampier, they waited until the ships came in from Jamaica to collect the logwood, and then they went aboard the ships and spent £30 or £40 on bouts of drinking and carousing. These bouts would last for three or four days at a time and were enlivened by the firing of the ship's guns, the necessary accompaniment whenever toasting someone's health.[16]

The logwood cutters had a reputation not unlike that of the original buccaneers who hunted cattle on the island of Hispaniola: hard men earning a difficult living in primitive conditions, unfettered by the constraints of civilized society. There were other similarities. Just as the Spanish drove out the hunters from Hispaniola and created a bunch of marauding pirates seeking revenge, so were the logwood cutters forced into piracy. Writing to the Council of Trade and Plantations in 1720, Jeremiah Dummer reported that, following the Treaty of Utrecht, the Spanish had seized the ships involved in the logwood trade in the bays of Campeche and Honduras and had so disrupted the trade that "the mariners who were employed in it to the number of 3000, have since turned pirates and infested all our seas."[17]

The situation was not quite as simple as that. As Captain Uring noted, many of the logwood cutters were former pirates, and it is evident that some men took time off from cutting logs to plunder passing merchantmen or to raid Indian villages along the coast. Moreover, it is unlikely that there were more than 1,000 men involved in the logwood trade. Dampier worked for a year among the logwood cutters in 1676, and reckoned there were 260 or 270 men in the area around the Laguna de Terminos, the principal center for the trade.[18]

It is little wonder that the logwood cutters took to drink or to piracy, because life on the Bay of Campeche was not pleasant. Most of the area consisted of mangrove swamps and mosquito-infested lakes and lagoons. The waters swarmed with alligators. Unpleasant parasites like guinea worms burrowed into the skin of feet and ankles, and everywhere there were biting and stinging flies. The men built themselves primitive huts on the banks of creeks where the logwood trees grew. They slept on wooden frames three feet off the ground because in the rainy season the whole area became flooded. They would climb off their beds into two feet of water and spend the day loading logs into canoes and taking them to where they could be collected by the ships. In the dry season they cut down the trees. This was hard work; the trees were five or six feet in circumference, and sometimes needed to be brought down by being blasted with gunpowder. The trunk was then cut into logs, and the bark was stripped off to expose the reddish brown heart. From this was extracted the valuable red stain used for dyeing cloth. The wood of the logwood tree (*Haematoxylon campechianum*) was also used for medicinal purposes.

Dampier reckoned the logwood trade to be one of the most profitable in England, but it never matched the profits of the slave trade or the tobacco trade. According to a government report, in the four years 1713 to 1716, some 4,965 tons of logwood were exported to England at not less than £60,000 per annum.[19] By comparison the colonies of Virginia and Maryland were together exporting 70,000 hogsheads of tobacco to England each year valued at £300,000 per annum. Log cutting was always a minor industry carried on by a few hundred ex-seamen and pirates in a remote corner of the globe.

Driven out of the Bay of Campeche, many of the logwood cutters headed for the Bahamas. The harbor at Nassau on the island of New Providence became the headquarters for another community of pirates, and acted as a meeting point for pirate ships operating throughout the Caribbean and the Atlantic Ocean. Their unofficial leader was Captain Jennings, "a man of good understanding and good estate." According to Johnson's *General History of the Pirates,* the pirate captains based at Nassau in 1716 included Benjamin Hornigold, Edward Teach, John Martel, James Fife, Christopher Winter, Nicholas Brown, Paul Williams, Charles Bellamy, Oliver la Bouche, Major Penner, Edward England, T. Burgess, Thomas Cocklyn, R. Sample, and Charles

Vane. Others who used Nassau's fine natural harbor as a rendezvous were Stede Bonnet, Howell Davis, Nichols, Miller, Napin, Fox, Porter, Macarty, Bunce, Leslie, John Rackam, and Mary Read and Anne Bonny.

The authorities were seriously alarmed by what was constantly referred to as a "nest of pirates." Reports of pirate attacks in the West Indies multiplied, and in London a report from the Council of Trade and Plantations warned that the Bahamas were so lacking in any form of defense that most of the inhabitants had fled, exposing the islands "to be plundered and ravaged by pirates, and in danger of being lost from Our Crown of Great Britain."[20]

On September 3, 1717, Mr. Secretary Addison reported that the King had ordered three measures to be taken against the pirates in the West Indies: the first was the sending of three warships to the Caribbean; the second was the issuing of a proclamation which assured His Majesty's pardon to those pirates who surrendered themselves; the third was the appointment of a governor of the Bahamas "who will be enabled to drive the pirates from their lodgement at Harbour Island and Providence."[21]

The man selected for this task was Captain Woodes Rogers, who was one of the heroes of the war against the pirates. Woodes Rogers was the son of a sea captain and was born in Bristol in 1679. He trained as a seaman but seems to have occupied a prominent position in the social life of Bristol. In 1705 he married Sarah, the daughter of Admiral Sir William Whetstone and in the same year was made a freeman of his native city.[22] In 1708 he organized and took command of a privateering voyage which was to take him around the world. The voyage was sponsored by the Mayor and corporation of Bristol, and Woodes Rogers had a commission from the Lord High Admiral to attack French and Spanish ships. He also secured the services of the fifty-six-year-old William Dampier as his pilot; the former buccaneer and explorer was an excellent choice as he had already circumnavigated the globe twice and was a highly experienced navigator. The expedition's two ships were the *Duke,* of 310 tons and thirty guns, and the 260-ton *Dutchess.* They set sail on August 2, 1708, and headed south for the Canary Islands.

Woodes Rogers proved a tough and capable commander. He put down several mutinies, survived storms and calms, and attacked and captured some twenty ships. In one pitched battle off the coast of California he was badly wounded: "I was shot thro' the left cheek, the bullet struck away great part of my upper jaw, and several of my teeth, part of which dropt down upon the deck where I fell."[23] A few days later, during an engagement with a massive 900-ton Spanish ship of sixty guns, he was hit again, this time by a wood splinter which cut through his ankle and knocked out part of his heel bone. He resolutely continued to give orders and to keep control of his sometimes unruly crews.

The expedition returned to England in 1711 with a rich haul of gold bullion, precious stones, and silks plundered from the vessels taken en route. The total value of the plunder was reckoned at £800,000. Two thirds of this went to the owners and sponsors, and the other third was divided among the officers and crew. Woodes Rogers wrote a candid and seamanlike account of his voyage, which was published in 1712 under the title *A Cruising Voyage Round the World*. It was widely read, and three editions were published within a few years of its first appearance. With his face badly scarred, and no doubt still limping from his wounded ankle, Captain Rogers returned to his family and his house in Queen Square, Bristol.

This was the man chosen to take up the post of Governor of the Bahamas. It was little wonder that the merchants of London and Bristol informed the King that they considered him "as a person every way qualified for such an undertaking."[24] His brief was to use whatever means he thought necessary to suppress piracy. He also took with him a Royal Pardon from the King which was to be granted to any pirates who surrendered to him before September 5, 1718.

Rogers set sail on April 11, 1718, on board the *Delicia,* a former East Indiaman, accompanied by HMS *Milford* and HMS *Rose* and two sloops. He arrived at the island of New Providence on July 26 to find a French ship burning in the harbor of Nassau. Pirates commanded by Vane had set the ship alight in order to drive out HMS *Rose,* which had pressed ahead of the squadron and arrived the previous evening. As the *Delicia* and HMS *Milford* sailed in, Vane decided that the odds were too great and fled. He fired his guns in a gesture of defiance and flew a black flag from the masthead of his sloop.

The new Governor landed and took possession of the fort, "where I read His Majesty's Commission in the presence of my officers, soldiers and about 300 of the people here, who received me under arms and readily surrendered, showing then many tokens of joy for the re-introduction of Government."[25] There was much to be done. He began by forming a council and appointed a secretary-general and a chief justice. He ordered repairs to the fort, which was in a crumbling condition, the seaward-facing bastion having recently collapsed. He arranged for the mounting of guns to defend the harbor. And he sent Captain Hornigold out to capture Vane and his pirates. Hornigold was a former pirate leader who had decided to surrender and accept the King's Pardon.

After chasing and losing Vane, whose sloop was a notably swift sailer, Hornigold continued his patrols. In October he captured a bunch of pirates at the island of Exuma, 130 miles southeast of New Providence. They were all men who had accepted the King's Pardon but had returned to piracy, and Governor Rogers determined to make an example of them. On Tuesday December 9, 1718, an Admiralty Court was held in His Majesty's Guard Room in Nassau.[26] Seven commissioners were assembled under the presidency of the Governor. They included William Fairfax, who was Judge of the Admiralty, three civilians, and Captain Wingate Gale, Captain Josias Burges, and Captain Peter Courant. The Register opened the proceedings by reading the Governor's special commission for assembling the court under the terms of the recent Act of Parliament for the suppression of piracy.

There were ten men on trial: John Augur, formerly master of the sloop *Mary* of Providence; William Cunningham, gunner of the schooner *Batchelors Adventure*; John Hipps, boatswain of the sloop *Lancaster*; and the mariners Dennis McKarthy, George Rounsivel, William Dowling, William Lewis, Thomas Morris, George Bendall, and William Ling. There was only one charge against the prisoners, but it was a damning one: having accepted the King's Pardon, they had returned to their former evil ways of robbery and piracy, and on October 6 had combined together "at a desolate island called Green Cay" to mutiny, and piratically steal and take the *Mary*, the *Batchelors Adventure*, and *Lancaster*, their cargoes and tackle; and further that they had marooned James Kerr, merchant, and others on Green Cay while they proceeded to the island of Exuma.

The prisoners pleaded not guilty, and evidence was taken from a number of witnesses. The prisoners were then examined individually.

Only one man, John Hipps, was able to prove that he was forced to join the pirates, and he was found not guilty. All the others were found guilty and condemned to death. The date of execution was fixed for ten o'clock on the morning of December 12. The official account of what took place is perhaps the most vivid of all the descriptions of pirate hangings:

> Wherefore about ten a clock the prisoners were released of their irons and committed to the charge and care of Thomas Robenson Esq, commissioned Provost Marshal for that day, who according to custom in such cases pinioned them and ordered the guard appointed to assist him to lead them to the top of the ramparts fronting the sea, which was well guarded by the Governor, soldiers and people to the number of about one hundred. At the prisoners request several prayers and psalms selected were read in which all present joined. When the service was ended, orders were given to the marshal, and he conducted the prisoners down a ladder provided on purpose to the foot of the wall, where was a gallows erected, and a black flag hoisted thereon and under it a stage, supported by three butts [large barrels] on which they ascended by another ladder, where the hangman fastened the cords as dexterously as if he had been a servitour at Tyburn. They had ¾ of an hour allowed under the gallows which was spent by them in singing of psalms and some exhortations to their old consorts, and other sort of spectators who got as near to the foot of the gallows as the marshal's guard would suffer them. Then the Governor ordered the marshal to make ready, and all the prisoners expecting the launch, the Governor thought fit to order George Rounsivel to be untied, and when brought off the stage, the butts having ropes about them were hauled away, upon which the stage fell and the eight swang off.[27]

Brief but equally graphic descriptions of each of the eight men executed were included at the end of Governor Rogers' report. We learn that John Augur was about forty years old, and was a well-known master of vessels at Jamaica before he commanded pirate ships. He appeared very penitent and did not wash or shave or change out of his old clothes before the execution. He had a glass of wine given him on the ramparts of the fort, and when he drank it he wished the Governor and the Bahama Islands good success. William Cunningham, aged forty-five, who had been a gunner with Blackbeard, was also very penitent and conscious of his guilt.

Dennis McKarthy behaved very differently. Aged twenty-eight and a former ensign in the militia, he put on clean clothes adorned with long blue ribbons at the neck, the wrists, knees, and cap. He mounted the ramparts cheerfully and said he could remember the time when there were many brave fellows on the island who would not suffer him to die like a dog. He pulled off his shoes and kicked them over the ramparts, saying that he had promised not to die with his shoes on. He leaped on the stage with as much agility as if he was about to take part in a prizefight, an illusion enhanced by the prizefighter's ribbons fluttering in the breeze.

William Dowling, aged twenty-four, was described as a hardened pirate who had lived a wicked life. William Lewis, aged about thirty-four, was also a hardy pirate and a former prizefighter. He refused to show any fear of death and demanded liquor to drink with his fellow prisoners on the stage and with the bystanders. Thomas Morris, aged twenty-two, was thought to be an incorrigible youth and pirate. He had frequently smiled during the trial, and he arrived on the ramparts dressed in a manner similar to McKarthy but with red ribbons instead of blue. Immediately before he was hanged he defiantly declared that he might have been a greater plague to these islands and now wished he had been so. George Bendall was aged eighteen and said he had never been a pirate before. He behaved in a sullen manner, and, according to the report, he had "villainous inclinations the most profligate youth could be infected with." William Ling, aged thirty, had little to say for himself, except that when Lewis demanded wine to drink, he answered that water was more suitable for them at a time like this.

The execution of the pirates at Nassau marked the end of New Providence as a pirate haven, but it did not mean the end of piracy in the Bahamas. Woodes Rogers had ambitious plans to strengthen the defenses of the island. He appointed three companies of militia to prevent surprise attacks. He had gun carriages made for unmounted guns, built a palisade around the fort, and cleared the streets, which had become overgrown with tropical vegetation. Unfortunately he had only a tiny force at his disposal, and many of the soldiers and sailors who had come out with him fell victim to fevers and diseases. Worse still, he felt that he had been abandoned by the authorities who had appointed him. He got no answers to his requests for aid from England, and felt increasingly isolated.

In February 1720 he wrote an angry letter to the Council of Trade and Plantations complaining that he had been "left in the utmost distress by HM. ships," who had abandoned him on the island with a few sick men to combat five hundred pirates.[28] The Governor of South Carolina confirmed Rogers' precarious position and warned the authorities in London that unless warships were stationed in the harbor at Nassau the pirates or the Spaniards would move in and make themselves master of the island. "The pirates yet accounted to be out are near 2,000 men and of those Vane and Thatch, and others promise themselves to be repossessed of Providence in a short time."[29] Rogers pressed on with plans to increase the island's defenses, but met with apathy and indifference from the inhabitants and continued silence from England. He wore himself out with his efforts, and after two years was forced by ill health to return to England. He was replaced as Governor by George Phenney, who lacked Rogers' indomitable spirit and fell victim to the corruption which was rife in the colony.

Dismayed by the reports from Nassau, Rogers petitioned the King to be reinstated as Governor. His petition was supported by twenty-nine influential names, including Sir Hans Sloane, Lord Montague, and the governors and former governors of several American colonies, including Alexander Spotswood of Virginia and Samuel Shute of Massachusetts. Phenney was recalled, and in the summer of 1729 Woodes Rogers sailed for New Providence accompanied by his son and daughter. He had increased powers, and was to receive a salary of £400 a year as Captain General and Governor-in-Chief. Once again he threw himself into schemes to improve the defense and welfare of the colony, including a scheme to encourage the planting of cotton and sugarcane. The main problem was the tiny population of the island, which consisted of 446 white men and women, 489 white children, 275 able blacks, and 178 black children.[30] He encountered opposition to his plans in the island's Assembly, but he did succeed in building a new barracks for the garrison of the fort. Again he was laid low by ill health, and in spite of a visit to South Carolina for a change of air he never recovered his old strength. He died at Nassau on July 15, 1732.

Before he left England for the last time in 1729, Rogers had commissioned a family portrait from William Hogarth, who was then a young man in his early thirties. The painting, which is now in the collections of the National Maritime Museum in London, is small but charming. The newly appointed Governor is shown seated outside the fort at Nassau, which he had repaired and which was the scene of the pirate trial and execution. He has a pair of dividers in his hand to symbolize his skills as a navigator, and by his side is a globe to represent his voyage around the world. His son William holds up a map showing part of the island of Providence. His daughter Sarah is seated with a spaniel beside her. Standing in the background is a maid with a bowl of fruit in her hands. On the castle walls above Woodes Rogers is a cartouche bearing the appropriately resolute and optimistic motto *"Dum spiro, spero"* ("While I breathe, I hope"), and in the harbor beyond is a ship firing a salute. The painting is a modest memorial to the man who drove the pirates from their headquarters in the Bahamas, and played a key role in bringing the reign of the pirates in the Caribbean to an end.

9

SLOOPS, SCHOONERS, AND PIRATE FILMS

THERE WERE three qualities required in a pirate ship: she had to be fast, seaworthy, and well armed. A fast ship enabled the pirates to catch their prey and to make a quick getaway, "a light pair of heels being of great use either to take or to escape being taken" in the words of Captain Johnson. For this reason, many of the pirates in the West Indies used the single-masted sloops built in Bermuda and Jamaica which had a well-deserved reputation for speed. The pirates kept them in good order, careening them regularly to keep the hulls smooth and clear of seaweed, and they could usually outsail any craft sent after them. When Vane's pirate sloops attacked shipping in the harbor of New Providence in the Bahamas in 1718, the authorities sent vessels to catch him, "but when they came out to sea, our sloops gave over the chase, finding he out-sailed them two foot for their one." [1]

The Barbary corsairs of the Mediterranean used oar-powered galleys rowed by slaves. These were long, slender craft which were renowned for their speed, and sailing ships becalmed in the light airs of the Mediterranean were at their mercy. Their oars acted like engines, enabling them to maneuver easily and to come racing alongside a victim. When the wind came up, the corsairs hoisted a large lateen sail on the single mast amidships. The galleys were armed with one or more big guns in the bows, and swivel guns mounted along the rails, but their principal armament was the complement of one hundred fighting men who swarmed aboard the victim and swept aside all opposition.

A pirate ship also had to be seaworthy—capable of riding out local storms, and able to make sea passages and, in some cases, ocean crossings. One of the most impressive aspects of the early-eighteenth-century pirates is the enormous voyages which they made in search of plunder. They cruised the North American coast from Newfoundland to the Caribbean. They crossed the Atlantic to the Guinea coast of Africa. And they rounded the Cape of Good Hope to Madagascar in order to plunder ships in the Indian Ocean.

The armament of the selected vessel was less important than speed and seaworthiness because guns could always be added later. Since this fitting out was carried out in a secluded location out of reach of the authorities, there are no accounts in official records, but a close reading of Johnson's *General History of the Pirates* suggests that it was normal practice for pirates to take over a ship and set the carpenter and gunners to work. Captain Edward England captured a ship called *Pearl,* "fitted her up for the piratical account," renamed her the *Royal James,* and set off to the Azores to plunder ships.[2] When Edward Lowther and his fellow mutineers seized the *Gambia Castle* in 1721, they "knocked down the cabins, made the ship flush fore and aft, prepared black colours, new named her the *Delivery,*" and sailed off to "seek their fortune upon the seas."[3]

The best account of alterations is in Johnson's chapter on Bartholomew Roberts. When Roberts and his men captured the *Onslow* in 1721, they decided to keep her for their own use. She was a handsome frigate-built ship, owned and operated by the Royal Africa Company. They set about "making such alterations as might fit her for a Sea Rover, pulling down her bulkheads, and making her flush, so that she became, in all respects, as complete a ship for their purpose as any they could have found; they continued to her the name of the *Royal Fortune* and mounted her with 40 guns."[4] As with Lowther's ship, the pirates removed the bulkheads or internal walls belowdecks, which were installed to hold the cargo. This created a clear space for working the guns, as in a man-of-war. The description of "making her flush" suggests that the pirates also removed the forecastle and lowered the quarterdeck. A flush-decked ship was one without a break or step in the weather deck. It would have provided the pirates with an unobstructed fighting platform. Basil Ringrose describes the buccaneers carrying out similar alterations to their ship in April 1681.[5]

Having cleared the decks, Roberts' men would have transferred guns from the first *Royal Fortune* and fitted them alongside the guns with which the *Onslow* was already equipped. It would have been necessary to cut some additional gunports, but this would not have been a problem for the ship's carpenters. The result was a formidable warship which would have been a match for the largest East Indiaman and would have made mincemeat of the average merchantman plying her trade across the Atlantic. It was Roberts' misfortune to encounter a naval ship manned by a determined commander within a few weeks of taking over the *Onslow*.

In addition to speed, seaworthiness, and armament, the size of the pirate ship was significant. Other things being equal, a large ship was faster and better able to ride out a storm than a small ship. A large ship could also provide a platform for more guns. But for a pirate there were some advantages in having a small ship. It was much easier to beach a small vessel, and to heel her over so that she could be careened. A vessel with a shallow draft could also hide among sandbanks and in creeks and estuaries which could not be navigated by a warship. Writing from New York in 1712, Governor Hunter noted, "This coast has been very much annoyed by a number of small privateers, who by the advantage of their oars and shoal water keep out of the reach of H.M. ships of war."[6]

Unlike the Royal Navy or the East India Company or the merchants of London or Boston, the pirates could not build a ship to order. They could only acquire vessels which came their way and, moreover, vessels which they were strong enough to overcome and capture. Since all their ships were stolen, they had to be opportunists. The majority of pirate ships were prizes, ships captured by force. Operating outside the law, the pirates could not, of course, go along to the prize courts to get their captured vessels valued and sold, which was the usual practice of privateer captains. Having looted a ship, the pirates would burn the vessel or set her adrift. However, if the pirate captain liked the look of the ship, he would either take her over for his own use or employ her as a consort.

A few pirate ships were taken by members of the crew plotting together and overcoming the captain and any men loyal to him. The most conspicuous example of this was Henry Avery, who was first mate of the merchant ship *Charles*. While she was anchored off Corunna with her captain asleep in a drunken stupor, Avery organized a mutiny and seized the ship. He renamed her the *Fancy* and sailed off to Madagascar to embark on an orgy of plunder that was to make him the most famous pirate of his day. The deposed captain of the ship was put ashore on the coast of Africa. There were forty-eight mutinies between 1715 and 1737, one third of which moved into piracy.[7] This would suggest that during that period no more than nineteen or twenty pirate ships were acquired through seizure by their own crews.

While most pirates remained faithful to one ship during their usually brief careers, some of the more successful pirates changed ships several times. Captain Vane, who was attacking shipping in the West Indies in 1718, began with the sloop *Ranger* of six guns and sixty men, but moved his command to a brigantine of twelve guns and ninety men. Captain Bellamy started his pirate career by taking over Hornigold's sloop *Mary Anne,* of eight guns, and died in a storm off Cape Cod while in command of the former slave ship *Whydah,* a hefty three-masted ship of 300 tons and twenty-eight guns.

Over the course of three years Bartholomew Roberts moved his command six times. His first command was the thirty-gun ship *Rover,* which he took over when the crew deposed Howell Davis from his post as captain. A few weeks later half the crew sailed away with the *Rover* while Roberts was on an expedition up an African river in a small sloop. Roberts crossed the Atlantic in the sloop and raided a harbor on the Newfoundland coast. He captured and took over a Bristol galley on which he mounted sixteen guns. With her, he managed to take a French ship of twenty-six guns which he named the *Fortune*. In 1720 he captured a French warship of forty-two guns which became the *Royal Fortune,* and in this formidable vessel he proceeded to wreak havoc among the shipping in the western Atlantic. He did not stop there, however: while cruising off the African coast in 1721, he captured the Royal Africa Company's ship *Onslow,* which as described, he adapted for his own use and also renamed the *Royal Fortune.*

An examination of the written evidence for the pirate attacks which took place in the Caribbean and along the North American seaboard between 1710 and 1730 shows that 55 percent of the attacks were made by pirates in sloops, 45 percent were carried out in ships, 10 percent in brigs or brigantines, 5 percent in schooners, 3 percent in open boats, and 2 percent in snows.[8] The typical pirate ship, then, was one denoted by that baffling word "sloop."

Nowadays the word "sloop" is a precise description for a sailing vessel with a fore-and-aft rig and one mast, on which is set a mainsail and a single foresail or jib. In the early eighteenth century the term was used more loosely and described a range of craft with a variety of rigs. In recent years maritime historians have traced the evolution of the sloop in America and northern Europe, and although some details remain hazy, there is enough evidence to be able to build up a reasonably accurate picture of the various types of sloop which would have been used by the pirates.

The sloops employed by the Royal Navy are a useful starting point because the Admiralty records include details of the measurements, tonnage, guns, and crew numbers for the sloops on the naval establishment.[9] A sloop first appears on the Navy List of 1656, and was a captured vessel named *Dunkirk* after her port of origin. She was forty feet on the keel with a beam of twelve feet and six inches, and she had two guns. Eighteen sloops were built in the Royal Dockyards during the Third Dutch War in the 1670s. Most of them carried four carriage guns and two swivel guns and were thirty-five to sixty feet on the keel and between 38 and 68 tons. The majority of them had two masts, with a large square mainsail and a square topsail on the mainmast, and a small foresail, with a bowsprit on which a spritsail was sometimes set. Several of these sloops appear in the drawings and paintings of the Willem van de Veldes.

By 1711 there were seven sloops on the establishment. The original Admiralty draft of HMS *Ferret* of 1711 has survived; this is the earliest-known plan of a British sloop and it provides a clear picture of her graceful lines. Her gundeck was sixty-five feet and seven inches in length, her keel length was fifty feet; the breadth inside her planking was twenty feet and ten inches, and she had a depth of hold of nine feet. Her burden was variously listed as 113 tons and 117 tons. She had eight oarports so that she could be rowed by sweeps in calms, and carried twelve guns. There is some difference of opinion about her rig. Howard Chapelle, the great American authority on ships, drew a reconstruction of the vessel with a single mast, presumably because the Admiralty plans only show chain plates and deadeyes for one mast. In a well-documented chapter on the sloop of war, corvette, and brig in *The Line of Battle: The Sailing Warship*, Robert Gardiner maintains that she would have had two masts and points out that the records show that she certainly had two masts by 1716.[10]

The best pictorial evidence for the rig of the sloops operating in American waters in the early eighteenth century is an engraving entitled "Sloop off Boston Light." It is by William Burgis and is dated 1729. Although intended as a portrait of the Boston lighthouse which was erected on Beacon Island in 1716, the picture clearly shows a British sloop at anchor. She has twelve guns and is flying a naval pennant from her masthead. W. A. Baker, in his book *Sloops and Shallops*, describes her rig as follows:

> Her loose-footed mainsail is of the short-gaff type with a long boom, and for headsails she has a staysail and jib; in light weather she probably carried a flying jib on the topmast stay as well. Although her standing yard is fitted with foot-ropes, the lower square sail may have been hoisted to the yard for setting, not furled upon the yard and let fall in the usual manner. A light square topsail would have been set flying on her topmast, which it may be noted, is fidded abaft the head of the lower mast.[11]

Baker draws attention to the 1717 "View of New York" by William Burgis, which depicts some twenty sloops with various types of rig. He also quotes a description of a sloop which was found upside down off Cape Cod in 1729. This is particularly fascinating because it describes the colors which the vessel was painted: "Rhode Island built, with a blue Stern, two Cabbin Windows, her Counter painted yellow with two black ovals, and he thinks her sides were painted yellow, her Keel was about 40 feet, and her bottom Tallow'd. Her Counter had been Cork'd and Pey'd with Pitch over the Paint & not scrap'd off. Her Mouldings were all white. She had lost her mast, bowsprit and rudder."[12]

The frequent attacks on merchantmen in the Caribbean by buccaneers and French privateers in the years around 1700 led to a demand for vessels fast enough to escape capture. The result was that shipbuilders in Jamaica developed a sloop which acquired an enviable reputation for seaworthiness and speed. The Jamaica sloop was built of red cedar and had a low freeboard and a steeply raked mast.

Similar in her lines and rig and equally renowned for her speed was the Bermuda sloop, which was built in considerable numbers and was much in demand by traders and privateers. Of the ten vessels provided with privateer commissions by the Governor of Jamaica in 1715, four are sloops, one is a galley, one a snow, and the remainder are not specified. Baker points out that the Bermuda sloop had many of the features shown in the plans of HMS *Ferret*. Certainly there is a strong resemblance between the *Ferret* and the drawing of a Bermuda sloop in Chapman's famous volume of ship plans *Architectura Navalis*, which was published in 1768.

From the existing evidence we cannot be certain exactly what type of sloop the pirates most frequently used, particularly as details are rarely given of their rig. However, we know that pirates needed vessels that were swift and well armed, so it would be reasonable to assume that many pirate sloops closely resembled the Bermuda sloops or the Jamaica sloops. By the time the pirates had fitted out these merchant vessels with more guns, they must have been almost indistinguishable from the naval sloops like HMS *Ferret*, and the sloop shown in the "View of Boston Light."

The word "ship" is used nowadays to describe any large, seagoing vessel, but in the days of sail it was a more precise term and described a sailing vessel which had three or more masts with square-rigged sails throughout. In the eighteenth century the great majority of warships and all the large merchant ships operated by the East and West India Companies were ships. Smaller vessels were rigged as brigs, brigantines, snows, sloops, and schooners.

A large number of pirates, including many of the better-known pirate captains, used ships. Some of these were large and powerful vessels of 200 tons or more and armed with thirty or forty guns. The average size of merchant ships coming out from London in the early eighteenth century was between 150 and 200 tons; vessels from English provincial ports averaged around 100 tons; the coasting vessels sailing to and from harbors like Boston, Charleston, and Port Royal, Jamaica, were mostly between 20 and 50 tons.[13] The pirate ships were therefore larger than many of their victims. However, the crucial difference between the pirates and the merchantmen lay in the number of guns and the size of the crews.

Even large merchant ships sailed with surprisingly small crews. Arthur Middleton, in his book *Tobacco Coast,* reproduces a detailed list of the ships in the tobacco fleet which sailed from Virginia to England on June 9, 1700. There were fifty-seven ships in the convoy, and the largest crew consisted of eighteen men, the smallest of ten men. The most heavily armed ship had ten guns, while the average number of guns per ship was six.[14] These figures are similar to those in an interesting list which appears in Johnson's *General History of the Pirates.* This gives details of nine ships which were taken by Captain England in the pirate ship *Royal James* on the west coast of Africa in the spring of 1719. The vessels ranged from a twelve-gun ship down to a two-gun sloop, with an average of four to six guns per ship. The average size of crew was sixteen men per ship.

These figures are in marked contrast to those of the pirate ships that preyed on them. Very few pirate ships had crews of fewer than 30; many had 150 to 200. This gave the pirates an overwhelming superiority when they came to boarding a victim, and no doubt the sight of more than 100 pirates armed to the teeth was enough to persuade most captains to surrender. However, the large numbers were not determined only by the need to outnumber the victim's crew in hand-to-hand fighting. A pirate ship, like a man-of-war, needed a large crew to work the guns.

A naval fifth-rate ship with thirty-two guns, for instance, had a total complement of 220 men. A fourth-rate ship of forty-four guns had a complement of 250 to 280 men. This puts the large crews of the pirate ships into perspective. There was no point in a pirate captain acquiring a ship of twenty guns and adding ten more if he did not have enough men to fire them. All except the very smallest of the guns mounted on gun carriages required a team of four to six men to load, aim, fire, and haul them back into position after the recoil. In addition, there had to be men to operate the smaller swivel guns and men to work the ship.

Henry Bostock, master of the sloop *Margaret,* was taken by Blackbeard off Crab Island on December 5, 1717. He was detained on board the pirate's ship for eight hours, and when he was interviewed a fortnight later, he was able to provide some useful details. Bostock reckoned "the ship to be as he thinks Dutch built, was a French Guinea man (he heard on board) that she had then thirty six guns mounted, that she was very full of men, he believes three hundred, that they told him they had taken her six or seven weeks before, that they did not seem to want provisions." [15]

Blackbeard and Hornigold had captured the ship in latitude 24 in the West Indies while she was en route for the French island of Martinique. Blackbeard took her over as his own ship, and named her the *Queen Anne's Revenge.* He must have trained his crew remarkably well, because shortly after acquiring the ship, he encountered HMS *Scarborough,* a fifth-rate ship of thirty-two guns, "who engaged him for some hours, but she finding the pirate well manned, and having tried her strength, gave over the engagement, and returned to Barbados, the place of her station." [16]

The following year Blackbeard carried out a remarkable raid on the town of Charleston, South Carolina. He sailed up to the harbor bar in the *Queen Anne's Revenge,* accompanied by three pirate sloops. For five days he blockaded the harbor, plundered any ships which came his way, and held the town to ransom. According to the report which Governor Johnson sent to London, the pirates:

> . . . appeared in sight of the town, took our pilot boat and afterwards 8 or 9 sail with several of the best inhabitants of this place on board and then sent me word if I did not immediately send them a chest of medicines they would put every prisoner to death, which for their sakes being complied with after plundering them of all they had were sent ashore almost naked. This company is commanded by one Teach alias Blackbeard has a ship of 40 odd guns under him and 3 sloops tenders besides and are in all above 400 men. [17]

One of the vessels in Blackbeard's flotilla on this occasion was the *Adventure* of ten guns. It was on board this relatively small sloop that Blackbeard fought his last battle when he was cornered by Lieutenant Maynard in Ocracoke Inlet in November 1718.

The only pirate ships which were comparable in size and force to Blackbeard's *Queen Anne's Revenge* were the ships of Bartholomew Roberts, William Moody, and Henry Avery. We have already seen that Roberts commanded a number of vessels. A Danish seaman who was a prisoner of Roberts gave a remarkably detailed account of the armament and crew of Roberts' largest ship, the first *Royal Fortune:*

... that the said Roberts ship is manned with about 180 white men and about 48 French Creole negros and has mounted 12, 8-pounders; 4, 12-pounders; 12, 6-pounders; 6, 8-pounders; and 8, 4-pounders; and in her main and foremast has 7 guns, 2 & 3-pounders, and 2 swivel guns upon her mizen.[18]

The London-born pirate William Moody, who was attacking shipping in the West Indies in 1718, commanded a ship called the *Rising Sun*. According to the deposition of John Brown, whose brigantine was captured by Moody while she was at anchor in the Bay of Caroline, the pirate ship was "mounted with thirty five guns, including swivel guns, having on board one hundred and thirty men."[19]

Lower down the scale, but nevertheless formidable ships in terms of firepower, were the commands of William Kidd, Edward England, Edward Low, and Sam Bellamy.

Captain Kidd's ship was the *Adventure Galley*, of 287 tons. She was built at Deptford in 1695, had a crew of 152, and carried thirty-four guns.[20] Like a number of ships at this particular period, she had oarports for sweeps (the long oars which could be employed in calms), which explains why she was called a galley, though she was in every other respect like a conventional three-masted ship. She would have looked very similar to the English ship the *Charles Galley* which was drawn and painted by the van de Veldes. The *Charles Galley* was built in 1676 for service in the Mediterranean against the Barbary pirates. She had thirty-two guns and her length on the keel was 114 feet, her breadth was 28 feet and 6 inches, and her depth was 8 feet and 7 inches. She was classed as a fourth-rate when she was launched.

Edward England's ship had twenty-six mounted guns and four swivel guns, and in 1718 "had on board about one hundred and thirty white men and about fifty others, Spaniards, Negroes and Indians."[21] Edward Low's ship the *Fortune* had twenty-eight guns and a crew of eighty men.

Perhaps the most interesting of the pirate ships is Sam Bellamy's *Whydah*. Her wreck was discovered off Cape Cod in 1984, and at the present time she is the only pirate ship to have been firmly identified. Archaeological excavation of the site has unearthed some fascinating material, and this, together with documentary research, has provided a vivid picture of the ship and her crew. The *Whydah* was named after the trading post of that name on the Gold Coast of west Africa. She was built in England, was commissioned in 1716, and was employed in the slave trade. She was a three-masted ship of 300 tons and about 100 feet in length. When captured by Bellamy, she was armed with ten guns, but the pirates converted her into a twenty-eight-gun ship with eighteen mounted guns and ten swivel guns. Twenty-seven guns have already been recovered from the wreck. There are five six-pounder guns, fifteen four-pounders, and seven three-pounders. In addition to a large quantity of round shot (cannonballs), the archaeologists have recovered bag shot, bar shot, expanding bar shot, and sixteen iron grenades.[22]

The pirate schooner, the favorite vessel of so many writers of fiction, appeared comparatively late on the scene. Although the Dutch were using two-masted vessels with fore-and-aft sails as yachts during the seventeenth century, the word "schooner" does not appear until 1717, when it is mentioned in two issues of the *Boston News Letter*. One of the earliest reports of pirates using a schooner appears a few years later. In August 1723 the *Boston Gazette* reported that Captain John Philmore, commander of a Cape Ann schooner, was taken by John Phillips in a pirate schooner off Newfoundland. In October of the same year the sloop *Content*, commanded by Captain George Barrow, was captured off Barbados by a pirate schooner of four guns and twenty-five men. But these reports are unusual, and it was not until the second half of the eighteenth century that the schooner rig became firmly established along the eastern seaboard of North America. By 1800 there were pilot schooners, naval schooners, and dozens of merchant schooners and fishing schooners. Among the most famous types were the Chesapeake Bay schooner, the Marblehead schooner, and the Grand Banks schooner, but by the time these fine craft appeared on the scene the great age of piracy in the Caribbean and along the North American coast was over.

However, occasional reports of pirate attacks in the Caribbean persisted in the nineteenth century, and it may have been these which caught the attention of the fiction writers. Two attacks, for instance, were widely reported and later published in book form. The first was the case of Aaron Smith, who was tried for piracy at the Old Bailey in December 1822. Smith was accused of seizing two merchant ships off

Cuba, but was able to prove in his defense that he had been captured by pirates the year before and forced to go along with them. After his acquittal he wrote a sensational account of his adventures entitled *The Atrocities of the Pirates: being a faithful narrative of the unparalleled sufferings endured by the author during his captivity among the pirates of the Island of Cuba; with an account of the excesses and barbarities of those inhuman freebooters.* Published in 1824, the narrative contains the most gruesome descriptions of pirate tortures. The vessel used by the pirates who captured Smith was a schooner.

Equally sensational was the story of Lucretia Parker, who witnessed a bloodthirsty attack by pirates while she was on board an English sloop en route from St. Johns to Antigua. The story was published in New York in 1826 under the title *Piratical Barbarity or the Female Captive.* Again, the pirates' vessel was a schooner. Perhaps it was one of these accounts which inspired Captain Marryat's story *The Pirate,* which was first published in 1836. It was one of more than fifteen sea stories by Marryat, who turned to writing after an adventurous and distinguished career in the Royal Navy. Apart from *Masterman Ready* and *Mr. Midshipman Easy,* his work is little known today, but he had many admirers in Victorian England. Marryat's book contains a wonderfully detailed and evocative picture of the pirate schooner *Avenger* as she lies at anchor in the calm waters of a small bay on the western coast of Africa:

> There she lay in motionless beauty, her low sides were painted black, with one small, narrow riband of red—her raking masts were clean scraped—her topmasts, her crosstrees, caps, and even running-blocks, were painted in pure white. Awnings were spread fore and aft to protect the crew from the powerful rays of the sun; her ropes were hauled taut; and in every point she wore the appearance of being under the control of seamanship and strict discipline. Through the clear smooth water her copper shone brightly; and as you looked over her taffrail down into the calm blue sea, you could plainly discover the sandy bottom beneath her and the anchor which then lay under her counter.

The schooner *Avenger* was formerly a slave ship, but had been taken over by Captain Cain and a murderous crew of pirates. She was armed with a long brass thirty-two-pounder gun amidships and had eight brass guns of smaller caliber mounted on each side of her decks. Her ropes were of manila hemp, her decks of narrow fir planks, and her bulwarks were painted bright green. Muskets and boarding pikes were ready to hand beside the mainmast.

The *Avenger* appears to have been the model for a succession of pirate ships in works of fiction, all of which have black painted hulls and a rakish air. The closest in appearance is the pirate ship in R. M. Ballantyne's *Coral Island,* an adventure story for boys which first came out in 1858. A junior version of *Robinson Crusoe,* it tells how three boys learn to survive when they are stranded on a deserted Pacific island. After several months alone they sight a sailing ship offshore. To their horror, they observe that "the flag at the schooner's peak was black, with a Death's-head and cross-bones upon it." Ralph, the narrator, is captured by the pirates and spends several weeks on board the schooner, which is described with as much loving detail as Captain Marryat's *Avenger.* Like the *Avenger,* the vessel is in immaculate condition with snow-white sails and polished brass: "everything from the single narrow red stripe on her low, black hull to the trucks on her tapering masts, evinced an amount of care and strict discipline that would have done credit to a ship of the Royal Navy."

Twenty-five years after the publication of *Coral Island,* the most famous of all the pirate vessels of fiction appeared on the scene. The *Hispaniola,* the star of Robert Louis Stevenson's *Treasure Island,* is another schooner. She is a vessel of 200 tons (exactly the same tonnage as the *Avenger*) and was bought at Bristol by Squire Trelawney. She sets sail for the West Indies and proves well able to cope with the heavy weather she encounters during the crossing of the Atlantic. Soon after she has dropped anchor off Treasure Island, the *Hispaniola* is seized by the pirates led by Long John Silver. Jim Hawkins gives Silver the slip and sets out to explore the island. After an encounter with the marooned seaman Ben Gunn, he returns to the beach: "the anchorage, under the lee of Skeleton Island, lay still and leaden as when we entered it. The *Hispaniola,* in that unbroken mirror, was exactly portrayed from the truck to the waterline, the Jolly Roger hanging from her peak."

Again there are echoes of Marryat in the description, though Stevenson never mentioned him as a source. He said that he drew on reminiscences of Poe, Defoe, Washington Irving, and "the great Captain Johnson's *History of the Notorious Pirates*."

The children who spend their summer holidays playing pirates in Arthur Ransome's *Swallows and Amazons* sail thirteen-foot dinghies, but in *Peter Duck*, which was published in 1932, the action revolves around a schooner on a treasure-hunting voyage to the West Indies. The children sail on the *Wild Cat* but are chased by a pirate schooner called the *Viper*. Like the majority of fictional pirate ships, she is painted black.

Not all the pirate ships created by writers of fiction were schooners. Captain Cleveland's vessel in Walter Scott's novel *The Pirate* of 1832 is a three-masted ship, but Scott based his story on the true life of Captain Gow, taking details from newspaper reports and trial documents. Captain Hook's vessel in *Peter Pan* is a brig, a two-masted vessel similar in size to a schooner but with square-rigged sails rather than fore-and-aft sails on both masts. J. M. Barrie provides a vivid description of her lying at anchor in a creek named after Captain Kidd, who was hanged at Execution Dock in 1719:

> One green light squinting over Kidd's Creek, which is near the mouth of the pirate river, marked where the brig, the Jolly Roger, lay, low in the water; a rakish-looking craft foul to the hull, every beam in her detestable, like ground strewn with mangled feathers. She was the cannibal of the seas. . . .

While writers on piracy have favored relatively small vessels like schooners and brigs, the directors of the swashbuckling pirate films usually selected large, three-masted ships and Spanish galleons. There were practical reasons for this: a big ship looked more impressive on the big screen; space was needed for the hero to engage in a duel with the villain; spectacular acrobatics in the rigging were more exciting and easier to stage in a large ship; and wide decks made it possible to film crowd scenes with several hundred seamen and pirates involved. The fact that few pirates operated anything approaching the size of some of the ships shown in the movies is another instance of the pirate myth taking over from reality.

As far as Hollywood was concerned, pirates provided an opportunity for buccaneering heroes to rescue beautiful women from picturesque villains in exotic locations. In common with westerns, they were a vehicle for exciting action sequences, but with swords instead of guns, and acrobatics in the rigging instead of chases on horseback. The filming of large sailing ships at sea posed problems, and sea battles were even more tricky, but much could be achieved with models and full-size mock-ups of one or two ships in the studio. The stories tended to be based on the privateers and buccaneers who operated in the Caribbean, rather than the Barbary pirates of the Mediterranean. The lives of Francis Drake and Henry Morgan provided useful material, and so did Captain Johnson's *General History of the Pirates,* but realism was never a major objective. The pirate films of the twenties, the thirties, and the early forties were escapist adventures and were not meant to be taken too seriously.[23]

The first swashbuckling pirate film of any note was *The Black Pirate,* a silent film made by United Artists in 1926. It starred Douglas Fairbanks, Sr., who was also the producer and the author of the story on which the screenplay was based. Fairbanks was forty-two but still capable of the dazzling swordplay and physical stunts which he had performed in a succession of spectacular movies from *The Mark of Zorro* to *The Thief of Bagdad.* He had wanted to make a pirate film for some time, and when the two-tone Technicolor process was introduced, he decided to use it for a film which incorporated excerpts from every pirate story imaginable. Fairbanks played the part of the Duke of Arnoldo, who takes on the identity of the Black Pirate in order to avenge himself on the pirates responsible for his father's death. He kills the pirate captain in a duel on a lonely beach and takes over command of his crew. In a spectacular debut as a pirate he captures a huge galleon single-handed; this involves disabling the galleon's rudder, scaling her stern, which is the height of a three-story building, swinging on a rope up to the masthead, and then performing a stunt which became legendary and was copied in at least two other films: digging his knife into the sail, he skims down the surface of the canvas, ripping the sail in half as he goes. He pauses briefly on the yardarm of the mainsail and then repeats the stunt and slithers down to the deck. He commandeers two swivel guns, turns them on the crew of the galleon, and forces them to surrender, to the cheers of the men on the approaching pirate ship. A beautiful princess (played by Billie Dove) is a prisoner on board the Spanish ship. Fairbanks, the Black Pirate, falls in love with her and tries to help her escape, but his plans are uncovered by the villainous pirate lieutenant and he is forced to walk the plank. He manages to swim ashore, and he returns with a band of followers who help him retake the ship. There are more sword fights, the pirates are defeated, and the princess is rescued. The critics were not impressed by the story, but loved the color and the action. "With its excellent titles and wondrous color scenes this picture seems to have a Barriesque motif that has been aged in Stevensonian wood," wrote Mordaunt Hall in *The New York Times*. "This is a production which marks another forward stride for the screen, one that the boy and his mother will enjoy and one that is a healthy entertainment for men of all ages."[24]

The Black Pirate led the way for a wave of pirate films. The best of these were based on the historical novels of Rafael Sabatini, in particular on his three sea stories: *The Sea Hawk,* which was first published in 1915, *Captain Blood* (1922), and *The Black Swan* (1932). Sabatini was born at Iesi in central Italy in 1875. His father was an Italian aristocrat and his mother an Englishwoman. He published his first novel in 1904 and thereafter his output averaged a book a year for the next forty years. In 1905 he married Ruth Dixon and moved to England, which became his home for the rest of his life. Sabatini's books have gone out of fashion today but were immensely popular in the period between the two world wars, and six of them were made into films. A silent version of *Captain Blood* was produced by Vitagraph in 1925, with J. Warren Kerrigan playing Blood. It was a lavish production and was well received by press and public alike. *Kine Weekly*'s critic noted that "Brisk action harmonizes perfectly with artistic conception and authentic verisimilitude,"[25] and the *Daily Graphic* thought the sea fight at the end was "the biggest and rowdiest thing yet seen on the silent screen."[26] But the Vitagraph film was totally eclipsed by the version produced by Warner Brothers in 1935. This version was remarkable for making stars of the two principal actors, and for being the first film with music by Erich Wolfgang Korngold, who went on to become one of the greatest of all film composers. The film also established its director, Michael Curtiz (later to make his name with *Casablanca*), as the master of the swashbuckling epic.

Jack Warner had originally intended to cast Robert Donat as Captain Peter Blood, but difficulties over the contract led to his withdrawal.

Warner's other choices for the part were Leslie Howard, Clark Gable, and Ronald Colman, but none of these was available and Michael Curtiz was ordered to set up screen tests for Errol Flynn, a twenty-six-year-old unknown who had arrived in Hollywood a few months before. The son of an eminent professor of marine biology from Australia, Flynn had led an action-packed life since leaving school in Sydney.[27] He had been manager of a copra plantation in New Guinea; he had gone gold prospecting and ocean voyaging, and had then spent a year as an actor in England with the Northampton Repertory Company. He had landed a small part with the Warner Bros. studio at Teddington, and on the strength of this he was sent to its Burbank studios in California. He had already been cast in a minor role in *Captain Blood,* but he showed up so well in the screen tests that it was decided to risk him in the lead part. The equally unknown Olivia de Havilland was cast opposite him in the part of Lady Arabella Bishop. She was only nineteen, but she had a timeless beauty which was ideally suited to costume dramas. Basil Rathbone was cast as the wicked French pirate Levasseur, and managed to steal every scene in which he appeared.

Warner's spent $1 million on the production of *Captain Blood.* Most of the filming took place in the studio, where sets were built to represent a Jamaican sugar plantation, the streets of Port Royal, and the deck of a three-masted ship. The sea battles were filmed using eighteen-foot ship models in the studio tank. The location sequences, notably the duel on the seashore between Flynn and Rathbone, were filmed at Laguna Beach. Curtiz was a perfectionist and would persevere day after day until he achieved the effects he wanted. "I don't understand why we are still shooting close shots of the guns firing, and broadsides," complained Hal Wallis, the producer. "There was nothing wrong with the ones we have."[28] There were also worries about the amount of violence in the film. Robert Lord, a screenwriter, sent a warning memo to Wallis: "Why do you have so much flogging, torturing and physical cruelty in *Captain Blood?* Do you like it? Does Mike like it or do you think audiences like it? Women and children will be warned to stay away from the picture—and rightly so."[29] But all went well and the film was a triumph. The overall profit was nearly $1.5 million, and the film was nominated for the best motion picture Oscar (which it lost to another maritime epic, MGM's version of

Mutiny on the Bounty, starring Clark Gable and Charles Laughton). Errol Flynn and Olivia de Havilland proved to be a magical combination and were so popular with the public that they subsequently starred together in nine other films, most memorably in the 1938 production of *The Adventures of Robin Hood.*

In 1924 First National Pictures produced a silent film of Sabatini's novel *The Sea Hawk,* with Milton Sills in the title role. This was one of the few Hollywood productions to feature the Barbary pirates, because in Sabatini's story the hero is an English aristocrat who is falsely accused of murder and is sold into slavery. He becomes a galley slave on a Spanish ship, is rescued by Barbary corsairs, and joins their company. He is soon leading the corsairs into battle and acquires a formidable reputation as the Sea Hawk. The character was evidently inspired by the lives of the Elizabethan noblemen Sir Francis Verney and Sir Henry Mainwaring, both of whom became pirates. When Warner Bros. took over First National, it decided to remake *The Sea Hawk,* using some of the lavish costumes and sets which had been made for the 1939 production of *The Private Lives of Elizabeth and Essex.*

Seton Miller was commissioned to write a new script, and a decision was made to revise Sabatini's story entirely. The hero was to be Captain Thorpe, the commander of a privateer in the service of Queen Elizabeth I who fights the hated Spanish in the Caribbean. Although Drake was the model for Captain Thorpe, Miller was aware that he must be careful how he portrayed a national hero. "Although I based Thorpe's character on Drake, Hawkins and Frobisher," he wrote in a memo, "I believe it is a mistake to openly identify Thorpe with Drake in a subtitle. The raid on Panama is from Drake, but otherwise Thorpe's adventures vary so widely from Drake's history that the British may resent taking large dramatic liberties with their naval hero, where they wouldn't with a presumably fictitious character."[30] With Europe and America engaged in the war with Nazi Germany, the film became a propaganda vehicle, with Spain cast in the role of Germany and some rousing patriotic speeches by Thorpe.

Once again Michael Curtiz was asked to direct, Korngold was commissioned to write the music, and Errol Flynn was cast in the title role. This time Brenda Marshall was the heroine, and Flora Robson was flown over from England to play the part of Queen Elizabeth. Warner's had recently built a deep-water tank in one of its studios, and this was used for the sea battle sequences. Two full-size galleons were constructed and floated in the tanks, which were twelve feet deep. Hydraulic jacks were used to rock the ships from side to side, and a painted sea and sky cyclorama provided the background.

The Sea Hawk was released in 1940. It was a box-office success, and in spite of the enormous sums spent on the production (said to be $1.75 million), it made a profit of $977,000.[31] Over the years the film has provoked mixed reactions from the critics. Some consider it to be one of the greatest swashbuckling films of all time; others have found it stagy and mannered, with an overwritten script. What is in no doubt is the performance of the principal actors: Flora Robson was magnificently regal as Queen Elizabeth, and Claude Rains was convincingly evil as the Spanish Ambassador; but the star was Errol Flynn, who was in peak form. He was consistently late on the set and frequently forgot his lines, but his looks and performance were not yet affected by his famously debauched lifestyle. He strode the deck of his ship with a commanding step and flashing eyes, and his duel with the traitorous Lord Wolfingham in the candlelit halls of the palace is one of the great set pieces of the cinema.

Very few pirate films have matched the style and the panache of those which starred Douglas Fairbanks, Sr., and Errol Flynn, although there were some fine productions. Some of the most notable were *The Black Swan* of 1942, starring Tyrone Power and Maureen O'Hara, which was based on Sabatini's story of Henry Morgan's buccaneers; the 1938 version of *The Buccaneer,* produced by Cecil B. DeMille and starring Fredric March; and the best pirate film of the fifties, *The Crimson Pirate,* with Burt Lancaster looking his most heroic and performing his own stunts, and Eva Bartok as a spirited heroine.

Robert Newton created a memorable pirate chief in the otherwise undistinguished *Blackbeard the Pirate* (1952), and Jean Peters was a dashing female pirate in *Anne of the Indies,* which also starred Louis Jourdan as a French naval officer and James Robertson Justice as a one-eyed Scottish pirate. The life of Captain Kidd, which seems to have all the elements for a great movie, has been the subject of some of the worst of all the pirate films. Charles Laughton reduced the part to a hammy caricature with a cockney accent in the 1945 version of *Captain Kidd,* and went on to star in the even worse *Abbott and Costello Meet Captain Kidd* of 1954. *Captain Kidd and the Slave*

Girl, which was made the same year, was a modest-budget film with competent acting but it took some liberties with history by getting Anne Bonny to fall in love with Captain Kidd, by introducing the long-dead buccaneer L'Ollonais into the story, and by throwing in appearances by Blackbeard, Henry Avery, and Calico Jack.

More than seventy films have been made about pirates, buccaneers, and corsairs. While some film directors and producers have gone to considerable lengths to build pirate ships, stage elaborate sea battles, and film in appropriate locations in the West Indies and elsewhere, it is curious how few of the films follow the historical events with any accuracy. Most are based on works of fiction, or plunder the histories of the real pirates with a cavalier disregard for the facts. There is nothing wrong with this. Robert Louis Stevenson, Walter Scott, Lord Byron, Daniel Defoe, and Rafael Sabatini have entertained generations of readers with the adventures of their fictitious pirates, and there is no reason why the filmmakers should not do the same. But the fact remains that the lives of some of the real pirates and the men who hunted them down are as fascinating and as full of drama as any of the works of fiction.

Captain Kidd
and
Buried Treasure

CHESAPEAKE BAY lies on the eastern seaboard of North America and is a vast inland sea surrounded by innumerable creeks and estuaries. In November 1720 the ship *Prince Eugene* of Bristol entered the bay and headed for the entrance to the York River. Instead of proceeding a few miles upstream to Yorktown, she dropped anchor at the mouth of the river. That night the ship's longboat was lowered over the side. Six bags filled with silver coins were stowed in the stern sheets of the longboat, and six heavy wooden chests were stowed amidships. The boat was rowed ashore in the darkness. The wooden chests were unloaded and carried up the beach and buried in the sand. When the longboat returned to the anchored ship, Captain Stratton gave the orders to get under way. The anchor was heaved up, the sails were set, and the *Prince Eugene* slowly made her way up the river, towing the longboat astern.

One of the members of the crew was Morgan Miles, a twenty-year-old Welshman from Swansea. When the ship reached Yorktown, he slipped ashore and informed the authorities that his captain had traded with a pirate in Madagascar.[1] He told them that the *Prince Eugene* had sailed to the pirate harbor at Sainte Marie in the north of the island and met up with Captain Condell, the commander of the pirate ship *Dragon*. A boatload of brandy had been sent across to the pirates, followed by other goods from the merchant ship's cargo. He had observed Stratton drinking with the pirate captain under a tree, and had seen a great quantity of Spanish silver dollars brought on board the *Prince Eugene*. The ship's carpenter had been ordered to make some chests to hold the money.

Captain Stratton was arrested in Yorktown, interrogated, and imprisoned. A few weeks later he was sent back to England on board the British warship HMS *Rye*. Another member of the crew, Joseph Spollet from Devon, told the authorities that he understood that the value of the Spanish silver which Stratton had acquired from the pirates was £9,000 (the equivalent of more than £500,000).[2] There is no record of what happened to the buried chests of silver. Presumably they were recovered by the authorities in Yorktown and confiscated.

Although buried treasure has been a favorite theme in the pirate stories of fiction, there are very few documented examples of real pirates burying their loot. Most pirates preferred to spend their plunder in an orgy of drinking, gambling, and whoring when they returned to port. The case of Captain Stratton described above is one of the rare instances of treasure being buried, and although the treasure in question was looted by pirates, Stratton himself was a dishonest sea captain rather than a pirate. Another case which is well documented took place 150 years earlier. Following his attack on the mule train at Nombre de Dios, Francis Drake and his men made their way to the coast and found that their ships had been forced to sail down the coast to avoid a Spanish flotilla. Drake ordered his men to bury their huge haul of gold and silver, and while some of his crew stayed behind to guard the buried hoard, Drake and the others set off in a makeshift raft to contact his ships. After six hours' sailing they sighted the ships and were picked up. That night they returned to the spot where the treasure had been buried, retrieved it, and set sail for England. While Drake's raid at Nombre de Dios made his name and his fortune, the incident of the buried treasure never attracted much attention.

The pirate who seems to have been largely responsible for the legends of buried treasure was Captain Kidd. The story got around that Kidd had buried gold and silver from the plundered ship *Quedah Merchant* on Gardiners Island near New York before he was arrested. Because of the extraordinary attention given to Kidd's exploits in the Indian Ocean and his subsequent trial and execution, he became one of the most famous pirates of history and the matter of the buried treasure received more attention than it ever deserved. The irony of it all is that Kidd never intended to become a pirate and to the end maintained his innocence of all wrongdoing. It was his misfortune to became a pawn in a political game involving players in London, New York, and India.[3]

Kidd was a victim of circumstance, but he was also the victim of defects in his character. He seems to have had some of the same traits as Captain Bligh of the *Bounty.* He was a good seaman, but he had a violent temper and a fatal inability to earn the respect of his crew. Unlike Bligh, who was a small man, Kidd was large and powerful and bullied his men. He was constantly engaged in arguments and quarrels. A local agent who met him at the Indian port of Carwar described him as a "very lusty man, fighting with his men on any occasion, often calling for his pistols and threatening any one that durst speak anything contrary to his mind to knock out their brains, causing them to dread him. . . ."[4] He annoyed dockworkers and sea captains by his arrogant manner and his habit of boasting about his grand connections. He deluded himself about his motives and his actions when he turned pirate in the Indian Ocean, and no doubt deserved the biting comment which was made by a Member of Parliament at the time of his trial: "I thought him only a knave. I now know him to be a fool as well."[5]

William Kidd was born about 1645 at Greenock, the Scottish port on the Firth of Clyde. His father was a Presbyterian minister. Nothing is known of his early years except that he went to sea, and by 1689 had become the captain of a privateer in the Caribbean. While in command of the ship *Blessed William,* he joined a squadron led by Captain Hewetson of the Royal Navy which raided the French island of Marie Galante and then fought a pitched battle with five French warships off the island of St. Martin. Unfortunately, Kidd's crew were more interested in buccaneering than in fighting for their country, and soon after they dropped anchor at Nevis, they seized Kidd's ship and sailed away without him. However, the Governor of Nevis was grateful for Kidd's actions against the French and presented him with a recently captured French vessel, which was renamed the *Antigua.*

In 1691 Kidd arrived in New York in command of his new vessel. On May 16 he married a wealthy widow, Sarah Oort, and in due course they moved into a fine house in Pearl Street at the southern end of Manhattan Island, near the quays of the old harbor. For the next four years Kidd developed business interests, cultivated friendships with politicians and merchants, and did some occasional privateering. He seems to have become bored with this life, and in 1695 he sailed for England, hoping to make his fortune from privateering.

With the help of Robert Livingstone, a New York entrepreneur who arrived in London around the same time, Kidd set about looking for sponsors who would put up the money for a privateering voyage. After much lobbying they gained the support of Lord Bellomont, a Member of Parliament and a staunch supporter of the ruling Whig party. Bellomont was in need of money and was to play a key role in the story because he had recently been nominated Governor of Massachusetts Bay. The three men devised an unusual scheme for making money: they would form a syndicate, buy a powerful ship, and dispatch it to the Indian Ocean to capture the pirates who were plundering shipping and selling the stolen goods to merchants in New York. Bellomont agreed to find financial backers for the venture, while Kidd undertook to command the ship and to recruit the crew under the usual privateering system of "no purchase, no pay."

Bellomont persuaded four other Whig peers to become financial backers: the Lords Somers, Orford, Romney, and Shrewsbury. Edmund Harrison, a wealthy City merchant and a director of the East India Company, also agreed to participate, and they approached the Admiralty for a privateering commission. At this date England was still at war with France, so there was no problem about obtaining a letter of marque which authorized the capture of French ships. This did not extend to the capture of pirate ships, but the shortcoming was overcome by issuing a patent under the Great Seal signed by the Lord Keeper of the Great Seal, who happened to be Lord Somers. This second commission authorized Kidd to hunt down "Pirates, Freebooters, and Sea Rovers" and in particular four pirates who were named in the document: Captain Thomas Tew, John Ireland, Thomas Wake, and William Maze, or Mace.

The most surprising part of the whole deal was that the King himself was persuaded to take part in the venture. William III gave formal approval to the scheme and signed a warrant which authorized the partners to keep all the profits from Kidd's captures, thus bypassing the usual arrangement whereby all prizes must be declared in the

Admiralty Courts. The King was induced to agree to this unusual arrangement because Lord Shrewsbury arranged for him to reserve a share of 10 percent.

The vessel selected for the privateering voyage was the thirty-four-gun *Adventure Galley*. On April 10, 1696, the *Adventure Galley* anchored in the Downs, and the Thames pilot was dropped off. After a brief stop at Plymouth they set off across the Atlantic to New York, where Kidd hoped to make up the crew numbers needed. News of the privateering voyage rapidly circulated on the waterfront, and he had no problem in recruiting 90 more men. When he left New York on September 6, 1696, there were 152 men in his crew. Governor Fletcher of New York described them as "men of desperate fortunes and necessitous of getting vast treasure."

They spent a day at Madeira to collect freshwater and provisions, then headed south. On January 27, 1697, they dropped anchor at Tulear (Toliara), a small port on the west coast of Madagascar. Kidd stayed here a month to give his men time to recover from the voyage. Several were sick with scurvy. He then sailed north to Johanna in the Comoros Islands and from there to the nearby island of Mohilla, where he careened his ship. While there he lost thirty men to tropical disease. The survivors were now becoming restless. He had taken on more men during his various stops in the Indian Ocean, and a number of former pirates had now joined the crew. The "no purchase, no pay" arrangement meant that they must capture a prize soon or go home penniless.

Kidd decided to head for the Red Sea and see whether he could intercept one of the ships of the pilgrim fleet. He told his crew he was heading for Mocha at the mouth of the Red Sea: "Come boys, I will make money enough out of that fleet." This was not part of his brief and was not covered by either of the privateering commissions which he carried, and so would be difficult to justify to his backers. The pilgrim fleet left Mocha on August 11, 1697, under the protection of three European ships, one of them, the thirty-six-gun *Sceptre,* commanded by Edward Barlow, recently promoted from first mate following the death of the captain. Barlow is much revered today among maritime historians for the vivid journal which he wrote and illustrated describing his life at sea.[6] Early on the morning of August 14, Barlow spotted the *Adventure Galley* closing with the convoy. Ominously, she was flying the red flag of piracy at her masthead. Barlow fired his guns in warning and raised the flag of the East India Company. The wind was light, so Kidd used his oars, steered toward a Malabar ship, and fired a broadside. Barlow was not prepared to lose one of his convoy. He lowered his boats and had his crew tow the *Sceptre* toward Kidd's ship. He ordered his men aloft to yell threats and fired off his guns. Kidd lost his nerve. He retreated out of range and after a while abandoned all hope of capturing a prize and sailed away.

His situation was deteriorating fast. His ship was leaking, supplies were short, and his crew were becoming mutinous. When they encountered a small trading ship off the Malabar coast, Kidd fired a shot across her bows and came alongside her. What happened next was the turning point in Kidd's voyage. The trader was flying English flags, and while Kidd was interviewing Captain Parker, her commander, some of Kidd's crew tortured Parker's men to find out where they had hidden their valuables. Several seamen were hoisted up on ropes and beaten with cutlasses. Kidd then seized provisions from Parker's vessel and forced him to stay on board and act as a pilot.

News of Kidd's attack on the pilgrim fleet and on the trading vessel began to circulate among the harbors of the region, and two Portuguese warships were sent out by the Viceroy of Goa to look for the *Adventure Galley*. For once things went Kidd's way. He was able to cripple the smaller of the two ships with his guns and to escape unscathed. But the lack of discipline and the piratical state of his crew were clearly demonstrated when they called in at the Laccadive Islands. The local boats were seized and chopped up for firewood, the native women were raped, and when their men retaliated by killing the ship's cooper, the pirates attacked the village and beat up the inhabitants. News of these atrocities reached the mainland and further added to the catalog of Kidd's misdemeanors.

Two further events sealed Kidd's fate. On October 30 an argument developed between Kidd and his gunner, William Moore. The men had been grumbling about the lack of prizes, and Kidd rounded on Moore, who was on deck sharpening a chisel, and called him a lousy dog. Moore replied, "If I am a lousy dog, you have made me so; you have brought me to ruin and many more."[7] Kidd was enraged by this remark. He picked up an iron-hooped bucket and thumped it down on the head of the gunner. Moore collapsed on the deck and was heard to say, "Farewell, farewell, Captain Kidd has given me my last."[8] The ship's surgeon took Moore below but could do nothing for him. His skull was fractured by the blow, and he died the next day. Kidd was unrepentant. He said he had good friends in England who would save him from the consequences.

On January 30, 1698, the *Adventure Galley* finally came across a prize worth taking. Off the port of Cochin on the Malabar coast of India she intercepted the 400-ton merchant ship *Quedah Merchant*. She had taken on a cargo of silk, calico, sugar, opium, and iron at Bengal and was heading north under the command of an English captain, John Wright. Kidd came alongside flying French flags. Most merchant ships on long voyages carried passes of several nationalities to avoid being claimed as a prize by privateers, and when Captain Wright saw Kidd's French flags he naturally produced a French pass. This played straight into Kidd's hand, because of course one of his letters of marque authorized him to attack and seize French ships. In fact the *Quedah Merchant* belonged to Armenian owners, and a considerable part of the ship's cargo was the property of a senior official at the court of the Mogul of India.

Kidd informed Captain Wright that he was claiming his ship as a prize, and without more ado he escorted her to the nearest port in order to sell some of her cargo and raise much-needed cash. The value of the *Quedah Merchant*'s cargo was estimated at somewhere between 200,000 and 400,000 rupees. Kidd sold the bulk of the goods at the port of Caliquilon for around £7,000, and then headed out to sea to look for more prizes. He captured a small Portuguese ship, looted her, and kept her as an escort. He chased the East India Company ship *Sedgewick* for several hours, but she escaped. He then headed back to Madagascar and, in April 1698, the *Adventure Galley* dropped anchor in the pirate harbor of Sainte Marie. Already at anchor was the pirate ship *Resolution* under the command of Robert Culliford, who had spent the last year plundering ships in the Indian Ocean. Culliford was one of a group of mutineers who had killed the captain of the East Indiaman *Mocha,* and taken her over. If Kidd had not already turned pirate, he should have arrested Culliford and seized his ship, because that was exactly what his commission authorized him to do. Instead Kidd assured him he meant him no harm and joined him for a drink.

Kidd remained at Madagascar for several months, recuperating from the weeks at sea and waiting for favorable winds. The men insisted on a final share-out of the plunder, and some deserted and joined Culliford. Kidd decided to abandon the leaking and rotten *Adventure Galley* and took command of the *Quedah Merchant,* which he renamed the *Adventure Prize.* In the early months of 1699 (there is no record of the exact date) he set sail with a very much reduced crew of twenty and a few slaves. He headed for the West Indies and reached the little island of Anguilla in early April. There he learned that the British government, at the request of the East India Company, had declared him a pirate. No pardon was to be extended to him, and he was to be hunted down and brought to justice. He hastily stocked up with food and water and, after a stay of no more than four hours, set sail for a safer haven.

He selected the Danish island of St. Thomas, which was commonly used by pirates as a place to sell their plundered goods, and sailed into the harbor there on April 6. He went to see the Governor of the island and tried to persuade him to offer him protection from the ships of the Royal Navy. Governor Laurents was not prepared to risk a naval blockade of his harbor and refused his request. This encounter was later reported in London with some additions to the story: "Letters from Curassau say that the famous pyrate Captain Kidd in a ship of 30 guns and 250 men offered the Governor of St. Thomas 45,000 pieces of eight in gold and a great present of goods, if he would protect him for a month, which he refused."[9]

Kidd returned to his ship, weighed anchor, and sailed onward. At the eastern end of the island of Hispaniola he sought refuge in the mouth of the Higüey River, where he moored his leaking ship to trees on the riverbank. Here he was joined by Henry Bolton, an unscrupulous trader with a shady past who had no qualms about dealing with the now-notorious pirate. Bolton and an associate agreed to buy the bales of cloth remaining in the hold of the former *Quedah Merchant,* and then bought the ship as well. Kidd purchased Bolton's sloop, the *Saint Antonio,* and moved on board with the remnants of his crew and the profits from his various transactions.

At this stage it became clear to Kidd that his situation was desperate. The British authorities throughout the Caribbean were on the lookout for him. Back in November Admiral Benbow had sent a letter to the governor of every American colony requesting them to "take particular care for apprehending the said Kidd and his accomplices wherever he shall arrive."[10] When the Governor of Nevis learned that Kidd was in the area, he sent HMS *Queenborough* to Puerto Rico to intercept him. Kidd decided that his only hope was to return to America and negotiate with his business partner Lord Bellomont, who was now Governor of New York, Massachusetts Bay, and New Hampshire. He set sail and headed north.

The *Saint Antonio* reached Long Island in June, and Kidd was reunited with his wife and two daughters after an absence of three years. Negotiations began with Bellomont in Boston, but the Governor was playing a tricky political game, having one eye on his own position and one eye on Kidd's treasure. Interviewed by Bellomont and subsequently by the Massachusetts Council, Kidd gave a detailed account of the goods and cash he had acquired from his captures. He listed the bales of silks, muslins, and calicoes; the tons of sugar and iron; fifty cannon; eighty pounds of silver and a forty-pound bag of gold. Bellomont was aware that if he handled the situation badly, Kidd was a serious danger to his career. The most satisfactory course of action was to arrest him for piracy, which would clear him of involvement in Kidd's exploits and enable him to take a portion of Kidd's treasure in his role as Vice Admiral of the colony. When Kidd arrived for another meeting with the Council at Boston, he found the constable waiting at the door. The constable stepped forward to arrest him and Kidd ran inside the building, yelling for Lord Bellomont. The constable ran after him, seized him, and marched him off to the town jail, with Kidd shouting and protesting as they went. Although he had earlier promised Kidd that he would obtain the King's Pardon for him, Bellomont was able to justify his change of heart because he had received specific instructions from England to arrest Kidd. Abandoned by the only man who could have saved him, Kidd faced a sealed fate. If he had hidden on one of the Caribbean islands or gone to earth on the mainland of America, he might have survived, as many other pirates managed to do, but he was now the scapegoat for all the acts of piracy committed by a generation of pirates in the Indian Ocean.

The news of Kidd's exploits had been followed closely in London, which was not surprising as a number of influential people, including the King, the Lord Chancellor, and several Whig politicians, had originally taken a stake in his venture. When it was learned that Kidd had turned pirate, there were many Tory politicians who saw an opportunity to create a major scandal and bring down key members of the government. Interest was heightened by rumors that Kidd's plunder was valued at more than £400,000. The East India Company demanded a share of the treasure to compensate for its losses in India and to repay some of the victims of Kidd's raids. In December the whole matter was debated in the House of Commons, and there was a vote of censure for the Whigs' handling of the affair. The Tories lost the vote, but the Secretary of State, Sir James Vernon, noted ominously, "Parliaments are grown into the habit of finding fault, and some Jonah or other must be thrown overboard if the storm cannot otherwise be laid."[11] Needless to say, it was Kidd who was to be the Jonah.

In September the news that Lord Bellomont had arrested Kidd reached London, and the Admiralty ordered a warship to be sent to Boston to bring him back to England. HMS *Advice* arrived at Boston in February 1700 during a spell of bitterly cold weather. Kidd was escorted on board, and together with thirty-one other prisoners, he began the voyage back to England. By the time the *Advice* anchored in the Thames he was very ill. However, he managed to write a letter to Lord Orford, one of the sponsors of the voyage, and gave a selective and flagrantly biased account of his actions in the Indian Ocean. He maintained that he had only taken two ships, both of which had flown French flags. He claimed that his crew had forced him to commit piracy and had robbed him and destroyed his logbook and all his records. He concluded: "I am in hopes that your lordship and the rest of the Honourable gentlemen my owners will so far vindicate me I may have no injustice."[12]

While the politicians, the lords of the Admiralty, the lawyers, and the merchants assembled their evidence and interviewed witnesses, Kidd was transferred from HMS *Advice* to the royal yacht *Katharine* at Greenwich. Worn down by months of solitary confinement and illness, and allowed no legal representation or even access to any relevant papers, he gave way to despair and contemplated suicide. Dreading the thought of death by hanging, he asked for a knife so that he could end his life. He was not to be allowed such a quick end to his troubles. On April 14 the Admiralty sent its barge down to Greenwich and Kidd was rowed upstream to Whitehall. That afternoon he was led into the Admiralty building in Whitehall and cross-examined by Sir Charles Hedges, the Chief Judge of the Admiralty, in the presence of Admiral Sir George Rooke, the Earl of Bridgewater, and other dignitaries. He repeated the arguments he had presented in his letter to Lord Orford. After seven hours of questioning, Kidd was led away to Newgate Prison, where he was to remain a prisoner for the next eleven months.

Even by eighteenth-century standards, Newgate was a nightmarish place in which to be confined. Situated on the corner of Holborn and Newgate Street, it was a forbidding stone building designed to house the criminal underworld of London while they awaited trial and death by hanging at Tyburn. Petty thieves and prostitutes rubbed shoulders with cutthroats and highwaymen. Wives and children were allowed to visit, and there was a relaxed attitude toward gambling, drinking, sex, and the keeping of pets and poultry, but this was offset by the severe overcrowding, the stinking smells, and the shrieks and shouts of the inmates. In 1719 Captain Alexander Smith described Newgate as a habitation of misery, "a bottomless pit of violence, a Tower of Babel where all are speakers and no hearers." [13]

On March 27, 1701, Kidd was allowed a brief respite from this hellhole. He was marched through the streets to Whitehall in order to be examined at the bar of the House of Commons, the first and only pirate in British history to have to explain his actions before the assembled Members of Parliament. He was hardly in a fit state to do so. Depressed, disheveled, and suffering the ill effects of more than two years of imprisonment in horrendous conditions, he must have been a pathetic sight. No records of the session have survived, and all we know is that an attempt to use the occasion to impeach Lord Somers and Lord Orford failed. A second examination by Members of Parliament followed on March 31, and Kidd was returned once again to Newgate.

By this time the lawyers had prepared their case. Henry Bolton, who had bought the *Quedah Merchant* from Kidd in Hispaniola, had been tracked down and brought to England for questioning. Coji Babba, an Armenian merchant who had been on board the *Quedah Merchant* during Kidd's attack and had lost all his goods, was sent from India by the East India Company so that he could give evidence for the prosecution. Kidd's two slaves Dundee and Ventura had been questioned, and piles of papers had been assembled from Lord Bellomont and everyone connected with the case. All that remained was the trial, which was scheduled to take place on May 8 and 9 at the Old Bailey.

Kidd had two weeks to prepare his defense. He asked for his papers to be sent to him, and in particular requested his two privateering commissions, his original orders from the Admiralty, and the two French passes he had been given by the captains of the *Quedah Merchant* and one of the other ships he had taken. Some documents were brought to him, but mysteriously missing were the French passes.

When the trial began before Lord Chief Baron Ward and four other judges, Kidd found himself facing a formidable list of charges. He was accused of the murder of William Moore, the man he had killed with the iron-hooped bucket; of piracy and robbery of the *Quedah Merchant;* and of piratically attacking and taking four other vessels and stealing their cargoes. On the matter of the murder charge, Kidd maintained that his crew was on the verge of mutiny at the time, that he was provoked by Moore, and that he had never intended to kill him. On the piracy charges, Kidd argued that he had a commission to take French ships, and insisted that if the French passes could be found, his innocence would be proved. However, the evidence assembled by the prosecution was formidable, and the witnesses for the prosecution were well briefed. Kidd blustered his way through the proceedings, but the verdict was inevitable. The jury found him guilty on all the charges, and the judge sentenced him to death by hanging. When he heard the sentence, Kidd said, "My lord, it is a very hard sentence. For my part, I am the innocentest person of them all, only I have been sworn against by perjured persons." [14]

But what of Kidd's plunder and the rumors of buried treasure? Kidd traded some of his cargo at a port in the Indian Ocean, and much of the rest he sold to Henry Bolton in Hispaniola. He bought the *Saint Antonio* for 3,000 pieces of eight, and acquired 4,200 pieces of eight in bills of exchange and 4,000 in gold bars and gold dust. He therefore sailed north with 8,200 pieces of eight in portable form, along with an unknown amount of goods and treasure loaded on his newly acquired sloop. When he arrived in New York, he may have handed some of his fortune to Mrs. Kidd and his friend Emott.

While preliminary negotiations were taking place with Lord Bellomont, Kidd moved his ship from New York harbor to the eastern end of Long Island, where he sailed back and forth near Gardiners Island. For some weeks the ship lingered between Gardiners Island and Block Island, and during this time three sloops came alongside to take off some of Kidd's crew, together with their sea chests and their share of the cargo. We know that Kidd sent Lady Bellomont an enameled box with four jewels in it. We also know that Mrs. Kidd sent a six-pound bag of pieces of eight to Thomas Way, and that Kidd sent several pounds of gold, believed to be worth £10,000, to Major Selleck in Connecticut. But the greatest amount came into the hands of John Gardiner, the proprietor of Gardiners Island, and it was this which was to lead to the legend of Kidd's buried treasure. On two occasions Kidd landed on the island; he bought food from Gardiner, and left behind five bales of cloth, a chest of fine goods, and a box containing fifty-two pounds of gold. This was probably his security in case things went wrong.

As soon as Kidd was safely locked up in Boston jail, Lord Bellomont made strenuous efforts to locate and retrieve the treasure, which was now scattered in various locations around New York, Boston, and the West Indies. Mr. Campbell's house in Boston was searched, and 463 ounces of gold and 203 ounces of silver were removed. John Gardiner sent Bellomont eleven bags of gold and silver. In the end 1,111 ounces of gold, 2,353 ounces of silver, forty-one bales of goods, bags of silver pieces, and various jewels were collected and sent on board HMS *Advice* for dispatch to England.[15] The total value of this was reckoned to be £14,000, a handsome sum, but nothing like the £40,000 Kidd had led Bellomont to expect, and a tiny fraction of the £400,000 Kidd was rumored to have plundered in the Indian Ocean. Although Henry Bolton had been arrested by the captain of HMS *Fowey,* there was no sign of the goods he had acquired from Kidd in the West Indies. The *Quedah Merchant,* abandoned in Hispaniola, was set on fire, and the burned-out hulk was left to rot on the shore of the river estuary. Over the years people have tried to find the remnants of Kidd's treasure and have carried out searches on Gardiners Island and many other locations, but without success.

We know more about Kidd's treasure than about any of the other pirates of his day simply because of the public interest surrounding his capture and trial. Other pirates of his day may have amassed more plunder than he did, but the evidence is fragmentary. Bartholomew

Roberts' biggest haul was probably the cargo of the Portuguese ship he looted in his first year of piracy. Blackbeard plundered around twenty ships during his two years as a pirate, but none of his prizes were spectacular in terms of treasure. After the battle at Ocracoke Inlet the loot recovered from his vessels and ashore in a tent was "25 hogsheads of sugar, 11 tierces, and 145 bags of cocoa, a barrel of indigo and a bale of cotton."[16] This, together with the sale of Blackbeard's sloop, came to £2,500—not a very impressive sum to have amassed during such a famous piratical career.

Captain England captured a number of rich prizes in the Indian Ocean. In 1720 he came across a Portuguese ship of seventy guns at anchor among the Mascarene Islands to the east of Madagascar. She had been badly damaged in a storm and put up no resistance when attacked by the pirates. Among the passengers on board was the Viceroy of Goa. According to Johnson's *General History of the Pirates,* the value of the diamonds on the ship was between $3 million and $4 million. He tells how the pirates sailed on to Madagascar, where they careened their ship and shared out the plunder, which worked out at forty-two diamonds a man. Henry Avery's capture of the *Ganj-i-Sawai* was in a similar league, and the treasure looted from her was variously estimated at between £200,000 and £350,000. Most pirates had to be content with very much more modest plunder.

Apart from Kidd's treasure, the best-documented booty from the great age of piracy is that looted by Sam Bellamy. Excavations on Bellamy's ship the *Whydah* have brought up from the seabed an impressive quantity of coins, gold bars, and African jewelry. There are 8,397 coins of various denominations, including 8,357 Spanish silver coins and 9 Spanish gold coins, which together add up to 4,131 pieces of eight. There are 17 gold bars, 14 gold nuggets, and 6,174 bits of gold, and a quantity of gold dust.[17] The African gold includes nearly four hundred items of Akan jewelry, mostly gold beads, pendants, and ornaments. No one will put a precise value on this and the press reports that the *Whydah* treasure is worth $400 million are wildly speculative, but the excavations have shown beyond doubt that some pirates really did lay their hands on large quantities of gold and silver.

The lure of treasure was always one of the most powerful motives for becoming a pirate. With riches like those acquired by Henry Morgan, Henry Avery, Captain Kidd, or Sam Bellamy a man could escape from the harsh life of the sea. He could squander his money on whores or pass his days drinking in some convivial tavern. He need never more risk death from malaria or yellow fever on the coast of Africa while his ship waited for a consignment of slaves. He could feast on fresh meat and good wine instead of moldering ship biscuits, salt pork, and evil-smelling beer.

Sailors were attracted by the tales of pirate kingdoms in Madagascar and the West Indies, where all men were equal, where everyone had a vote in the affairs of the pirate company, and where the plunder was fairly shared out. And for the more adventurous, piracy offered the chance to leave the gray, cold waters of the North Sea or the New-foundland Banks and explore the warm blue waters of the Caribbean.

Some men were driven to piracy from sheer necessity. Two of the most dramatic increases in pirate activity took place when peace was declared after long periods of naval warfare and large numbers of seamen were out of work. When fifty years of hostilities between En-gland and Spain were finally ended in 1603, hundreds of seamen from the Royal Navy and from privateers were thrown on the streets. Their only skill was in handling a ship, and many turned to piracy. For the next thirty years, shipping in the English Channel, the Thames estuary, and the Mediterranean was ravaged by pirates.

The second surge in piracy took place in the years following the Treaty of Utrecht of 1713, which brought peace among England, France, and Spain. The size of the Royal Navy slumped from 53,785 in 1703 to 13,430 in 1715, putting 40,000 seamen out of work.[18] There is no proof that these men joined the ranks of the pirates, and Marcus Rediker has pointed out that most pirates were drawn from the merchant navy, not the Royal Navy; but many contemporary observers believed that the rise in pirate attacks in the years after the Peace of Utrecht was due to the large numbers of unemployed seamen. They particularly blamed the Spanish for driving the logwood cutters out of the bays of Campeche and Honduras after the Treaty of Utrecht, and they also blamed the privateers. Many privateering commissions had been issued in the later years of the seventeenth century, particularly in the West Indies. Peace put an end to this, and the Governor of Jamaica warned London of the likely outcome: "Since the calling in of our privateers, I find already a considerable number of seafaring men at the towns of Port Royal and Kingston that can't find employment, who I am very apprehensive, for want of occupation in their way, may in a short time desert us and turn pirates."[19]

The speeches of condemned pirates awaiting execution provide a further insight into what induced men to take up piracy. Some blamed the cruelty of captains, but many blamed drink for leading them astray. Before he was hanged at Boston in 1724, William White said that drunkenness had been his ruin, and he had been drunk when he was enticed aboard a pirate ship. John Archer, who was hanged on the same day, admitted that strong drink had hardened him into committing crimes that were more bitter than death to him now. But it was the lure of plunder and riches which was the principal attraction of piracy, just as it has been for every bandit, brigand, and thief throughout history.

II

Hunting Down the Pirates

THE STORY OF Blackbeard and his grisly death has become so embroidered with legend that one is half inclined to put it all down to the fertile imagination of Captain Johnson. However, the salt-stained logbooks of the naval officers involved are a salutary reminder that Blackbeard was a real person. In the Public Record Office at Kew is the captain's log of HMS *Lyme,* which describes the dispatching of the expedition "in quest of ye Pirate Teach in N Carolina,"[1] and in the National Maritime Museum at Greenwich is the log which was kept by Robert Maynard, first lieutenant of HMS *Pearl* and the man who led the naval force which destroyed the most famous of all the pirates. Maynard's entry for November 17, 1718, reads:

> Mod gales & fair Weather, this day I recd from Capt Gordon, an Order to Command 60 Men out of his Majsties Ships Pearle & Lyme, on board two small Sloops, in Order to destroy Some pyrates, who resided in N Carolina, This day Weigh'd, & Sail'd hence with ye Sloops undr my Command, having on board Proviso of all species with Arms, & Ammunition Suitable for ye occasion.[2]

The man responsible for organizing the expedition in search of Blackbeard was Alexander Spotswood, the Governor of Virginia. Spotswood had received numerous complaints from the traders of

North Carolina of the pirates' activities. He believed that the government of that province was too weak to restrain them, and he was
particularly concerned that the pirates planned to fortify an island at
Ocracoke Inlet, making it into a general rendezvous for all the pirate
ships in the region. He issued a proclamation on November 24, 1718,
offering rewards for the conviction or killing of the pirates:

> . . . For Edward Teach, commonly called Captain Teach, or Black-
> Beard, one hundred Pounds, for every other Commander of a Pyrate
> Ship, Sloop, or Vessel, forty pounds; for every Lieutenant, Master,
> or Quarter-Master Boatswain, or Carpenter, twenty Pounds; for
> every other inferior Officer, fifteen Pounds, and for every private
> Man taken on Board such Ship, Sloop, or Vessel, ten Pounds;[3]

Spotswood approached the commanders of the two British warships
on the Virginia station, Captain Gordon of HMS *Pearl* and Captain
Brand of HMS *Lyme* and asked them whether they would be prepared
"to extirpate this nest of vipers." The captains pointed out that it was
not possible for their ships to navigate the shallow and difficult channels around Ocracoke, and they had no orders to hire and pay for
smaller vessels. Spotswood offered to put up the money for two sloops
and to send for pilots from Carolina. At this the captains agreed to
provide the men.[4]

Lieutenant Maynard, "an experienced officer and a gentleman of
great bravery and resolution,"[5] was appointed to lead the expedition.
He had under his command thirty-five men from the *Pearl*, and a
midshipman and twenty-five men from the *Lyme*. The hired sloops
were the *Ranger* and the *Jane*. Maynard took command of the *Jane*
and a Mr. Hyde was put in command of the *Ranger*. Neither of the
sloops had guns, so Maynard had to rely on small arms, swords, and
pistols.

Maynard found out from passing vessels that Blackbeard's sloop
Adventure was anchored on the inner side of Ocracoke Island, facing
the sheltered waters of Pamlico Sound. It was an ideal refuge, protected by numerous shoals and sandbanks. Maynard's sloops, guided
by the local pilots, arrived in the area at dusk on Thursday, November
21 and the decision was made to wait for the tide and make the attack
early the following morning.

At first light the sloops weighed anchor and crept toward the island.

There was very little wind, and Maynard ordered some of his men to take a small boat and row ahead of the sloop, taking soundings as they went. As they approached the pirate ship, they were greeted by a volley of shot. The boat hastily retreated to the protection of the sloops.

At this stage the odds were still in Maynard's favor. According to Captain Brand's report to the Admiralty, the pirate ship only had nineteen men on board, "thirteen white and six Negros." [6] Moreover, Blackbeard and several of his crew had spent much of the night drinking. However, the pirate captain knew the shoals and channels, and his ship was armed with nine mounted guns. With the alarm raised, he cut his anchor cable and headed for a narrow channel among the submerged sandbanks. Maynard hoisted the King's colors and set off in pursuit.

There was so little wind that the sloops had to use their oars to make any progress. At this point Maynard's sloops ran aground, and a shouted exchange took place between Maynard and Blackbeard. There are several versions of this. The briefest is Maynard's own account which simply reads. "At our first salutation, he drank Damnation to me and my Men, whom he stil'd Cowardly Puppies, saying, He would neither give nor take Quarter." [7] Johnson's version, which seems to have been based on the newspaper accounts, is more colorful:

Black-Beard hail'd him in this rude Manner: **Damn you for Villains, who are you? And from whence came you?** The Lieutenant make him Answer, **You may see by our Colours we are no Pyrates.** Blackbeard bid him send his Boat on Board, that he might see who he was but Mr Maynard reply'd thus; **I cannot spare my Boat, but I will come aboard of you as soon as I can, with my Sloop.** Upon this Black-beard took a Glass of Liquor, & drank to him with these Words: **Damnation seize my Soul if I give you Quarters, or take any from you.** In Answer to which, Mr Maynard told him, **That he expected no Quarters from him, nor should he give him any.** [8]

With the rising tide, and with the help of much heaving and pulling from his men, Maynard's two sloops floated free and began to row toward the *Adventure*. As they approached, Blackbeard fired a broadside from his guns, which he had loaded with swan shot, nails, and pieces of old iron. The effect was devastating. In Maynard's words, "Mr. Hyde was unfortunately killed, and five of his Men wounded in

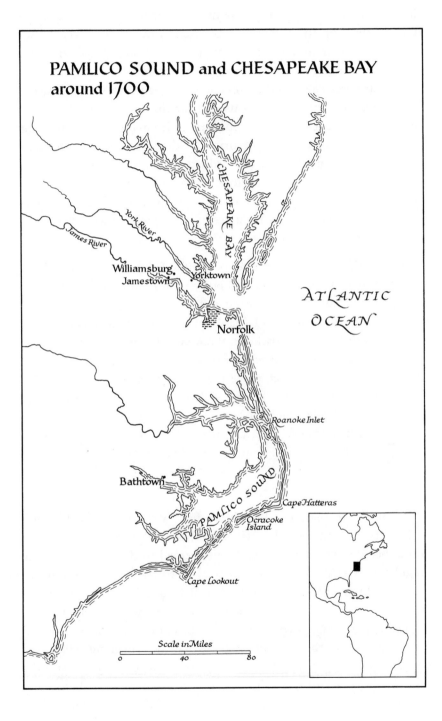

PAMLICO SOUND and CHESAPEAKE BAY
around 1700

CHESAPEAKE BAY

York River

James River

Williamsburg
Jamestown
Yorktown

ATLANTIC
OCEAN

Norfolk

Roanoke Inlet

Bathtown

PAMLICO SOUND

Cape Hatteras

Ocracoke
Island

Cape Lookout

Scale in Miles

0   40   80

the little sloop, which having nobody to command her, fell astern and did not come up to assist me till the Action was almost over."[9] According to the more detailed account in the *Boston News Letter*, six men were killed and ten wounded by the broadside.

Maynard pressed on in the *Jane* and succeeded in shooting away the *Adventure*'s jib and fore-halyards and forcing the vessel ashore. He ordered all except two of his men to hide in the hold with their weapons at the ready while he made his final approach. As the *Jane* came alongside his ship, Blackbeard naturally assumed his guns had killed most of her crew and decided to board Maynard's ship with ten of his pirates. They clambered aboard, and as they did so, the sailors emerged from hiding. The most complete account of what happened next appears in the *Boston News Letter:*

> Maynard and Teach themselves begun the fight with their swords, Maynard making a thrust, the point of his sword went against Teach's cartridge box, and bended it to the hilt. Teach broke the guard of it, and wounded Maynard's fingers but did not disable him, whereupon he jumped back and threw away his sword and fired his pistol which wounded Teach. Demelt struck in between them with his sword and cut Teach's face pretty much; in the interim both companies engaged in Maynard's sloop, one of Maynard's men being a Highlander, engaged Teach with his broad sword, who gave Teach a cut on the neck, Teach saying well done lad; the Highlander replied, If it be not well done, I'll do it better. With that he gave him a second stroke, which cut off his head, laying it flat on his shoulder.[10]

According to Maynard, Blackbeard fell "with five shot in him and 20 dismal cuts in several parts of his body."[11] Like Rasputin, that other bearded monster of history, he seemed to defy death until the highlander's fatal slash with his broadsword. It is not surprising to find that local legend has it that when Blackbeard's body was thrown overboard, the headless corpse swam around the sloop several times.

The death of the pirate captain did not immediately signal the end of the battle. All the accounts suggest that the remaining pirates put up a desperate fight. By the time the *Ranger* came alongside with the rest of the attacking party, the decks were running with blood and strewn with dead and dying men. There are differing accounts of the final casualty list. Captain Brand reported to the Admiralty that eleven seamen were killed (two from the *Lyme* and nine from the *Pearl*) and more than twenty were wounded. Some of the pirates jumped overboard and were killed in the water. One body was only discovered several days later because of the number of birds hovering overhead. The final death toll of the pirates varies between nine and twelve, with nine badly wounded men taken prisoner.

The casualties might have been higher because Blackbeard had instructed one of the blacks in his crew to set light to the gunpowder store and blow up the pirate ship if the lieutenant and his men boarded the vessel. Fortunately, two men from a trading sloop who had been drinking with Blackbeard the previous night were hiding below during the fight, and they prevented the black from carrying out his orders.

Maynard kept Blackbeard's head and slung it below the bowsprit of his sloop. The display of the gruesome trophy in this manner was very much in the spirit of an age when the heads of traitors were impaled on spears over the gateway to London Bridge and the corpses of criminals suspended in prominent places as a warning to others. Maynard also needed the head as proof that he had killed the notorious pirate, and could claim the reward. A similar action was reported in the *London Journal* on April 22, 1727: the head of Nicholas Brown, "a notorious pirate," was brought in to Jamaica by Captain Drudge, "a reward of £500 having been promised by the Government there for the taking him."

After the battle Maynard sailed across the sound to Bath Town to get help for the wounded. Some weeks later he set sail in the pirate sloop *Adventure,* accompanied by the hired sloop *Jane.* He headed north for Virginia to rejoin his ship HMS *Pearl* and to report the success of his mission to Captain Gordon, his commanding officer. On January 3, 1719, the two sloops sailed up the James River toward Williamsburg. It was a fine winter's day with a light wind ruffling the surface of the water. As he dropped anchor opposite HMS *Pearl,* Maynard ordered his men to fire a nine-gun salute. As the warship's great guns fired an answering salute, her crew could clearly see the bearded head of the most wanted pirate on the American coast hanging below the bowsprit of the pirate sloop. Later that day, in the column of his logbook headed "Remarkable Occurencies &c," Maynard noted in the matter-of-fact language expected of naval officers:

Little wind & fair weather this day I anchored here from N Carolina
in the Adventure Sloop Edward Thache formerly Master (a Pyrat)
whose head I hung Under the Bowsprete of the Said Sloop in order
to present it to ye Colony of Virginia & ye goods & Effects of the
Said Pyrat I Deliver'd to my Commanders Disposal.[12]

Because of his fearsome reputation, the death of Blackbeard and the
subsequent trial and execution of the remnants of his crew were regarded as a major coup in the war against the pirates. For the British
authorities, it was as significant in propaganda terms as the trial and
hanging of Captain Kidd back in 1701.

Blackbeard's last stand at Ocracoke Inlet became a pirate legend,
with the fight between Lieutenant Maynard and the awesome figure
of Blackbeard on the deck of a ship depicted as a classic confrontation
between the forces of good and evil. The newspapers of the day reported the battle in some detail, and Captain Johnson's *General History of the Pirates* included a vivid account which has provided the raw
material for numerous books on piracy, and has inspired several plays,
ballads, and films. Eighty years after Blackbeard's death a melodrama
by James Cross entitled *Blackbeard, or the Captive Princess* was first
performed on the London stage; it was a popular favorite for many
years. Described as "A serio-comic ballet of action, in two acts," the
scenario consisted of ten pages of songs and detailed stage directions.
It opened at the Royal Circus in Lambeth on Easter Monday 1798
and was repeated for a hundred nights for the rest of the season. The
story was based on the historical accounts of Blackbeard's last days,
but took considerable liberties with the characters involved and with
the locations. The love interest was supplied by the introduction of a
beautiful princess borrowed from the story of Henry Avery, and the
production was enlivened by complicated scenic effects, numerous
rousing songs, and the noises of fifes, drums, pistol shots, and cannon
fire.

The first scene takes place in the pirate's cabin, where Blackbeard
and some of his men are carousing. Blackbeard's black servant Caesar
spies a sail on the horizon through his telescope, and the crew prepare
for action. The ship is taken and two captives are brought belowdecks.
The first is Ismene, a Mogul Princess, and the second is her lover,
Abdallah. The action moves to the waterfront on the island of Mada-

gascar, where Blackbeard's wife, Orra, is awaiting the pirates' return. A black boy sings a ballad, there is a slave dance, and then Blackbeard comes ashore from his state barge accompanied by the captive Princess, who is now the object of his lust. In a room in Blackbeard's fort, Orra accuses Ismene of stealing her husband's affection, but the Princess declares that she detests the pirate. Orra arranges for them both to escape. The scene changes to the West Indies, where the two women are being pursued along a track by Blackbeard and Caesar. Orra is stabbed to death by Blackbeard, and Caesar fights and wounds Abdallah. Back on board the pirate ship *Revenge*, Blackbeard is attempting to ravish the Princess Ismene, but he is interrupted first by the ghost of Orra and then by the news that an enemy is in sight. Blackbeard learns that "The Enemy is British and will Die or Conquer." Down in the powder magazine, Caesar is preparing to blow up the ship but is prevented by the combined efforts of Ismene and Abdallah. In the final scene Lieutenant Maynard's ship, the *Pearl*, is alongside the pirate ship. There is a fight between Maynard and Blackbeard. Maynard is wounded, but Abdallah enters and overcomes Blackbeard, who throws himself into the sea. The pirates surrender, Princess Ismene and Abdallah embrace, and the curtain falls to shouted "Huzzas of victory."

The play was frequently revived and adapted during the course of the nineteenth century. No doubt much of its popularity was due to its maritime theme and its patriotic songs, which delighted a British audience during those anxious years when Nelson and the navy seemed the only defense against Napoleon and a French invasion. The play's triumphal ending reminded the London audience that British sailors would always overcome the enemies of Great Britain. A version of the play became one of the most popular scenes for the Pollock's Toy Theatre, and can still be bought today.[13] As for the village of Ocracoke in North Carolina, the story of Blackbeard has proved a useful tourist attraction. Visitors to the island will find an inn called Blackbeard's Lodge, a pirate souvenir shop called Teach's Hole, and the Jolly Roger Pub.

PIRATE ACTIVITY reached a peak in the years around 1720: from Boston to Barbados, the reports were the same. A letter from Governor Johnson of South Carolina to London in May 1718 expressed a view that was common throughout the colonies: "The unspeakable calamity this poor province suffers from pirates obliges me to inform your Lordships of it in order that his Majesty may know it and be induced to afford us the assistance of a frigate or two to cruise hereabouts upon them for we are continually alarmed and our ships taken to the utter ruin of our trade."[14] Lieutenant General Mathew reported from the island of St. Kitts in September 1720 that the pirates "were actually coming into Basse Terre Road" and burning ships under the very guns of the battery.[15]

"I think the pirates daily increase, taking and plundering most ships and vessels that are bound to this island,"[16] wrote the Commander in Chief of Jamaica in December 1717. He warned that no ships bound for Great Britain dared to stir without the protection of a convoy. Governor Shute of Boston put it bluntly: "the pirates still continue to rove these seas, and if a sufficient force is not sent to drive them off our trade must stop."[17]

It has been estimated that there were between fifteen hundred and two thousand pirates operating in the Caribbean and North American waters around this time.[18] The average pirate ship had a crew of around eighty men, so that there must have been between fifteen and twenty-five pirate ships cruising the area. At first sight this seems a tiny number to cause such alarm and to threaten the trade of the colonies. But it has to be remembered that the islands and coasts which were their hunting grounds were sparsely populated and extremely vulnerable to determined raids by heavily armed ships. The population of Port Royal, Jamaica, in 1700 was around three thousand; New York was a city of eighteen thousand people, and Charleston had around five thousand. The entire population of Newfoundland at this time was no more than two thousand.[19] As we have already seen, the majority of merchant ships sailing in and out of these and other colonial ports had crews of ten to twenty men and were rarely armed with more than eight or ten small guns. Two pirate ships armed with a total of fifty guns had the firepower of a small army, and were invincible against any force less than a naval warship.

The authorities in London were well aware of the piracy problem, and indeed had taken some steps to tackle piracy and some of the worst abuses of privateering. But wars in Europe inevitably had a higher priority than piratical raids in the colonies. Until the Treaty of

Utrecht was signed in 1713 and settled the long-standing struggle between Britain and France, the Lords of the Admiralty had more pressing calls on the ships of the Royal Navy. However, a series of measures were taken between 1700 and 1720 which were to prove remarkably effective. One of the most surprising aspects of the great age of piracy is how suddenly the pirate threat collapsed. From the peak of two thousand pirates in 1720, the numbers dropped to around one thousand in 1723, and by 1726 there were no more than two hundred.[20] The incidence of pirate attacks declined from between forty and fifty in 1718 to half a dozen in 1726.

The problem was tackled in a number of ways: by the introduction of legislation; by issuing pardons to pirates in the hope that they would abandon their lives of crime; by stepping up naval patrols in the worst affected areas; by promising rewards for the capture of pirates, and licensing private ships to attack and capture pirates; and by the trial and execution of captured pirates. Some of these measures were more effective than others, but the combined effect of all of them was to eliminate piracy as a serious threat to trade in the Atlantic and the Caribbean.

Until 1700 the legal procedure for dealing with captured pirates was governed by an Act passed by Parliament in 1536, "for the punishment of pirates and robbers of the sea."[21] This decreed that all cases of piracy on the high seas or in any harbor or river over which the Lord High Admiral had jurisdiction must be heard before the Admiral and three or four common law judges appointed by the Lord Chancellor. This meant that piracy was no longer subject to the rules of civil law but came under the jurisdiction of the High Court of the Admiralty. The problem for the colonial governors was that the captured pirates must be brought to London to be tried before the Court of Oyer and Terminer sitting in the Old Bailey. The occasional hanging of a bunch of pirates on the Thames at Execution Dock provided an entertaining spectacle for the inhabitants of Wapping and Rotherhithe, but had a minimal effect on the crew of a pirate ship anchored off the coast of Africa or cruising the Bahamas under the heat of the Caribbean sun.

The breakthrough came with the "Act for the More Effectual Suppression of Piracy" of 1700. This ended the requirement that pirates must be returned to England for trial and enabled Vice-Admiralty Courts overseas to hold trials. It authorized the use of the death penalty, and stipulated that those found guilty must be executed on or near the sea. Seamen who resisted pirate attack were to be rewarded by receiving a percentage of the cargo they had saved.

The Act provided the legislative machinery, but it was not immediately followed by a spate of executions because the pirates had to be caught before a trial could be set up. One of the first trials to take place outside England was the result of a pirate captain and his crew returning to the very harbor from which they had seized a ship during a mutiny. In May 1704 John Quelch sailed into Marblehead in Massachusetts after several months of plundering shipping along the coast of Brazil. A few days later Quelch and twenty-five pirates were arrested and imprisoned in the jail at Boston. The trial began on June 13 before a Court of Admiralty under the presidency of Joseph Dudley, Captain General and Governor-in-Chief of the provinces of Massachusetts Bay and New Hampshire.[22] It was held in the Town House in Boston at the top end of the street now called State Street. Quelch and six of his crew were sentenced to death. The date of execution for the condemned men was set for Friday, June 20, and in the intervening period the pirates were subjected to a barrage of sermons and prayers and exhortations from the Reverend Cotton Mather.

On the day of execution the pirates were taken in procession from the prison to the waterfront, accompanied by the Provost Marshal, the town constables, and forty musketeers. The gallows had been erected on the shore near Hudson's Point, so the pirates were rowed across the harbor in a boat with the chaplain. A description of the final scene was recorded by Judge Sewell in his diary:

> When I came to see how the river was covered with people, I was amazed. Some say there were 100 boats. . . . When the scaffold was hoisted to a due height, the seven malefactors went up: Mr. Mather prayed for them, standing upon the boat. Ropes were all fastened to the gallows (save King who was reprieved). When the scaffold was let to sink, there was such a screech of the women that my wife heard it sitting in our entry next the orchard, and was much surprised at it; yet the wind was sou-west, our house a full mile from the place.[23]

Thirteen of Quelch's crew were reprieved and subsequently pardoned. This was a pattern which was often repeated. After the grim formalities of a pirate trial the court often reprieved some of the accused men, even if they were found guilty. The younger members of the crew, who might be boys of fifteen and sixteen, were the most likely to be pardoned.

The granting of pardons to pirates on the loose was one of the measures designed to curb piracy. On September 5, 1717, King George I issued a royal proclamation which declared that any pirates who surrendered themselves to the authorities within a limited time "should have His most gracious Pardon."[24] The proclamation was sent out to the governors in the West Indies and the American colonies, who then had the responsibility of contacting the pirates. The first reactions to the proclamation were encouraging. Governor Bennett of Bermuda dispatched a sloop to the pirates in Providence and the news was accepted "with great joy" by the three hundred pirates gathered there. Most agreed that they would surrender themselves to the Governor. Captain Jennings and seven other pirates duly arrived in Bermuda and gave themselves up. They were issued with a form of certificate devised by Bennett.[25]

Governor Peter Heywood of Jamaica sent out two ships which contacted Hornigold and one or two of his consorts. The pirates sent the following letter in reply: "This is to acquaint your Excellency that wee have mett with Capt Cook who hath brought us the wellcome Tydings of an Act of Grace from his Majesty King George which wee embrace and return his Majesty our hearty thanks for the same. God save the King."[26]

Captain Woodes Rogers, who arrived in Nassau as Governor in July 1718, had some success with the pardons. According to Johnson's *General History of the Pirates,* all the pirates "at this colony of rogues" submitted and received certificates of pardon except Captain Vane and his crew. The pirates must still have been coming in six months later, because in January 1719 Woodes Rogers informed Secretary Craggs in London that Captain Congon, who commanded two pirate ships, had offered to surrender and "embrace H. M. gracious pardon."[27]

The test of this particular measure was whether the pardoned pirates abandoned piracy for good, and whether the number of pirate attacks was significantly reduced. The records suggest that the royal proclamation may have helped in certain areas such as the Bahamas, but had little effect elsewhere. Governor Shute reported from Boston that the

King's proclamation had not produced the hoped-for effects and the pirates were still out in force. Governor Johnson, who had recently been humiliated by Blackbeard's blockade of Charleston, declared, "I don't perceive H.M. gracious proclamation of pardon works any good effect upon them, some few indeed surrender and take a certificate of there so doing and then several of them return to the sport again. . . ."[28]

Further evidence of the British authorities' determination to wipe out piracy was the announcement of substantial rewards for seamen who captured pirates. In 1717 a royal proclamation was issued which offered a reward of £100 for the apprehending of a pirate commander, £40 for a pirate officer, £30 for "an inferior officer," and £20 for a private seaman.[29] Alexander Spotswood's 1718 offer of a reward for the capture of Blackbeard was clearly drawn from this earlier proclamation. But what the merchants, the councils, and the governors in the colonies wanted most was more warships. The response from Britain was limited, but warships were eventually sent out, and the subsequent battle between the Royal Navy and the pirates provides one of the most exciting episodes in the history of piracy.

In the year 1718 the Royal Navy had on its books sixty-seven ships of the line, fifty fifth-rate and sixth-rate warships, seven sloops, and some thirteen thousand seamen.[30] This was a formidable fighting machine and was the British authorities' most effective weapon against the elusive pirates. Even the smallest of the ships of the line had fifty guns and was equal in force to Blackbeard's *Queen Anne's Revenge,* the largest of the pirate ships. As described in the previous chapter, most pirate ships were sloops of ten to twenty guns, and in an encounter with a third-rate ship of seventy guns they would have been blown out of the water.

The navy was capable of sending a squadron of ships anywhere in the world, and frequently did so. In 1702, for instance, Admiral Benbow was in the West Indies in command of six ships of the line, which included his flagship, the *Breda,* of seventy guns, and the *Ruby* of forty-eight guns. Sailing off the coast of South America near Cartagena, they encountered a smaller French squadron. The resulting action, which became known as the Battle of Santa Marta, was indecisive and chiefly memorable for the heroic conduct of Benbow. His right leg was smashed by chain shot, but he refused to leave the quarterdeck. He later died of his wounds. Stevenson immortalized him by giving his name to the inn kept by Jim Hawkins' father in *Treasure Island*.

Six years later Commodore Charles Wager was cruising the same waters when he intercepted the Spanish treasure fleet off Cartagena. Wager had four ships under his command: the *Expedition* of seventy guns, the *Kingston* of sixty guns, the *Portland* of fifty guns, and a fire ship. The Spanish convoy consisted of two sixty-four-gun ships, two fifth-rates, and eight smaller vessels. After a ninety-minute action, the *San Joseph,* the largest of the Spanish ships, blew up and sank, taking nearly six hundred men down with her and a vast quantity of treasure. Another Spanish ship was captured, and a third ran ashore.

The pirates were no match for naval squadrons of this strength, and one of the reasons that they got away with murder and plunder for so many years was that the Admiralty never mobilized this sort of force against them. The policy was to station a guardship at certain strategic locations, and to provide warships to protect convoys of merchant ships crossing the Atlantic. In 1715 there was one sixth-rate ship of twenty-four guns at New York, one on the Virginia station to guard the Chesapeake, one on the New England station, and one for Maryland. To patrol the West Indies there was one twenty-gun ship for the Leeward Isles, two ships on the Barbados station, and one forty-two-gun ship and two small fourteen-gun sloops for Jamaica.[31] This was totally inadequate, and a glance at a map of the pirate hunting grounds shows why.

The American coast from Boston to Charleston, South Carolina, is a network of river estuaries, bays, inlets, and islands. It was impossible for four ships to provide anything more than a token protection for such a vast and complex shoreline. The Caribbean posed an even greater problem. Not only were there hundreds of undefended islands, but many were uninhabited and poorly charted. These provided innumerable hiding places for ships. Lieutenant General Hamilton spelled out the difficulties in a report from Antigua to the Council of Trade and Plantations. He pointed out that it was impossible for one man-of-war to guard an area with "the islands lying separate and at so great a distance from each other." Pirates and privateers were able to play hide-and-seek with the navy: "They narrowly watch the motion of the man of war, that when she is to windward, they are commonly to leeward and appear even at the mouths of our very harbours." [32]

The coast of Africa had fewer hiding places, but like the West Indies, it frequently proved a death trap for European seamen. Malaria, dysentery, yellow fever, and other diseases lay in wait for the crews of ships who spent time in the tropics. The horrors of the slave trade are well known, but what is not so well known is that white seamen died in the same proportion as black slaves. According to one estimate, one white man in three died in his first four months in Africa. [33] Within a few weeks of their arrival on the African coast in 1721 the crew of HMS *Weymouth* were so stricken by illness that the warship could not put to sea, and was unable to take part in the search for the pirate ships of Bartholomew Roberts. The West Indies was no better. In 1716 HMS *Scarborough* buried twenty men and had forty sick while stationed at Barbados, so that she was "but in ill state to go to sea." [34] In 1726 a Caribbean expedition led by Admiral Hosier suffered losses which were to cause future generations of seamen to regard a West Indian posting with horror. Over the course of two years Hosier's squadron of 4,750 men lost more than 4,000 dead from fever. [35]

Apart from the size of the area which had to be protected and the ravages of sickness in tropical locations, the navy also had the problem which has always faced the forces of law and order when confronted by well-armed rebels, guerrillas, or terrorists: knowing where and when the next attack might take place. One solution was to increase the number of warships and to order their commanders to give top priority to the tracking down of pirates. In September 1717 Mr. Secretary Addison wrote from his office in Whitehall to the Council of Trade and Plantations that in view of the reports of piracy in the West Indies, "H.M. has signified his pleasure to the Lords of the Admiralty that one fourth-rate and two fifth-rate men of war be ordered to those seas to suppress the pirates, and protect the trade." [36]

The lists drawn up by the Admiralty showing "The present Disposal of all His Majesties Ships & Vessels in Sea Pay" clearly indicate their Lordships' recognition that the pirates must be taken seriously. As already stated, in 1715 there were four ships stationed on the east coast of America and five in the Caribbean. In 1719 there was still only one ship for New York, and one for New England; but Virginia, which had been plagued by Blackbeard and his consorts, was allotted two ships instead of one. Two forty-gun ships and a sloop were allotted to Jamaica with instructions "to correspond and act in concert against the pirates" with the two warships on the stations at Barbados and the Leeward Isles; and an additional three warships were sent "to suppress the Pirates in the West Indies, particularly about the island of Jamaica." [37]

In November 1717 the *Boston News Letter* was able to report that HMS *Phoenix* and HMS *Pearl* had arrived at New York, and in August the following year HMS *Pearl* and HMS *Lyme* were convoying merchantmen off the coast of Delaware. The stage was set for a series of dramatic battles against the pirates.

The first of these battles was the action at Ocracoke Inlet which put an end to the activities of Blackbeard and his men. This was a major victory for the authorities in the propaganda war, but it did not have a significant effect on the operations of the other pirates, which continued unabated. The greatest blow to the pirate community was the capture of the crew of Bartholomew Roberts on the west coast of Africa.

On February 6, 1721, HMS *Swallow* weighed anchor at Spithead and set sail for Africa. She was accompanied by HMS *Weymouth,* and was responsible for a convoy of six merchantmen: the *Whydah,* the *Martha,* the *Cape Coast,* and three sloops. [38] The *Swallow* was a powerful two-decker of fifty guns built at Chatham Dockyard and launched two years previously. She was commanded by Captain Chaloner Ogle, an experienced and resourceful officer "from an ancient and respectable family" [39] who was soon to receive a knighthood for his successful actions against the pirates.

The convoy reached the mouth of the Sierra Leone River on April 9 and on June 18 anchored off Cape Coast Castle, where they were given a salute of fifteen guns. Leaving the merchantmen to unload their cargoes and take on board slaves, the two warships sailed south to the Isle of Princes, where there was a small fort and a good harbor 200 miles from the fever-ridden coast. After seven weeks here they sailed to the island of St. Thomas, and then spent the next four months patrolling the coast. [40]

On January 7 the *Swallow* was back at Cape Coast Castle, where Captain Ogle learned from the Governor that two pirate ships were

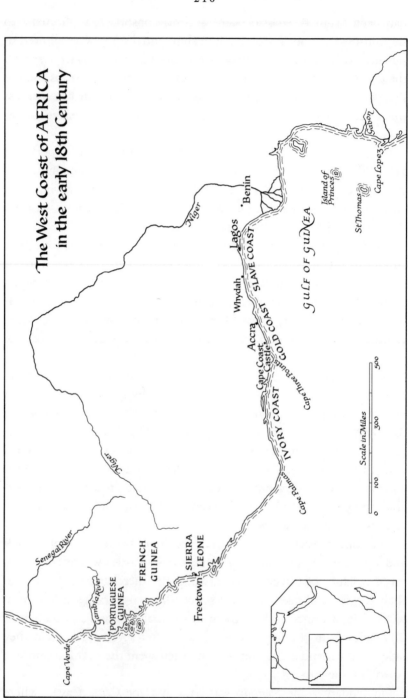

The West Coast of AFRICA in the early 18th Century

operating in the area. By this time the crew of the *Weymouth* were so stricken by tropical diseases that she was scarcely fit to put to sea, so the *Swallow* set off on her own in search of the pirates. On January 15 she called in at Whydah, a busy trading post and center for the slave trade some two hundred miles along the coast. Here, her crew saw the results of the pirates' raids at first hand, for the place was still reeling from an attack by Bartholomew Roberts three days before.

Roberts had left the West Indies six or seven months earlier and headed for the African coast in command of the *Royal Fortune*, the forty-two-gun French warship he had captured in 1720, and the brigantine *Good Fortune*. In spite of (or perhaps because of) a successful season of plunder, the pirates had become increasingly unmanageable: "being almost always mad or drunk, their behaviour produced infinite disorders, every man being in his own imagination a captain, a prince or a king."[41] It is easy to see how the round of looting, casual violence, and incessant drinking broke down any semblance of discipline and produced what Johnson describes as "a company of wild ungovernable brutes." When they were some four hundred leagues off the African coast, the crew of the brigantine, commanded by Captain Anstis, voted unanimously to leave Roberts, and departed in the middle of the night.

Roberts put a brave face on this flagrant threat to his authority and sailed on in the *Royal Fortune* till he reached the Senegal River on a part of the African coast in the hands of the French. There he was challenged by two French ships patrolling the area to prevent foreign interlopers attempting to trade. When Roberts hoisted the black flag and ran out his guns, the ships surrendered without a fight. Roberts took his two prizes down the coast to Sierra Leone, where he adapted them for his own use. The larger vessel of sixteen guns was christened the *Ranger*, and the other ship, which was armed with ten guns, was named the *Little Ranger* and put to use as a store ship.

The *Royal Fortune* anchored in the Sierra Leone River in June 1721, and from the trading post on the banks of the river Roberts learned that HMS *Swallow* and HMS *Weymouth* had paid a visit there a month before but were not due back till the end of the year. The pirates mistakenly believed that this gave them a clear run, so after careening and refitting their ships, they sailed southeast along the African coast, plundering as they went. At Sestos they exchanged the *Royal Fortune* for a fine frigate-built vessel called the *Onslow*. She was the property of the Royal Africa Company and had been captured while her captain and most of her crew were ashore. Roberts adapted her for his own use and renamed her the *Royal Fortune*. It was in this ship, accompanied by the *Ranger*, that Roberts attacked the shipping at Whydah on January 12, 1722.

There were eleven or twelve ships at anchor when he sailed in with black pirate flags and pennants flying. All of the ships surrendered, and their commanders agreed to ransom their vessels, except Captain Fletcher, the commander of the English slave ship *Porcupine*, who refused. This so enraged the pirates that they decided to burn his ship. One of the pirates covered the deck of the *Porcupine* with tar to make her burn more easily, and they set her alight. What horrified the onlookers, and made a considerable impression on the officers of the *Swallow* when they later heard what happened, was the cruel fate of the blacks on board. The pirates were in too much of a hurry to release the eighty slaves on the ship who were chained together in pairs. The wretched captives were "under the miserable choice of perishing by fire or water: those who jumped over-board were seized by sharks, a voracious fish in plenty in this Road, and in their sight, torn limb from limb alive."[42] Before leaving the anchorage at Whydah, Roberts seized the finest of the French ships for his own use. She was known as a fast sailer and had previously operated out of St. Malo as a privateer.

Captain Ogle reckoned that Roberts' next move would be to find a suitable place in the Bight of Benin to convert the captured ship for his own use: "Therefore I judged they must go to some place in the Bight to clean and fit the French ship before they would think of cruising again, which occasioned me to steer away into the Bight and look into those places which I knew had depth of water sufficient. . . ."[43]

The *Swallow* headed south, and after three weeks' search she located the pirates at daybreak on February 5. Three of Roberts' vessels were anchored in the lee of Cape Lopez. There was a strong wind blowing from the southeast, and before she could get within gunshot of the pirates, the *Swallow* was forced to bear away to the northwest to avoid running onto a sandbank called the Frenchmans Bank. The pirates, seeing a ship approach and then veer away, assumed she was alarmed by their presence. Roberts ordered his thirty-two-gun consort the *Ranger* to give chase.

Realizing that the pirates had not recognized the *Swallow* as a British warship, Captain Ogle deliberately slowed her progress to enable the pirates to catch up. He maintained the same course but spilled the wind from his sails by bracing the yards, leading the mainsheets aft, and bringing the tacks of the mainsail and foresail on board. By 10:30 A.M. the *Ranger* was close enough to fire her chase guns. The crew of the *Swallow* saw that the pirates had rigged their spritsail yard under the bowsprit ready for boarding; they also noted that she was flying an English ensign as well as a Dutch pennant and the pirate black flag.

At 11:00 A.M. the pirates were within range of musket shot, and Captain Ogle ordered the helmsman of the *Swallow* to starboard her helm. The warship swung across the path of the *Ranger*, opened her gunports, and ran out her lower guns. The deafening boom of the *Swallow*'s broadside was the first warning the pirates had that their supposed victim was heavily armed and prepared to fight. The *Ranger* swept across the bows of the warship, and it was some time before the *Swallow*'s gunners could bring their guns to bear again. When they did so, the outcome was inevitable. An hour and a half after the first shots had been fired, the pirates surrendered. The main topmast of their ship had been brought down, and twenty-six of her crew were killed or wounded, including her commander, Captain Skyrm, who had one leg shot off during the action. According to the *Swallow*'s logbooks, the pirate ship "hauled down his black flag the moment he made us to be a Kings ship but it was hoisted again afterwards."[44] Johnson notes that at the end of the action the pirates threw their flag overboard so it could not be displayed in triumph over them.

That night there was a tropical storm with thunder and lightning and heavy rain. The British sailors worked through the night and all the next day, repairing the damage to the pirate ship, securing the prisoners, and dealing with the dead and wounded.

At two in the morning of February 7 the *Ranger*, with a prize crew on board, set sail for the Isle of Princes, while the *Swallow* headed back to Cape Lopez. They arrived during the evening of the ninth and could see in the distance two ships at anchor. There was not enough daylight to attack, so Captain Ogle was forced to stand off. The weather deteriorated, and they had to contend with fresh gales and rain while they beat to windward.

At first light on the morning of February 10 the *Swallow* bore away for Cape Lopez, and her crew prepared for the final confrontation with the pirates. As they drew closer, they could see three ships at anchor: Roberts' ship the *Royal Fortune,* the *Little Ranger,* and a pink. According to Johnson, the pink was the *Neptune* of London, commanded by Captain Hill. Roberts had invited Hill on board his pirate ship, and when the warship was sighted, they were having breakfast together in the great cabin of the *Royal Fortune.* The identity of Captain Hill is a mystery. He does not appear to have been a pirate, and Captain Ogle's report suggests that his ship was in the employment of the Royal Africa Company. He played no part in the subsequent action, but took the opportunity to plunder the cargo of the *Little Ranger* while the *Royal Fortune* was at sea. The pirates who survived the battle were furious because all their sea chests were broken open and looted of any valuables. "The pirates informed me," wrote Captain Ogle, "that they had left in their chests aboard considerable quantities of gold."[45]

As the warship approached the anchorage, Captain Ogle hoisted a French ensign, which confused the pirates, who debated whether she was the *Ranger* returning, a Portuguese ship, or a French slave ship. A seaman called Robert Armstrong, who was a deserter from the *Swallow,* identified her correctly, but the pirates continued to have doubts until the warship ran out her guns and hoisted the King's colors. Bartholomew Roberts must have realized that the situation was desperate, but he put on a crimson waistcoat and breeches, a hat with a red feather, slung a pair of pistols on a silk sling over his shoulders, and issued orders with a bold unconcern for the likely outcome.

At 10:30 A.M. the *Royal Fortune* slipped her anchor cable and got under way. The clearest account of what happened next is to be found in the evidence which the *Swallow*'s officers gave at the trial of the pirates two weeks later:

About eleven a clock she being within pistol shot abreast of us, and a black flag, or pendant hoisted at their main topmast head, we struck the French Ensign that had continued hoisted at our staff till now, and displayed the Kings Colours, giving her at the same time our broadside which was immediately returned by them again but without equal damage, their mizen top-mast falling and some of their rigging being disabled.

The pirate sailing better than us, shot ahead above half gun shot, while we continued firing (without intermission) such guns as we could bring to bear . . . till by favour of the wind we came alongside again, and after exchanging a few more shot, about half past one, his main-mast came down, being shot away a little below the parrel.

At two she struck, and called for quarters, proving to be the *Royal Fortune* of 40 guns, formerly the *Onslow,* and the prisoners assured us that the small ship remaining in the road . . . was called the *Little Ranger* and did belong to their company. . . . The total of the men on board were 152 of which 52 were negroes.[46]

What this report does not mention is that the battle was fought in driving rain with "lightning and thunder and a small tornado." Roberts himself was killed by one of the broadsides from the *Swallow,* his throat torn out by grapeshot. He collapsed across the blocks and tackles of a gun, where he was found by a member of his crew, who burst into tears when he found he was dead. His body was thrown overboard, as he had frequently requested during his lifetime. Two other pirates were killed, and ten wounded. The *Swallow* did not suffer a single casualty.

Just as Blackbeard had wanted his ship blown up rather than surrendered, so some members of Roberts' crew threatened to do the same. At the trial it was discovered that James Philips, a morose and drunken pirate, was down in the hold when the *Royal Fortune* surrendered. He had a lighted match and intended to set the magazine on fire, "swearing very prophanely lets all go to hell together."[47] He was prevented from doing so by two seamen recently captured by the pirates.

The *Swallow* returned to Cape Lopez to find that the *Little Ranger* was deserted and had been looted of most of her contents. Captain Hill's pink had vanished, and it was therefore assumed that he and his crew were responsible.

For the next few days the *Swallow*'s crew were busy carrying out repairs, careening their ship, and collecting wood and water. They were hampered by a succession of tornadoes, thunderstorms, and continual downpours of rain. On February 18 they set sail in company with the *Royal Fortune* and the *Little Ranger.* They sailed first to the Isle of Princes to collect the *Ranger,* and then all four ships sailed to

Cape Coast Castle. As the *Swallow* anchored off the castle on March 16, she was given a salute of twenty-one guns. The next day the prisoners were sent ashore and locked up in the castle. The subsequent trial became a landmark in the war against the pirates. It resulted in fifty-two men being hanged and seventeen being sentenced to imprisonment in the Marshalsea Prison.

After the trial Captain Ogle had instructions to proceed to the West Indies before returning to England. He took two of his prizes with him as far as Jamaica. On August 20, 1722, the island was hit by a massive hurricane. All the merchant ships in the harbor at Port Royal were sunk or driven ashore, including the *Royal Fortune* and the *Little Ranger,* which were swept onto the rocks under Saltpan Hill and broken to pieces in less than an hour. The *Swallow* was only saved by the exertions of her crew, who managed to lay additional anchors and cut away the masts to prevent her heeling over.

Soon after his return to England, Captain Chaloner Ogle received a knighthood in recognition of his success against the pirates. In 1739 he became a Rear Admiral and he finished his career with the rank of Admiral of the Fleet.

There is an interesting postscript to this saga. On April 3, 1725, more than three years after the event, the *London Journal* reported that the officers and men of the *Swallow* who were responsible for taking Bartholomew Roberts and his men on the coast of Guinea had been paid the bounty money at the declared rate due to them under the royal proclamation for taking pirates. "It is remarkable that none of the Officers and crew of the said ship knew they were entitled to the said bounty, till the publishing of a book entitled, A General History of Pirates, where the said Proclamation is taken notice of." This, of course, was Captain Johnson's famous work, which was first published in 1724.

THE BATTLES which destroyed Blackbeard and Bartholomew Roberts and their crews were the most dramatic of the naval actions against the pirates, but they were not isolated incidents. In June 1718 HMS *Scarborough,* the ship which had been worsted by Blackbeard's ship two years earlier, captured the pirate ship *Blanco* of six guns, commanded by the French pirate Le Bour. It was not an unqualified success because of the eighty pirates on board only seventeen were captured, and the captain and the remainder escaped. In May 1722 the Governor of Jamaica, Sir Nicholas Lawes, reported that HMS *Launceton* of forty guns, under Captain Candler, had been dispatched to the southwestern end of Hispaniola to protect shipping from pirates, and had captured a Spanish pirate ship commanded by Mathew Luke, an Italian. The captured pirates were put on trial in Jamaica, and forty-one of the fifty-eight crew were hanged.

In May 1723 Governor Hart reported from St. Kitts that HMS *Winchelsea*, commanded by Captain Orme, had taken Captain Finn and eight of his pirate crew on the island of Tobago. This was evidently considered a coup because Finn was known to have been an associate "of the infamous Roberts the Pyrate," and had been commander of the brigantine *Good Fortune*. The captured pirates were put on trial, and six of them were hanged "at the high water mark in the town of St. Johns in Antigua."[48] Governor Hart further reported that Captain Brand, the commander of HMS *Hector*, was pursuing the rest of the pirates on the island of Tobago. "It is to the indefatigable care of Capt. Brand and Capt. Orme in pursing the pirates wherever they hear of them, that the trade in these parts is so well secured from that pest, for which they can't be too much commended. . . ."[49]

But apart from the bloody battles which ended the careers of Blackbeard and Roberts, the naval action which attracted most attention was the fight between Captain Solgard of HMS *Greyhound* and two ships commanded by Edward Low, the most brutal of the pirates of this period. The action was fought in the seas to the east of Long Island and lasted for more than eight hours. HMS *Greyhound* was a twenty-gun ship and relatively new, having been launched at Deptford in 1720. The two pirate ships were the sloop *Fortune* of ten guns, commanded by Low, and the sloop *Ranger* of eight guns, commanded by Captain Harris.

Solgard located the pirates at 4:30 A.M. on June 10, 1723.[50] Whether by chance or design is not clear, but he repeated the maneuver which had enabled Ogle to catch Roberts' consort off guard: he tacked and headed away from the pirates, which encouraged them to give chase. This gave Solgard time to clear his ship for action.

At 8:00 A.M. the ships were closing and the pirate sloops each fired a gun and hoisted a black flag. As the warship showed no sign of surrendering, they hauled down the black flags and replaced them with red flags to signal no quarter would be given. The *Greyhound* held her fire until the pirate sloops were abreast of her, when she let loose with round shot and grapeshot. For an hour or so the shooting continued, but the pirates then decided they had had enough and pulled away from the warship with the help of their oars. Captain Solgard put eighty-six of his men on the oars and set off in pursuit. At 2:30 P.M. they caught up with the pirate sloops and bombarded them with grapeshot, bringing down the mainsail of the *Ranger*. At four o'clock her crew surrendered. Low turned tail and fled. Solgard had to secure his prisoners, and although he chased Low, they lost sight of him near Block Island.

The captured pirates were tried before an Admiralty Court held in the Town House of Newport, Rhode Island. The president of the court was William Dummer, Lieutenant Governor of Massachusetts. Twenty-six pirates were hanged on July 19, 1723, on the shore of Newport harbor at Gravelly Point. Governor Burnet of New York wrote a letter to Lord Carteret in London which must have greatly cheered the lords of the Admiralty:

> I have the honour to acquaint your Lordship with the good news that the station ship for this place under the command of Captain Solgard, has on the 10th of this instant engaged two pirate sloops at once, of about 70 men and 8 guns a piece, under the command of one Low, and after having disabled one towards night, she struck to the man of war, but night coming on, he lost sight of the other, which he writes me word, he has intelligence by which he believes he shall find her to the eastward of Boston. This blow, with what they have received from Captain Ogle will I hope clear the seas of these accomplished villains. These last have been remarkably cruel and have done vast damage in the West Indies.[51]

Solgard's victory was on a much smaller scale than Sir Chaloner Ogle's crushing defeat of Roberts' ships, but it made a greater impression because it took place in American coastal waters rather than off the distant shores of Africa. A month after the battle the grateful Corporation of New York gave Captain Solgard the freedom of the city and presented him with a gold snuffbox handsomely engraved with the city arms on one side and a picture of the *Greyhound*'s fight with the pirate sloops on the other.[52]

SINCE THE TIME OF Henry VIII it was the custom during times of war to give license or "letters of marque" to private merchant ships. These authorized the captain of a named vessel to attack and capture the ships of an enemy nation. It was a cheap and easy way of augmenting the Royal Navy, and the owners and captains of the privateers received a proportion of the value of any captured vessel. In 1677 the Vice-Admiralty Court in Jamaica, which had been set up to deal with the prizes of privateers and naval ships in time of war, was given a special commission to try pirates. But the example was not extended to the other colonies, although some governors and councils did occasionally take the law into their hands and executed pirates.

The Prize Act of 1692, along with twenty-two instructions issued by the Privy Council, provided much-needed regulation for the conduct of privateering, an activity which had hitherto been subject to abuse and often amounted to outright piracy. The captors of ships were given a statutory right to their prizes, but the prizes had to be declared in the appropriate courts. The division of the prize money between the Crown, the shipowners, and the ship's officers and men was laid down. The effect of the Act, as Ritchie has pointed out, was that "it was now much easier to identify the privateers; for anyone who lacked the required passes, certificates, regulations, bonds, and even flags, was a pirate."[53]

The Treaty of Utrecht put a stop to the issuing of licenses against French and Spanish ships, but it did not stop the practice altogether. The pirates had become the new enemy, and the governors of the colonies in America and the West Indies on several occasions issued licenses to private ships authorizing them to capture pirates.

In November and December 1715 the Governor of Jamaica, Lord Hamilton, commissioned ten ships, which ranged in size from the *Diligence Galley* of 90 tons to the 20-ton sloop *Mary*.[54] One of the ten commanders who were commissioned was Jonathan Barnet, who was captain of the *Tyger*, a 90-ton snow. He is of particular interest for two reasons: firstly because his commission and instructions have been

preserved; and secondly because he was responsible for capturing Calico Jack and the female pirates Mary Read and Anne Bonny.

Barnet's instructions begin with a preamble which explains that the
frequent attacks by pirates on the high seas in the West Indies has
made it necessary "besides His Majesty's Ships of War to fit out and
commission other Private Men of War." It goes on to authorize him
and the snow *Tyger* "by force of arms to seize, take and apprehend all
pyratical ships and vessels with their commander officers and crew."[55]
There follow specific instructions which include bringing in any captured pirates to Port Royal, keeping a journal of all proceedings, and
flying a Union Jack of the same design as that worn by naval ships
except for a white escutcheon or square in the middle of the flag.
Barnet is next referred to by the new Governor of Jamaica, Sir Nicholas
Lawes, in his report to London dated November 13, 1720, in which
he briefly describes the action which led to the capture and eventual
trial of "Calico Jack" Rackam:

> About a fortnight ago a trading sloop belonging to the island being
> well manned and commanded by a brisk fellow, one Jonathan Bar-
> net, did us a very good piece of service. He was met by pirate vessel
> at the leeward part of this island commanded by one Rackum in
> which were 18 pirates more whom he took and are now in gaol.[56]

Two other privateer actions against pirates are of particular interest.
In August 1718, two months after Blackbeard's blockade of Charleston, two pirate ships under the command of Vane and Yeats appeared
off the harbor bar and proceeded to plunder shipping coming in and
out of the port. Among the vessels taken were the ship *Coggershall* of
Ipswich, which was laden with logwood, a sloop from Barbados, and a
large brigantine from the Guinea coast, with ninety blacks on board.
The Governor and Council of South Carolina were so alarmed by this
latest threat to their trade and the flagrant insults of the pirates that
they commissioned two sloops to go out against them: the *Henry* of
eight guns, commanded by Captain Masters, and the *Sea Nymph* of
eight guns, commanded by Captain Hall. The expedition was led by
Colonel William Rhett, who had volunteered his services.

They failed to find Vane, but while they were searching the coast
south of Charleston, they came across a pirate ship and two of her
prizes at anchor in the Cape Fear River.[57] A confused action took

place, complicated by the fact that the pirates and the privateers went aground on shoals in the river. At one point the *Henry*, with Colonel Rhett on board, was stranded by the ebb tide for nearly six hours and exposed to derisive insults and sporadic fire from the pirates. However, the rising tide floated Rhett's two sloops an hour before the pirates floated off, which enabled the crew of the *Henry* to carry out repairs and prepare to move in for the kill. They were about to board the pirate sloop when a white flag was sent up and the pirates surrendered. Casualties were heavy: the privateer ships lost fourteen men killed and had sixteen wounded in the action; the pirates had seven killed and five men wounded. However, Colonel Rhett found that the captain of the pirate ships was Major Stede Bonnet, who had sailed as a consort of Blackbeard and was one of the big names in the pirate community. Some weeks later Bonnet and thirty-three members of his crew were put on trial in Charleston. The subsequent hanging of Bonnet and thirty others was another landmark in the war against the piracy.

A third privateer action which resulted in the death of a well-known pirate and the capture of his crew took place on the shore of a remote island ninety miles off the coast of South America. In October 1722 the sloop *Eagle* was sailing from the island of St. Kitts to the port of Cumana in Venezuela.[58] Her course took her close by the island of Blanco, where her captain, thirty-two-year-old Walter Moor, saw a sloop aground in a sandy bay. Knowing the island to be uninhabited and not a place where law-abiding traders would normally call, he suspected the vessel to be a pirate. No doubt thinking of the reward if he captured her, Moor prepared to attack. As he approached the beach, he saw that the sloop was heeled over for careening, with her guns ashore. He challenged her to show her colors. The mystery vessel hoisted a St. George's flag and fired at the *Eagle*. At this hostile response, Captain Moor prepared to board her, but before he could do so, the pirates cut their anchor cables and hauled the stern of their sloop ashore. Not wanting to run aground, Moor anchored the *Eagle* in the shallows opposite the pirate ship and proceeded to pound her with his guns until she surrendered.

Before Moor and his men were able to take possession of the ship, the pirate captain and ten or twelve of his crew climbed out of the cabin windows and escaped ashore. The island was densely wooded with *Lignum vitae* trees and thick shrubs and undergrowth, so that the men Captain Moor sent in pursuit of the pirates had difficulty finding them. After searching the island for five days, they captured five men. Some of the pirates had remained with the ship, so that the total number captured was twenty-four. From the prisoners they learned that the pirate captain was George Lowther, but he eluded capture. It was Lowther who had recently attacked the *Princes Galley* of London, tortured her crew, forced the surgeon's mate and a carpenter to join the pirates, and plundered her cargo.

The *Eagle* sailed on to Cumaná, where Moor reported to the Governor. The captured pirate sloop was officially condemned and handed over to Moor and his crew. The Governor sent a small sloop with twenty-five men to the island of Blanco to round up the remaining pirates: they captured four of them, but Lowther, three men, and a small boy could still not be found. It was later learned that Lowther committed suicide; Captain Moor "was informed that George Lowther of the said pirate sloop had shot himself on the Island of Blanco, and was found dead with his pistol busted by his side."[59] On March 11, 1724, a Court of Admiralty was held on the island of St. Kitts, and the remnants of Lowther's crew were put on trial.[60] The two young seamen from the *Princes Galley* who had volunteered to join the pirates were found guilty but were reprieved. Eleven pirates were hanged on March 20.

In retrospect it is surprising how effective the Royal Navy and authorized privateers were in hunting down the pirates. The pirates' cruising grounds extended for thousands of miles, and there were so many places in the Caribbean and along the coasts of North America and Africa where they could hide their ships. And yet, without radios and telephones, the news of a pirate's whereabouts would be passed among the thousands of ships and small craft plying among the islands and up and down the coast. The information would eventually reach the governor of a colony, the captain of a naval ship, or an agent of the Royal Africa Company or the East India Company. A warship would be dispatched, and a patient search made until the pirate was tracked down. It took Captain Ogle in HMS *Swallow* nearly eight months to find Bartholomew Roberts, but in the end the plunderings of the most successful of all the pirates were brought to an end. Already the world was becoming too small for a wanted pirate to be able to find a safe hiding place.

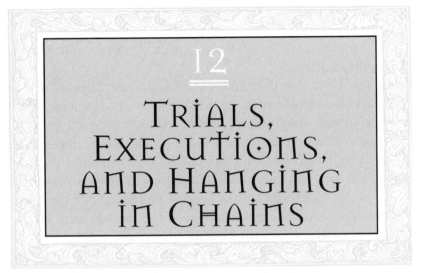

12

TRIALS,
EXECUTIONS,
AND HANGING
IN CHAINS

FOR MORE THAN four centuries pirates were hanged at Execution
Dock on the north bank of the Thames. The exact spot is shown
on old maps of London and lies a mile downstream from the Tower
of London on a bend of the river at Wapping. Today the riverside pub
the Captain Kidd overlooks the original site of the gallows.

In the early years of the eighteenth century, when Captain Kidd,
John Gow, and other notorious pirates were hanged there, the waterfront at Wapping was a jumble of wharves, wooden cranes, and timber
yards. Beyond the wharves were narrow streets lined with the houses
of seamen, dockers, shipwrights, and their families. The main port of
London was a little further upstream and centered on Custom House
Quay. There the ships were moored three and four deep, creating a
forest of masts and weather-beaten sails as far as Old London Bridge.

The gallows was set up on the shore near the low-tide mark. After
the pirates had been hanged, their bodies were slowly submerged by
the swirling waters of the incoming tide. It was usual to allow three
tides to pass over them before the bodies were taken away. The reason
why pirates on both sides of the Atlantic were hanged "within the
flood marks" was to stress the point that their crimes had been committed within the jurisdiction of the Lord High Admiral. He was
responsible for the punishment of all felonies committed on the high

seas and waterways up to the low-tide mark. Above the tide line, the civil courts took over.

The foreshore along the banks of the Thames was composed of mud and gravel and smelled of rotten wood and weed and sewage, but it was firm enough to walk on at low tide, and even to drive a horse and cart across. When an execution was due to take place, large crowds gathered on the shore and in boats and ships moored out in the river. The condemned man had to travel in a procession from the Marshalsea Prison on the south bank, across London Bridge and past the Tower to Execution Dock. The procession was led by the Admiralty Marshal or his deputy, who carried the silver oar which represented the authority of the Admiralty. The pirate traveled in a cart and was accompanied by the prison chaplain. When the procession reached the riverside, there was a pause and the pirate was given the chance to address the crowds. Some, encouraged by the chaplain, mumbled a few words of repentance; others spoke defiantly, and occasionally at some length.

The gallows was a simple structure of two wooden uprights joined at the top by a crossbeam. A ladder was leaned against the gallows, and the rope with the hangman's noose was suspended from the beam. The pirate was helped up the ladder by the executioner, the noose was placed around his neck, and when the Marshal gave the signal, the executioner pushed him off into space. The drop was not always enough to cause death instantly, and it was not unusual for relatives or friends to pull on the pirate's legs to put him out of his agony. Sometimes the rope broke, and the half-conscious man was hauled back up the ladder to be hanged a second time.

After the submerging by the tides, the body was either taken away and buried in an unmarked grave or sent to Surgeon's Hall for dissection, or hung in chains. The dissection of executed criminals had been authorized in Henry VIII's reign and was common practice by the eighteenth century. This was the fate of a gang of pirates who operated from Hastings and were hanged in 1768. There were instances where a hanged man survived the execution. William Duell was hanged in 1740 and taken to Surgeon's Hall for dissection. As his body was being washed, it was observed that he was still breathing. A surgeon bled him and in two hours he had recovered and was sitting up in a chair. He was sent back to Newgate Prison, and the authorities evidently decided that one hanging was enough. His sentence was commuted to transportation to the colonies.[1]

After the public hanging at Wapping it was the custom to display the corpses of the more notorious pirates at places along the river where they would be seen by the crews of all ships entering and leaving the port. The body of Captain Kidd was suspended on a gibbet at Tilbury Point on the lower reaches of the Thames. Here it was a prominent landmark and would have remained visible for an hour or more as the ships navigated Sea Reach, that broad stretch of the river which curves around the desolate point. Further upstream, opposite the town of Woolwich, the body of John Prie, pirate and murderer, was hung in chains in 1727.[2] Following the capture and trial of Captain Gow and his crew in 1725 it was ordered that Gow and his lieutenant be hung in chains, one of them opposite Deptford and one opposite Greenwich.[3]

On the other side of the Atlantic the seaman faced further reminders of the fate of those who took up piracy. Outside the harbor of Port Royal, Jamaica, were two small islands or cays. On Deadman's Cay the body of Calico Jack Rackam was hung from a gibbet following his execution in November 1720. Four months later the body of Captain Vane was displayed on the nearby islet of Gun Cay. In Antigua, some six hundred miles to the east, Captain Finn and four pirates were hanged in 1723. The judgment of the Admiralty Court was that the body of Captain Finn be hung in chains on Rat Island, which lies in the middle of St. Johns harbor.[4]

On the east coast of America pirates were executed at Charleston, South Carolina, at Williamsburg in Virginia, and at Newport, Rhode Island, but it was at Boston that the seaman would have seen most evidence of pirate hangings. In June 1724 the *Boston Gazette* reported, "On Tuesday the 2nd instant, were executed here for piracy John Rose Archer, Quarter-Master, aged about 27 years, and William White, aged about 22 years: After their Death, they were conveyed in boats down to an island where White was buried, and the Quarter-Master was hung up in irons, to be a spectacle, and so a warning to others." Three years later the body of William Fly was suspended from a gibbet on the island of Nick's Mate at the entrance to the Charles River.

To ensure that the displayed bodies remained intact for as long as

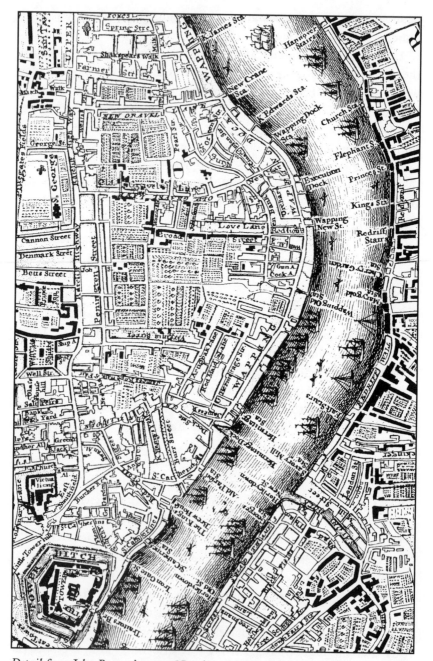

Detail from John Rocque's map of London of 1769. Condemned pirates were taken in procession from the Marshalsea Prison, past the Tower of London (bottom left) to Execution Dock, which can be seen on the bend of the river between the New Stairs and Dock Stairs in Wapping.

possible, the corpses were coated with tar. This was normally used to preserve the wooden hulls of ships and would have been reasonably effective in preventing the ravages of the weather. It may also have discouraged the attentions of carrion crows and gulls. Once coated with tar, the body was fitted into a specially made harness of iron hoops and chains which held the head, body, and legs in place. An example of a set of irons and chains dated 1742 has been preserved in the Town Hall of Rye in Sussex. It would have taken a blacksmith some time to make and explains why this was the most costly item on the list of expenses incurred during the hanging and gibbeting of Archer and White at Boston. The hire of a boat and the cost of laborers to set up the gibbet and dig the grave of White came to £3.15s.8d, but it cost £12.10s "To Makeing of the Chains for John Rose Archer one of the Pyrats and the hire of a man to fix him on the Gebbet att Bird Island."[5]

The bodies selected for long-term display in or outside ports were a tiny proportion of the total number of pirates who were executed. In the years between 1716 and 1726 more than four hundred men were hanged for piracy,[6] an average of forty men each year. In 1723, when the war against the pirates was at its height, no fewer than eighty-two men were hanged. Back in 1617 Sir Henry Mainwaring complained that men were encouraged to become pirates because it was the custom "that none but the Captain, Master, and it may be some few of the principal of the company shall be put to death."[7] This was no longer the case in the early eighteenth century. When Captain Thomas Green and seventeen members of his crew were tried for piracy at Edinburgh in 1705, all except one were hanged. Thirty of the thirty-four members of Major Stede Bonnet's crew were hanged in 1718. Forty-one of the fifty-eight members of Matthew Luke's crew were hanged in Jamaica in 1722. Fifty-two of Bartholomew Roberts' crew were hanged on the African coast in 1723. And twenty-five of the thirty-four pirates captured by Captain Solgard were executed at Newport, Rhode Island, in the same year. Of twenty-seven trials held between 1700 and 1728, in only five cases were the executions restricted to the ringleaders.[8] Bearing in mind that the total number of pirates operating around the shores of the Atlantic in 1720 was around two thousand men, we begin to see why the great age of piracy came to a rapid end. The hunting down of pirates by the Royal Navy, and the subsequent mass hangings of those captured, effectively eliminated most of the pirate leaders and decimated the ranks of the pirate community.

But it was not simply the numbers of pirates executed which contributed to their downfall. The publicity surrounding the trials and the public nature of the executions ensured that seamen and their families were keenly aware of the penalty for piracy. The pronouncements of the judges, prosecutors, and clergy stressed the wicked nature of their actions and made it plain that pirates were enemies of all mankind. The trials, hangings, and the heavy condemnation of piracy by Church and State acted as a powerful deterrent to anyone tempted to join the pirates.

Most trials lasted no more than one or two days, even when twenty or thirty prisoners were involved. There were no doubt practical reasons for hurrying things along. Following the Act of 1700 which authorized the setting up of Vice-Admiralty Courts in the colonies, it was usual for the colonial governor to preside over pirate trials, assisted by a group of local worthies and the captains of naval ships stationed in the area. The governors had many other duties to attend to, the captains would have been reluctant to leave their ships for more than a few days, and prominent citizens and merchants would have wanted to get back to their businesses and their estates. But the principal reason for the pace of the proceedings was the absence of arguments for the defense. In accordance with the usual practice of the day, the accused men had no legal representation and had to conduct their own defense. Since the majority of men on trial were seamen with little or no education, they were ill equipped to make a good case. Sometimes they offered nothing in their defense at all; sometimes they simply said that they were drunk at the time; mostly they claimed that they were forced men—that their ships had been captured by pirates and they had been compelled to sign the pirate articles. This was difficult to prove and relied on statements from other members of the pirate crew, or on the observations of the crews of attacked ships. Seamen, by the very nature of their roving existence, were unable to call on previous captains and shipmates to testify to their good character. Occasionally the sentencing of a prisoner was delayed to enable witnesses to be produced. In 1719 a Court of Admiralty was held at the Old Bailey to try three men, Laws, Caddiz, and Tyrril, for piracy. Laws and Caddiz were found guilty and sentenced to death, "but the trial of Tyrril is again deferred till April next, part of his witnesses being beyond the sea."[9] But this was rare, and the courts were not usually prepared to hold up the proceedings.

The odds were always weighted heavily in favor of the authorities, who were keen to use the propaganda value of the trials and executions as a weapon in the war against pirates. After the hanging of forty-one pirates in Jamaica in 1722, Governor Lawes wrote to London, "I make no question but the example that has been made of these rogues will defer others in these paths."[10] It is noticeable that the authorities invariably fielded a strong team for pirate trials. When Quelch and twenty-four members of his crew were tried in Boston in 1704, the President of the Admiralty Court was Joseph Dummer, Captain-General and Governor-in-Chief of the provinces of Massachusetts Bay and New Hampshire. He was assisted by two Lieutenant Governors, Thomas Povey and John Usher; by Nathaniel Byfield, Judge of the Admiralty; Samuel Sewell, First Judge of the Province of Massachusetts Bay; by Mr. Brenton, Collector of HM Taxes; Mr. Addington, Secretary to the Province; and by twelve members of HM Council of Massachusetts Bay. Bellamy's crew faced a similar heavyweight assembly at Boston in 1717. Samuel Shute, the Governor, presided, and he was assisted by Lieutenant Governor William Dummer; John Menzies, the Vice-Admiralty Judge; the captain of HMS *Squirrel;* the Collector of Plantation Duties; and seven members of the Council.[11]

The most extraordinary array of legal dignitaries was that assembled in London for the trial of Captain Kidd and nine members of his crew in 1701. The trial was held at the Old Bailey, and no fewer than six judges were concerned in the proceedings: Lord Chief Baron Ward, Baron Hatsell, Mr. Justice Turton, Mr. Justice Gould, Mr. Justice Powell, and Sir Salathiel Lovell, the Recorder of London. The counsel for the Crown consisted of Sir John Hawles, the Solicitor General, assisted by Dr. Newton, the Chief Advocate to the Admiralty, and Mr. Coniers, Mr. Knapp, and Mr. Cowper. In many ways Kidd's trial was not typical. Kidd was kept in prison for nearly two years before trial, which was very unusual in piracy cases; and for reasons already explained (see chapter 10) the proceedings were turned into a show trial.

One feature which Captain Kidd's trial did share with other pirate trials was that Kidd was indicted for murder as well as piracy. Kidd maintained that he was provoked by Moore, the ship's gunner he killed with a bucket, and had struck out in the passion of the moment, but his judges considered there was no provocation and the twelve-man jury found him guilty of murder. While piracy and murder both carried the death penalty, the courts regarded murder as the more serious charge, and when it could be proved, the prisoner had little or no hope of a reprieve. In sentencing Major Stede Bonnet, the judge declared, "But to theft, you have added a greater sin, which is murder. How many you may have killed of those that resisted you in the committing of your former piracies, I know not. But this we all know, that besides the wounded, you killed no less than eighteen persons out of those that were sent by lawful authority to suppress you. . . ."[12] When Thomas Green and eighteen of his crew were tried in the Admiralty Court of Scotland in 1705, Green was charged with murdering ten members of the crew of the ship *Worcester* in addition to the charge of piracy. At his trial in 1726 William Fly was accused of murdering John Green, master of the snow *Elizabeth,* and Thomas Jenkins, the mate, by throwing them overboard.

Some details of the proceedings in the trials of Calico Jack and the female pirates in Jamaica and the trial presided over by Governor Woodes Rogers at Nassau have already been noted, but one of the most significant of all pirate trials took place on the west coast of Africa in 1722. The records of the trial have been preserved and are worth examining because they show the workings of a Vice-Admiralty Court and provide valuable information about the attitude of the authorities to piracy at this date.[13] The trial followed the capture of Bartholomew Roberts' pirate ships by Captain Chaloner Oglē.

The operations of Ogle's ship HMS *Swallow* resulted in the rounding up of 268 men. Of these, 77 were black Africans, and 187 were white men, which included a number of seamen and passengers recently captured by Roberts during his raids along the African coast. Captain Ogle took all of them to the trading post at Cape Coast for trial by a Vice-Admiralty Court. Apart from nineteen men who died of their wounds before the trial, all the white men taken by HMS *Swallow* were examined by the court. The majority were subjected to individual cross-examination. Within three weeks of the formal opening of the proceedings, fifty-two men had been hanged, twenty had been condemned to penal servitude in Africa, and seventeen had been sentenced to imprisonment in London's Marshalsea Prison.

The setting for the trial was the castle at Cape Coast. This was a massive structure of medieval appearance with four great towers or bastions, battlemented walls fourteen feet thick, and some seventy great guns, most of which faced seaward and commanded the anchorage in front of the castle. Built by the Swedes in 1652, the castle was taken over by the English in 1664 and became the overseas headquarters of the Royal Africa Company. The agent-general of the company was based here, as well as a small army of merchants, clerks, workmen, and soldiers. The permanent garrison varied between fifty and one hundred men, depending on the ravages of disease and the supply of reinforcements from England.[14]

In startling contrast to the daunting edifice of the castle with its spacious rooms, warehouses, and workshops, a beautiful garden was situated a short distance away. It much impressed Captain Uring when he visited Cape Coast on one of his voyages. He described the garden as "abounding with all manner of fruits that the country produces, as China and Seville oranges, lemons, citrons, melons, pomegranates, cocoa-nuts, tamarinds, pine apples, grapes, limes, guavas, and the casava tree, all planted between the hills in exact order in walks, containing an extent of about twenty acres of ground."[15] As he walked among the rows of fruit trees under the tropical sun, it must have been easy to forget the primary purpose of the castle and the small town which it guarded. In common with Whydah, Elmina, Accra, and a succession of trading posts along the west coast of Africa, Cape Coast was established for the export of gold, ivory, redwood, and slaves. On the Gold Coast and what was sometimes called the Slave Coast, the principal export was black African slaves, who were shipped to the plantations in North America and the West Indies. It has been calculated that during the eighty years of its existence the Royal Africa Company alone delivered 100,000 slaves to the colonies. At the time of Bartholomew Roberts' raids along the African coast, around 36,000 Africans were being transported across the Atlantic each year from the various trading posts.[16] It was no doubt in the cells and compounds used for holding slaves before shipment that the men captured by HMS *Swallow* were imprisoned before trial.

The trial began on March 28, 1722, in the great hall of the castle. As captor of the pirates, Captain Ogle was disqualified from sitting in judgment, and so Captain Herdman, the commander of HMS *Weymouth,* was appointed President of the Court. There were six commissioners: The Honorable James Phipps, General of the Coast; Mr. Edward Hyde, Secretary to the Royal Africa Company; Mr. Henry Dodson and Mr. Francis Boye, merchants; and to make up the required number, Lieutenant Barnsley and Lieutenant Fanshaw were summoned to join the commissioners. The heavy naval presence (the key witnesses were from the *Swallow*) may explain the brisk, seamanlike conduct of the proceedings. Legal jargon was kept to the minimum, and there seems to have been a genuine attempt made to give the prisoners a fair hearing.

There were two principal charges against the defendants. The first was that they had wickedly united together against His Majesty's trading subjects: "Ye have twice been down this coast of Africa; once in the beginning of August, and a second time in January last, sinking, burning and destroying such goods, and vessels as then happened in your way."[17] The second charge was that they had attacked His Majesty's ship *Swallow* and were thus "Traitors, Robbers, Pyrates and Common Enemies of Mankind."

After the Register of the Court had read out the charges, the eighty men captured from the *Ranger* were asked how they pleaded. All pleaded not guilty. Three members of HMS *Swallow*'s crew, Lieutenant Isaac Sun, Ralph Baldrick, the boatswain, and Daniel McLaughlen, then described the events of February 5, when their ship was attacked by the *Ranger.* The prisoners agreed that they were on board the *Ranger* when she assaulted the King's ship and that they had all signed the pirate articles. Most of them claimed that they were forced men, and had never fired a gun during the action, and that any assistance they had given was through terror of death. At this point in the proceedings the court came to the "merciful resolution" that further evidence should be brought against each person singly.

Similar charges were brought against eighty men from the *Royal Fortune,* and they too pleaded not guilty. The court then examined each man in turn and listened to the statements of witnesses such as Captain Traherne, whose ship, the *King Solomon,* had been taken by the pirates. After the evidence for each of the accused was heard, the verdict was given: he would be pronounced guilty, or sentenced to the Marshalsea, or acquitted. It is revealing to see on what grounds some men were found guilty and some innocent of the charges.

The majority of those found guilty and subsequently hanged were condemned for being "active and forward" or "brisk and lively," which in most cases meant that they had been with the pirates for a year or more and took an active part in working the ship. All those who were seen to be armed with pistols or cutlasses during an attack were found guilty, and so were those who fired the ship's guns or were observed looting and plundering. Four men were found guilty because they were seen carousing and drinking with the pirates. Three men were condemned because they had joined the pirates voluntarily. James Skyrm, who was the captain of the *Ranger,* and the men who had been elected quartermaster, boatswain, and boatswain's mate were found guilty. Given the reputation of pirates and the previous record of Roberts' crews, it is surprising that only four men were condemned for acting cruelly or threatening violence. The guilty men were sentenced by the President of the Court in the following words:

> Ye and each of you are adjudged and sentenced to be carried back to the place from whence you came, from thence to the place of execution without the gates of this castle, and there within the flood marks to be hanged by the neck, till you are dead, dead, dead. And the Lord have mercy upon your souls. After this ye, and each of you shall be taken down and your bodies hung in chains.[18]

The fifty-two men condemned to death were hanged in batches at intervals throughout the month of April: six on the third; six on the ninth; fourteen on the eleventh; four on the thirteenth; eight on the sixteenth; and fourteen on the twentieth.

Imprisonment in the Marshalsea was reserved for those who were so constantly drunk that they were not fit for duty; for "a half-witted fellow . . . ever in some monkey-like foolish action," and for a prisoner who was accused by Elizabeth Trengrove, a passenger in the *Swallow,* of being "very rude, swearing and cursing and forcing her hooped petticoat off."[19]

The court acquitted all those who could prove that they had been forced to join the pirates. The most interesting of these was Henry Glasby, who had been chief mate of the ship *Samuel* of London, commanded by Captain Cary. He had been captured during the attack and abused and wounded when he refused to sign the pirate articles. When the pirates called in at Hispaniola, he had run away, using a pocket compass to find his way through the woods. However, he was so daunted by the barbarity of the island that he decided to make his way back to the pirate ship. Roberts subsequently forced him to become master of the *Royal Fortune,* but several witnesses gave evidence of his good character and swore that he never fired the guns and that he restrained the pirates from cruel actions.

THE ADMIRALTY COURTS ensured that all present at a pirate trial were aware of the wickedness of piracy and the evil nature of those who practiced it. The job of the clergy was to extract confessions of guilt from the condemned men, and to persuade them to repent and to see the error of their ways. This was not always easy. Many pirates had no time for religion and even less for the clergy; this is nowhere better illustrated than in the case of Captain Alexander Dolzell, who was convicted of piracy at the Old Bailey in December 1715.

While held in the dungeon at Newgate Prison, Dolzell and two men convicted with him were visited constantly by the Reverend Paul Lorrain, who was the "Ordinary," or prison chaplain. He instructed them in the Christian religion, "which they little knew, and had less practised." On the three Sundays before the execution he preached to them in the morning and afternoon, concentrating his attention on the universal use of prayer. Captain Dolzell was a hardened criminal. He had been convicted of high treason while a privateer a few years before and had spent some time in Newgate under sentence of death. He had then obtained a free pardon and been released. In November 1720 he had attacked the crew of a French vessel anchored off Le Havre. The crew were tied up, and one of them was thrown overboard and drowned. Dolzell, a forty-two-year-old Scotsman described by the Ordinary as pernicious and dangerous, refused to look at the Bible and threatened to tear it up, and on one occasion he said he would kick the Ordinary down the stairs:

He was so brutish and so obstinate that he would not be satisfied with anything I offered to him in this matter, saying, he hated to see my face, and would not attend in the Chapel (where I performed Divine Service) nor receive any public or private admonition from me, but with his dying breath declared that I was the cause of his death, and he would do me some mischief or other before he died, or haunt me afterwards.[20]

In the last moments of his life Dolzell had a change of heart. As Lorrain offered up final prayers on the scaffold, Dolzell said he repented and apologized for his rude and unjust behavior. The Ordinary was not impressed: "whether that repentence was sincere, and not too late, is much to be doubted."

Paul Lorrain was the chaplain to Newgate Prison for twenty-two years and had ministered to Captain Kidd in 1701. Kidd was an educated man and had no grudge against the church, but he proved almost as recalcitrant as Dolzell because he believed himself to be innocent of the charges of murder and piracy brought against him. Every day and sometimes twice a day Lorrain visited Kidd and the condemned men. On the Sunday after the trial Lorrain preached a sermon which would have given little comfort to the prisoners: his text was "And they shall go away into everlasting punishment."

In spite of all his efforts, Lorrain found that Kidd was not prepared to confess to the crimes of which he was convicted. On the day of the execution the Ordinary took Kidd along to the prison chapel for more prayers and exhortations, but "the hardness of Capt. Kidd's heart was still unmelted." However, Kidd did promise that he would make a full confession beneath the gallows. Lorrain preceded the pirates to Execution Dock and mounted the scaffold hoping to secure the wretched man's confession at last. Kidd disappointed him: "I found to my unspeakable grief, when he was brought thither, that he was inflamed with drink, which had so discomposed his mind, that it was now in a very ill frame and very unfit for the great work, now or never to be performed by him."[21] Kidd made a long and rambling speech to the crowd. He repeated that he had struck William Moore in a passion and had never intended to kill him. He expressed his sorrow at being unable to take his leave of his wife and children who lived in New York, and said he was more unhappy at the effect on his wife of the news of his shameful death than he was of his own misfortunes. He urged all seamen and particularly captains to take warning from the events which had led to his miserable fate.

When Kidd was turned off the scaffold, the rope broke and he fell to the ground still conscious. The indefatigable Lorrain seized the opportunity to make another attempt at extracting a confession from him: "When he was brought up and tied again to the tree, I desired leave to go to him again, which was granted. Then I showed him the great mercy of God to him in granting him (unexpectedly) this further respite that so he might improve the few moments now so mercifully allotted to him in perfecting his faith and repentance. Now I found him in much better temper than before." [22] The scaffold having collapsed, Kidd had to be launched the second time from the top of a ladder. Lorrain climbed halfway up the ladder so that he could continue with his prayers and exhortations. As Kidd swung off to his death, the Ordinary at last felt he had done his job and left the scene "with a greater satisfaction than I had before that he was penitent."

It would be hard to match the conscientious efforts of the Ordinary of Newgate, but there was an American preacher who was equally persistent in persuading uncouth pirates to show a suitable degree of penitence. The Reverend Cotton Mather was the clergyman in charge of the Second North Church in Boston from 1685 to 1722. He came from a family of distinguished Puritan leaders and statesmen and was inspired with religious fervor from a young age. He entered Harvard College at the age of twelve and preached his first sermon at the age of sixteen. Endowed with enormous energy, he set himself punishing goals. He read fifteen chapters of the Bible every day. He preached, fasted, prayed, cared for the poor and sick, and produced a constant stream of books and pamphlets. Living at a time and in a place where piracy was a serious threat to seamen and shipping, he was constantly warning his congregations of the wickedness of pirates, and he played a significant role in a number of pirate trials and executions.

While Quelch and his crew were in jail following their trial, Mather was one of several ministers who endeavored to bring the pirates to repentance. "There were sermons preached in their hearing every day; and prayers daily made with them, and they were catechised; and they had many occasional exhortations." [23] He and another minister walked with them in the procession to the scaffold, and from a boat in the river opposite the place of execution, he gave the final prayers before the pirates were hanged.

When the crew of Bellamy's ship *Whydah* were rounded up and brought to Boston for trial it was Mather whom the pirates asked to see. He prayed with them and lectured them and reminded them that "All the riches which are not honestly gotten must be lost in a shipwreck of honest restitution, if ever men come into repentance and salvation."[24] As the eight condemned men walked in procession to the scaffold, Mather spoke to each of them in turn. Later he published his conversations in a pamphlet which included the text of one of his sermons.[25] While Mather no doubt edited his recollections of the conversations, they clearly reveal his religious zeal, and provide some insight into the minds of the pirates as they walked to their death.

"How do you find your heart now disposed?" Mather asked Thomas Baker, a twenty-nine-year-old Dutchman who was a tailor by trade.

"Oh! I am in a dreadful condition! Lord Jesus, Dear Jesus, look upon me!"

"You are sensible that you have been a very great sinner."

"Oh! Yes I am! And is it possible that such a sinner should ever find mercy with God? Oh God, wilt thou pardon such a sinner!"

"My friend, this is the very first thing that I am to advise you of. There is a pardon to be had! Mark attentively every word that I speak unto you. I perceive you are in very great agony, but the strait gate must be entered with such an agony."

Cotton Mather left Baker and proceeded to question Simon Van Vorst, a young man of twenty-four who had been born in New York and later traveled out to the West Indian island of St. Thomas:

"Of all your past sins, which are they, that now lie most heavy upon you?"

"My undutifulness unto my parents; and my profanation of the Sabbath."

"Your sinning against a religious education is a fearful aggravation of all your sins. I pray you, to count it so."

"I do sire."

"But I wish that you, and all your miserable companions here, were more sensible of the crime for which you are presently to be chased from among the living. You are murderers! Their blood cries to Heaven against you. And so does the blood of the poor captives (fourteen score, I hear) that were drowned when the Whydah was lost in the storm which cast you on shore."

"We were forced men."

"Forced! No; there is no man who can say he is forced unto any sin against the glorious God. Forced! No; You had better have suffered any thing than to have sinned as you have done. Better have died a martyr by the cruel hands of your brethren than have become one of their brethren. Say now; what think you of the bad life, wherein you have wandered from God? Can you say nothing that your worthy parents (whom you have killed!) may take a little comfort from! Have some light in their darkness?"

"I am heartily sorry for my very bad life. I die with hope that God Almighty will be merciful to me. And I had rather die this afternoon, I would choose death rather than return to such a life as I have lived; rather than repeat my crimes."

" 'Tis a good and a great speech; but such as I have heard uttered by some, who after a reprieve, (which you cannot have) have returned unto their crimes. I must now leave you in the hands of Him who searches the heart; and beg of him, Oh! May there be such an heart in you!"

The conversation with John Brown, a twenty-five-year-old Jamaican who had been taken by pirates off Cuba, went as follows:

"Brown, in what state, in what frame, does thy death now within a few minutes of thee, find thee?"

"Very bad! Very bad!"

"You see yourself then a most miserable sinner?"

"Oh! most miserable!"

"You have had a heart wonderfully hardened."

"Ay, and it grows harder. I don't know what is the matter with me. I can't but wonder at my self!"

"There is no help to be had, anywhere, but in the admirable Saviour, whom I am now to point you to."

"Oh! God be merciful to me a sinner!"

"A sinner. Alas, what cause to say so! But I pray, What more special sins, lie now as a more heavy burden on you?"

"Special sins! Why, I have been guilty of all the sins in the world! I know not where to begin. I may begin with gaming! No, whoring, that led on to gaming; and gaming led on to drinking; and drinking to lying, and swearing and cursing, and all that is bad; and so to thieving; and to this!"

As in the case of Quelch and his men, Mather addressed his final prayers to Bellamy's crew from a boat which was lying off the shore on which the gallows had been erected. The capture of William Fly and his men in 1726 provided another opportunity for the Reverend Cotton Mather to preach on the evils of piracy and to counsel the condemned men.[26] As always, he recorded his conversations and sermons and had them printed. Fly was not cooperative. He refused to go the meeting-house where Mather preached on the Sunday before the execution, and he showed a total lack of the penitence required of him. With brave defiance, Fly walked to the place of execution with a nosegay in his hand, calling out to people in the crowd as he went. He mounted the stage with a spring in his step, reproached the hangman for not understanding his trade, and showed him how to manage the ropes in the most effectual manner. His indomitable spirit in the face of the condemnation of the court and the admonitions of Cotton Mather is remarkable, but was not unusual. A surprising number of pirates showed defiance at the end and refused to die in the contrite and penitent manner expected of them. Governor Hart commented after the execution of eleven pirates at St. Kitts in 1724 that they "behaved themselves with greater marks of sorrow and contrition than is usually found amongst those wretched set of people."[27]

The dying speeches and confessions of criminals hanged in England and the colonies were usually printed and sold in considerable numbers in the days following the execution. The largest single source of such speeches is the eighteenth-century periodical which was entitled *The Ordinary of Newgate, His Account of the Behaviour, Confession, and Dying Words of the Malefactors Who Were Executed at Tyburn*. Most of these are biographies of thieves and murderers hanged at Tyburn, but the speeches of a number of pirates are included. In Boston, as already described, the Reverend Cotton Mather recorded and published the final words of the pirates who were hanged during his years as a minister there. Similar accounts were published in the other ports and harbors where pirates were hanged.

Coached by the clergy during their last hours in prison, the condemned men spoke in heavily religious language full of regret for their sins. But in spite of the editing by priests and printers, some of the speeches provide a moving testament to those seamen who took to piracy to escape from the harsh life on the merchant ships, or signed the pirate articles while they were blind drunk and found themselves committed to a life from which there was no escape.

Among the dying words of the pirates captured by Captain Solgard of HMS *Greyhound* is a poem. It was written by John Fitz-Gerald, a twenty-one-year-old Irishman from County Limerick who was hanged with his comrades at Charleston, South Carolina, on July 19, 1723.[28] It is not a great poem, but it is as good an epitaph as any for the men who were hanged for piracy around the shores of the Atlantic.

> In youthful blooming years was I, when I that practice took;
> Of perpetrating piracy, for filthy gain did look.
> To wickedness we all were bent, our lusts for to fulfil;
> To rob at sea was our intent, and perpetrate all ill.
>
> I pray the Lord preserve you all and keep you from this end;
> O let Fitz-Gerald's great downfall unto your welfare tend.
> I to the Lord my soul bequeath, accept thereof I pray,
> My body to the earth bequeath, dear friend, adieu for aye.

Afterword
The Romance
of Piracy

Men and women who were attacked by pirates found it a terrifying and deeply shocking experience. There was the violence and the noise of the approach as the pirate ship fired warning shots and swung alongside with her heavy sails flapping thunderously. There was the confrontation with tough and brutal young men armed with knives, cutlasses, and boarding axes who deliberately knocked down or slashed at anyone who showed resistance. There was a confused and frightening phase during which the pirates ransacked the ship, interrogated the captain and crew, and frequently employed torture to extract information. And all too often the attack ended with some of the victims lying dead on the deck or with their bleeding bodies being thrown over the side to the sharks.

It is not so different today in some parts of the world. Piracy is a regular occurrence on the coast of Brazil, in the Caribbean, on the west coast of Africa, and above all in the Far East, particularly in the Malacca Strait, which has the greatest concentration of merchant shipping in the world. In 1992 there were more than ninety attacks on shipping in the international waters between Singapore and Sumatra. Most of the pirates in that region operate from the narrow, winding channels in the islands of Indonesia. They use converted fishing boats with outriggers and powerful engines and make their attacks at night, approaching their targets from astern, often undetected on the ships' radar. Once alongside they throw up ropes with grapnel hooks or shin up bamboo poles and clamber aboard. The small crews on today's merchant ships have no chance against half a dozen determined men armed with machetes, knives, and pistols. The pirates force the captain to open the ship's safe, and having seized the contents, they steal any loose valuables in the crew's cabins. Within ten or twenty minutes they have completed their work and are over the ship's side. By the time the authorities have been alerted they are racing back to their bases among the islands. There are also highly organized gangs armed with machine guns and assault rifles who attack in high-speed motorboats and commandeer the ships themselves. They carry forged papers, and sell off the entire cargo at a suitable port, making millions of pounds from the transaction.[1]

There is nothing romantic about modern piracy, and as in earlier times, it is not uncommon for the captain and crew to be seriously wounded or killed if they fail to cooperate. Since piracy is simply armed robbery on the high seas, and has been accompanied by a catalog of cruelties and atrocities, it is surprising that it should have acquired a comparatively glamorous image. Part of the explanation may be found in the exotic locations where many of the pirates operated. The cruising grounds of the most notorious seventeenth- and eighteenth-century pirates were the tropical waters of the Caribbean, the west coast of Africa, and the Indian Ocean. Coral islands, lagoons, and sandy beaches fringed with coconut palms have an extraordinary attraction for those brought up in colder northern latitudes, and this is why even a small-time pirate like Calico Jack, who attacked fishing boats in the seas around Jamaica, has more appeal than a bank robber or a thief who specializes in raids on main-street banks or stores. There is also the romance of the sea. The mythical voyages of Odysseus, the travels of Columbus, Magellan, and Captain Cook, and the sea stories of Conrad and Melville have fascinated generations of land-based readers. The pirates who roamed the seas in search of plunder share in this fascination.

Another part of the explanation may be the anarchic nature of piracy. Most people are condemned to lives of monotony. Year in and year out, workers in offices, factories, and large and small companies follow the same daily routine. They catch the same bus or train; they drive along the same route and suffer the same delays and traffic jams. They endure hours of boredom, often doing a job which gives them little or no satisfaction. They come home to face the predictable problems of family life or the loneliness of a flat in some dreary location. What greater contrast could there be with a life of piracy? The pirates escaped from the laws and regulations which govern most of us. They were rebels against authority, free spirits who made up their own rules. They left behind the gray world of rainswept streets and headed for the sun. We imagine them sprawled on sandy beaches with a bottle of rum in one hand and a lovely woman by their side, and a sleek black schooner moored offshore waiting to carry them away to distant and exotic islands.

There is a less obvious explanation for the attraction of the pirates. In his lengthy poem *The Corsair* Lord Byron created a pirate who was aloof and alien, "A man of loneliness and mystery" with a cruel past and an untamed spirit. As all women know and some men can never understand, the most interesting heroes of literature and of history have been flawed characters. The British nation admired and honored the Duke of Wellington, but when news of Lord Nelson's death at Trafalgar reached London, men and women wept in the streets. Yet Nelson was a vain, impetuous, and diminutive figure who abandoned his wife and embarked on a passionate and ill-advised affair with the voluptuous Lady Hamilton. Heathcliff, Rochester, and Rhett Butler have a greater appeal, particularly for women, than the stalwart, manly heroes of the type created by writers like John Buchan. So it is with the pirates. They are seen as cruel, domineering, drunken, heartless villains, but it is these very vices which make them attractive. A degenerate and debauched man is a challenge which many women find hard to resist. They want to give him the love they feel he is missing and they want to reform his evil ways. There is also the powerful attraction of the strong and ruthless man who sweeps a woman off her feet and against all opposition carries her away to another life. This is, of course, the basic plot of most of the romantic novels which have ever been written, but it does help to explain why pirates (or the fictional image of pirates) have always had as great an attraction for women as they have for men.

The real world of the pirates was harsh, tough, and cruel. Pirates were mostly young men in their twenties and were far more likely to be ex-seamen than they were to be aristocrats or educated men. Pirate captains were often vicious and sadistic villains whose careers rarely lasted more than two or three years. They were more likely to drown in a storm or suffer death by hanging than they were to live out their days in luxury on the riches they had plundered. Those who spent time among the pirates were horrified by their foul language, their drunken orgies, and their casual brutality.

The passing of time has mellowed the harsh picture which is revealed in the depositions of seamen who were attacked by pirates, and in the journals of men like Dampier and Ringrose who voyaged with the buccaneers. The melodramas of the Victorian era transformed pirates into stage villains who were frightening but not entirely believable. Gilbert and Sullivan's *Pirates of Penzance* and Barrie's *Peter Pan* took this image a step further, creating pirates who were entertaining caricatures. The novels of Walter Scott, Captain Marryat, R. M. Ballantyne, and Robert Louis Stevenson redressed the balance and made it clear that pirates were ruthless in their pursuit of treasure and were capable of cruelty and murder, but however vivid the descriptions of the writers, we are aware that their pirates are fictional characters. The films of the thirties and forties took the pirate stories of fact and fiction and added glamour. The swashbuckling heroes played by Douglas Fairbanks, Sr., and Errol Flynn were handsome and chivalrous but bore little resemblance to the pirates of the Caribbean on whom they were based.

The fact is that we want to believe in the world of the pirates as it has been portrayed in the adventure stories, the plays, and the films over the years. We want the myths, the treasure maps, the buried treasure, the walking the plank, the resolute pirate captains with their cutlasses and earrings, and the seamen with their wooden legs and parrots. We prefer to forget the barbaric tortures and the hangings, and the desperate plight of men shipwrecked on hostile coasts. For most of us the pirates will always be romantic outlaws living far from civilization on some distant sunny shore.

Appendix I

Trials and Executions of Pirates, 1700–1730

DATE OF TRIAL	PIRATES ON TRIAL	LOCATION OF TRIAL AND EXECUTION	NUMBER HANGED	NOTES
1701, May 18	24 Frenchmen from the pirate ship *La Paix*	London Execution Dock	24	
1701, May 8	Capt. Kidd and 9 men from *Adventure Galley*	London Execution Dock	9	Kidd's body hung in chains at Tilbury Point
1704, June 13	Capt. Quelch and 25 men from the *Charles*	Boston Charles River	7	
1705	Capt. Green and 17 men from the *Worcester*	Edinburgh Leith Sands	17	
1715, Nov. 9	Capt. Dolzell and 2 men	London Execution Dock	1	
1717, June	De Mont, De Cossey Rossoe, and Ernandos	Charleston, S. Carolina Charleston harbor	4	Judge Trot was President of the Vice-Admiralty Court
1717, Oct. 18	8 men from Capt. Bellamy's ships	Boston Charles River	6	Survivors of the shipwreck on coast of Cape Cod
1718, Dec. 9	10 pirates captured by Capt. Hornigold	Nassau, Bahamas Nassau waterfront	8	Capt. Woodes Rogers presided over this trial
1718, March 12	15 men from Blackbeard's sloop *Adventure*	Williamsburg, Virginia Gallows Road	13	Israel Hands and Samuel Odell were reprieved
1718, Oct. 28	Major Stede Bonnet and 34 men from his crew	Charleston, S. Carolina Charleston harbor	30	
1719	The pirates Laws, Caddiz, and Tyril	London Execution Dock	3	
1719, February	Capt. Worley and 1 man	Charleston, S. Carolina Charleston harbor	2	
1720, Nov. 16	Capt. Rackam and 10 men	Spanish Town, Jamaica Gallows Point	10	Rackam's body hung in chains on Deadman's Cay

DATE OF TRIAL	PIRATES ON TRIAL	LOCATION OF TRIAL AND EXECUTION	NUMBER HANGED	NOTES
1720, Nov. 28	Mary Read and Anne Bonny	Spanish Town, Jamaica	—	Both reprieved on being found to be pregnant
1721, March 22	Capt. Vane and 1 man	Spanish Town, Jamaica Gallows Point	2	Vane's body hung in chains on Gun Cay, off Port Royal
1721	Richard Luntly, carpenter	Edinburgh Leith Sands	1	
1722	Italian pirate Capt. Luke and 57 men	Jamaica Gallows Point	41	Captured by HMS *Launceton* off Hispaniola
1722, Oct. 11	10 pirates from Capt. Blanco's crew	Nassau, Bahamas	5	All the men executed were Spanish
1722, March 28	Crew of Bartholomew Roberts' pirate ships	Cape Coast Castle Waterfront by castle walls	52	77 men acquitted; 37 were sent to prison[1]
1723, July 5	Capt. Massey	London Execution Dock	1	
1723, July 10	Capt. Harris and 36 men from the *Ranger*	Newport, Rhode Island Newport harbor	26	Pirates captured by Capt. Solgard of HMS *Greyhound*
1723	Capt. Finn and 5 men	Antigua, West Indies St. Johns harbor	5	Finn's body hung in chains on Rat Island in the harbor
1723, July	Capt. Philip Roche	London Execution Dock	1	
1724, March 11	16 men from Capt. Lowther's crew	St. Kitts, West Indies	11	These were the pirates captured by Walter Moore, master of the *Eagle*
1724, May 12	Archer, White, and 14 men	Boston Charles River	2	Archer's body hung in chains on Bird Island

DATE OF TRIAL	PIRATES ON TRIAL	LOCATION OF TRIAL AND EXECUTION	NUMBER HANGED	NOTES
1725, May	Capt. Gow and 7 men from the *Revenge*	London Execution Dock	8	Bodies of Gow and Williams, his lieutenant, hung in chains at Greenwich and Deptford
1726	Capt. Lyne and 19 men	Curaçao	18	
1726, July 4	William Fly and 15 men	Boston Charles River	3	Fly's body hung in chains on island called Nick's Mate
1727, July	John Prie	London Execution Dock	1	Prie's body hung in chains opposite town of Woolwich
1729	John Upton	London Execution Dock	1	

NOTES

[1] Captain Ogle found 187 white men and 77 black men alive on board Bartholomew Roberts' pirate ships. The black slaves were not put on trial. Of the white men 52 were hanged, 20 were sentenced to seven years' servitude in the mines at Cape Coast, 2 were respited pending the King's pleasure, 17 were condemned to imprisonment in the Marshalsea, 77 were acquitted, and 19 died before coming to trial (Captain Ogle's letter of April 5, 1722. ADM.1/2242, PRO).

Appendix II

Pirate Attacks, 1716–1726

This list is confined to incidents in the Caribbean and east coast of North America where some details were reported of the type of pirate vessel, and the number of her guns and crew.

DATE OF ATTACK	PIRATE CAPTAIN	SHIP TYPE	GUNS	CREW	LOCATION OF ATTACK
1716, October	Jennings	Sloop	—	134	New Cuba
1717, May	Bellamy	Ship	30	200	Off South Carolina
1717, July	La Bouche	Ship	20	170	Latitude 36
1717, August	Napin	Sloop	12	100	En route to Boston
1717, August	Nichols	Sloop	6	80	En route to Boston
1717, October	Teach	Sloop	12	150	En route to Philadelphia
1717, November	Kentish	Ship	22	150	Nevis
1717, November	Edwards	Sloop	8	50	Nevis
1717, December	Teach	Ship	36	300	Near Crab Island
1717, December	+ consort	Sloop		—	Puerto Rico
1718, January	Lobdin	Brigantine	10 + 2S	90	Barbados
1718, February	England	Ship	26 + 4S	180	Jamaica
1718, April	Vane	Sloop	6	60	Bahamas
1718, April	(not known)	Sloop	11	25	Rhode Island
1718, April	Teach	Ship	40	300	Island off Turneff
1718, April	+ consort	Sloop	10		Island off Turneff
1718, May	Teach	Ship	40	300	Off Providence
1718, May	+ consort	Sloop	12	115	Off Providence
1718, June	Teach	Ship	40	300	Charleston, South Carolina
1718, June	+ consorts	3 sloops	—	100	Charleston, South Carolina
1718, October	Vane	Brigantine	12	90	Rhode Island
1718, October	Yeats	Sloop	8	20	Rhode Island

DATE OF ATTACK	PIRATE CAPTAIN	SHIP TYPE	GUNS	CREW	LOCATION OF ATTACK
1718, December	Moody	Ship	24	—	St. Christophers
1718, December	Frowd	Brigantine	8	—	St. Christophers
1718, December	(not known)	Sloop	6	—	St. Christophers
1719, February	England	Ship	24 + 2S	200	Antigua
1719, March	Moody	Ship	35	130	Bay of Carolina
1719, March	Frowd	Brigantine	4	60	Lat. 35, Long. 38
1720, July	Roberts	Ship	26	200 on both	Newfoundland Banks
1720, July	+ consort	Sloop			Newfoundland Banks
1720, September	Rackam	Sloop	4 + 2S	12	Off Jamaica
1721, April	Roberts	Ship	32 + 9S	228	Leeward Islands
1721, April	Stidien	Brigantine	24 + 6S	140	Leeward Islands
1723, September	Lowther	Sloop	8	30	Barbados
1723, October	(not known)	Schooner	4	25	Barbados
1725, June	Pyme	Sloop	10 + 16S	—	Latitude 40
1726, June	Fly	Snow	6	23	Off Philadelphia

NOTES
S = Swivel guns (so 10 + 2S means 10 mounted guns on gun carriages and 2 swivel guns on the rails of the vessel)

Appendix III

Extracts from "The present Disposal of all His Majesties Ships and Vessels in Sea Pay" issued by the Admiralty Office[1]

1 May 1715

RATE	SHIPS	NO. OF MEN	NO. OF GUNS	WHERE AT PRESENT
4	Southampton	—	—	Coming from Newfoundland and the Straights
5	Folkestone	160	42	
6	Deal Castle	100	24	} Coming from Jamaica
	Biddeford	100	20	
5	Speedwell	105	28	Barbadoes
6	Phoenix	100	24	New England
	Seaford	100	24	New York
	Success	115	20	Virginia
	Nightingale	115	24	Maryland
	Valeur	100	24	Attends on Maryland
	Sea Horse	100	20	The Leeward Islands
	Solebay	100	24	To go from New England to New York
5	Dolphin	110	30	Gone to the Isle of May
4	Anglesea	185	46	Gone to Carthagena
	Warwick	130	30	} Barbadoes
5	Roebuck	160	42	
	Diamond	160	42	} Jamaica
sloop	Tryal	60	14	
	Jamaica	60	14	Attends on Jamaica

NOTES
[1] These lists of ships do not include "Ships at Home," "Guardships at Chatham, etc." or ships "Going on Foreign Voyages."

1 May 1718

RATE	SHIPS	NO. OF MEN	NO. OF GUNS	DISPOSITION	
4	Dragon	240	50	} Newfoundland, &c.	
6	Rye	115	20		
5	Diamond	160	40		
	Ludlow Castle	160	40	} Jamaica	To correspond and act in concert against the Pirates
sloop	Swift	40	6		
5	Scarborough	125	30	Barbadoes	
6	Seaford	100	20	Leeward Islands	
5	Pearle	160	40	} Virginia	To correspond and act in concert against the Pirates
6	Lyme	115	20		
	Phoenix	100	20	New York	
	Squirrel	100	20	New England	
	Winchelsea	115	20	On a survey in the West Indies	

Ordered Home

RATE	SHIPS	NO. OF MEN	NO. OF GUNS	DISPOSITION
4	Newcastle	240	50	From Newfoundland
5	Adventure	160	40	Jamaica
	Shoreham	125	30	Virginia
sloop	Tryal	60	6	Leeward Islands

1 May 1719

RATE	SHIPS	NO. OF MEN	NO. OF GUNS	DISPOSITION	
5	Milford	155	30	To suppress the Pirates in the West Indies, particularly about the Island of Jamaica	
6	Rose	115	20		
sloop	Shark	80	14		
5	Diamond	160	40		
	Ludlow Castle	160	40	} Jamaica	To correspond and act in concert against the Pirates
sloop	Happy	80	14		
5	Scarborough	125	30	Barbadoes	
6	Seaford	100	20	Leeward Islands	
5	Pearl	160	40	} Virginia, and to come home with the Trade by the last of July this month	
6	Lyme	115	20		
	Phoenix	100	20	New York	
	Squirrel	100	20	New England	
	Deal Castle	100	20	Gone to the Plantations with Proclamations, &c, and to bring home the Governor of New York	

1 May 1720

RATE	SHIPS	NO. OF MEN	NO. OF GUNS	DISPOSITION
4	Mary	320	60	
5	Adventure	190	40	
	Mermaid	135	30	Jamaica
sloop	Happy	80	14	
5	Roy'l Anne Galley	190	40	Cruising against the Pirates on the Coast of Guinea
	Lynn	190	40	
	Milford	155	30	Barbados
6	Rose	115	20	Leeward Islands
sloop	Shark	80	14	
6	Rye	115	20	Virginia
	Flamborough	115	20	Carolina
	Phoenix	100	20	New York
	Squirrel	100	20	New England
5	Kinsale	135	30	To North America with Dispatches

To correspond (Virginia, Carolina, New York, New England)

Appendix IV

Extract from the logbook of William Dampier while en route from the coast of Mexico to the island of Guam in the Pacific Ocean, 1686.

DAY	COURSE	DISTANCE	S.	W.	LATITUDE	WINDS
1	SW 5 W	106	68	81	R. 19 : 2	NW : NNW
2	SW 1 W	142	98	101	R. 17 : 2	N b W
3	W by S	102	19	100	Ob. 17 : 6	N
4	W 12 S	140	29	136	Ob. 16 : 37	N : NNe
5	W 20 S	160	54	150	Ob. 15 : 43	N
6	W 10 S	108	18	106	Ob. 15 : 25	NE
7	W 15 S	89	23	86	Ob. 15 : 2	NE : ENE
8	W 2 S	64	5	63	R. 15 : 57	ENE
9	W 4 S	94	6	93	Ob. 14 : 51	ENE
10	W 5 S	138	12	137	Ob. 14 : 39	ENE
11	W 5 S	124	10	123	Ob. 14 : 29	ENE
12	W 5 S	179	14	169	R. 14 : 15	ENE
13	W 5 S	170	14	169	R. 14 : 15	ENE
14	W 5 S	180	15	177	R. 13 : 46	ENE
15	W 6 S	174	18	172	R. 13 : 28	ENE cloudy

A table of each day's run during the first half of April 1686, reproduced from William Dampier's book *A New Voyage Around the World*. Dampier describes the table as follows:

> The table consists of 7 Columns. The first is of the days of the month. The 2d Column contains each days course, or the point of the Compass wee ran upon. The 3d gives the distance or length of such course in Italian or Geometrical miles, (at the rate of 60 to a degree) or the progress the Ship makes every day; and is reckoned always from noon to noon. But because the course is not always made upon the same Rhumb in a direct line, therefore the 4th and 5th Columns show how many miles we ran to the South every day, and how many to the West; which last was our main run in this Voyage. . . . The 6th Column shews the lat. we were in every day, where R. signifies the dead Reckoning, by the running of the Logs, and Ob. shews the lat. by observation. The 7th Column shews the Wind and Weather.

Notes

Where only the surname of the author of a cited book is given, the full title and place and date of publication will be found in the Bibliography.

Key to Abbreviations Within Notes

ADM   Admiralty and Navy Board records
CO   Colonial Office records
HCA   High Court of Admiralty records
CSPC   Calendar of State Papers: Colonial, America and West Indies
NMM   National Maritime Museum
PRO   Public Record Office

Introduction

1. John Turner, *Sufferings of John Turner, Chief Mate of the Ship* Tay *Bound for China and Their Seizure and Captivity Among the Ladrones* (London, 1809).

2. Lucretia Parker, *Piratical Barbarity or the Female Captive* (New York, 1826), p. 15.

3. John Robert Moore was Professor of English at Indiana University. He announced his discovery that Captain Charles Johnson was really Daniel Defoe at a meeting of the Modern Language Association in 1932. His two key books on Defoe and Johnson were *Defoe in the Pillory and Other Studies* (1939) and *Daniel Defoe, Citizen of the Modern World* (Chicago, 1958).

4. Letter of February 3, 1814, from John Murray to Byron, quoted in Rutherford, p. 69.

Chapter 1

1. This account of Stevenson is drawn from: Colvin (1911 edition); Bell; McLynn; and the introduction and notes in the Oxford University Press World Classics edition of Robert Louis Stevenson, *Treasure Island* (Oxford, 1990).

2. Quoted in Emma Letley's Introduction to *Treasure Island* (op. cit.), p. vii.

3. Robert Louis Stevenson, *My First Book* (first published in *The Idler*, August 1894), reprinted in *Treasure Island* (op. cit.), p. 197.

4. Quoted in Emma Letley's Introduction to *Treasure Island* (op. cit.).

5. McLynn, p. 266.

6. Bell, p. 281.

7. Johnson, p. 121.

8. Bell, p. 103.

9. Letter to W. E. Henley, May 1883, in Colvin, p. 116.

10. CO.1/57, f 381, PRO.

11. Captain Chaloner Ogle's letter to the Admiralty. ADM.1/2242, PRO.

12. Johnson, p. 344.

13. Ned Ward, *The Wooden World Dissected* (London, 1707), p. 82.

14. *The Post-Man,* issues of 21 to 24 September (London, 1717).

15. PRO, HCA 1/42/26v, and PRO, HCA 1/41/189v. For further details see correspondence from Cheryl Fury and J. D. Alsop in *The Mariners Mirror,* volume 80 (London, 1994), pp. 341–42.

16. Dampier, volume II, p. 223.

17. Senior, p. 15.

18. Rediker (Cambridge, 1989; paperback edition), p. 258.

19. Quoted in Harland, p. 177. Harland's book is a detailed survey of ship handling and the language used by seamen throughout the Western world when working their ships.

20. For further details of seamen's clothes see: Rodger (op. cit.), pp. 64–65; Rediker, p. 11; Ritchie, p. 114; Dudley Jarrett, *British Naval Dress* (London, 1960); Commander W. E. May, *The Dress of Naval Officers* (London, 1966).

21. Senior, p. 37.

22. Johnson, p. 243.

23. CO.323/3, f 56(ii), PRO.

24. Ordinary of Newgate, *His Account of the Behaviour, Confession, and Last Speech of Capt. Alexander Dolzell,* 1715 (London, 1715). A copy is in the Caird Library, NMM.

25. Johnson, pp. 84–85.

26. CO.152/12, no. 67(iii), PRO.

27. Lee, p. 233.

28. Johnson, p. 243.

29. Drury, *Madagascar* (London, 1897).

30. Rediker, pp. 12, 260; and Rodger, p. 114.

31. Earle, pp. 65–66.

32. These figures are based on lists of men on trial for piracy which are given in trial documents, Colonial Office Documents, *Johnson's General History of the Pirates,* and in contemporary newspapers.

33. CO.152/13, f 282, PRO.

34. CSPC, volume 1720–21, no. 758.

35. CO.23/1, part 3, f 49 (ii), PRO.

36. CO.1/57, f 381, PRO.

37. Dampier, volume I, p. 33.

38. Exquemelin, part IV, p. 366.

39. CO.38/24, no. 145, PRO.

40. G. E. Manwaring and W. C. Perrin, *The Life and Works of Sir Henry Mainwaring,* 2 volumes (Navy Records Society, London, 1920–21).

41. William Lithgow, *Rare Adventures and Painfull Peregrinations* (London, 1632).

42. Johnson, p. 111.

43. This account of J. M. Barrie and *Peter Pan* is taken from: Green; Haill; Birkin; and the Oxford University Press World Classics edition of J. M. Barrie, *Peter Pan in Kensington Gardens* and *Peter and Wendy* (Oxford, 1991).

44. Haill, p. 14.

45. The details of Avery's life are taken from: Hill, pp. 99–105; Daniel Defoe, *The King of the Pirates, Being on Account of Famous Enterprises of Captain Avery, with the Lives of Other Pirates and Robbers* (London, 1724); Johnson; and an excellent summary in Ritchie, pp. 85–89.

46. Hill, p. 102.

47. Johnson, p. 57.

48. There is a useful entry on Charles Johnson in the *Dictionary of National Biography.*

49. Before *The Pirates of Penzance* had its premiere in London, a performance was given at the Royal Bijou Theatre at Paignton in Devon on December 30, 1879, to establish the British copyright, and a few hours later a performance was given at the Fifth Avenue Theatre in New York in order to establish the American copyright.

Chapter 2

1. A graphic description of Nombre de Dios in 1570 by Juan López de Velasco is quoted by Andrews, p. 19.

2. The details of Drake's raids are taken from: Kenneth Andrews, *Drake's Voyages* (London, 1967); Wilson; Williams, *The Sea Dogs;* and Neville Williams, *Francis Drake* (London, 1973).

3. Williams, *The Sea Dogs,* p. 90.

4. The experienced Portuguese pilot Nuno da Silva spent fifteen months on board and gave a detailed description of her sailing qualities. Wilson, p. 45.

5. Williams, *The Sea Dogs,* p. 130.

6. Ibid. p. 130.

7. The brief account of Cortés and Pizarro is taken from J. H. Parry, *The Age of Reconnaissance* (London, 1963), and *The Times Atlas of Exploration,* edited by Felipe Fernandez-Armesto (London, 1991).

8. Figures compiled by Earl J. Hamilton in *American Treasure and the Price of Revolution in Spain* are quoted in *The New Cambridge Modern History* (Cambridge, 1957), p. 452.

9. The standard work on historical coins is the handsome book produced by the British Museum and Spinks: J. Cribb, B. Cook, and I. Carradice, *The Coin Atlas: The World of Coinage from Its Origins to the Present Day* (London, 1990).

10. Peter Wood, *The Spanish Main* (Amsterdam, 1979), p. 18.

11. For useful introductions to Hawkins see Williams, *The Sea Dogs;* and Andrews.

12. Peter Wood, *The Spanish Main,* p. 56.

13. Ibid., p 64.

14. For a balanced assessment of Exquemelin, see Earle, *The Sack of Panama,* pp. 265–66.

15. "An advertisement to the reader concerning this second edition" (1684) quoted in Exquemelin, p. 1.

16. Exquemelin, p. 103.

Chapter 3

1. Pope, p. 347.

2. The account of Henry Morgan in this chapter is based on: Pope; Earle, *The Sack of Panama;* Exquemelin; and Pawson and Buisseret.

3. Pope, p. 343

4. Ibid., p. 261.

5. Ibid., p. 342.

6. Ibid., p. 343.

7. On November 21, 1671, Morgan signed a deposition giving his age as thirty-six, which would make his year of birth 1635. He was born either in the village of Penkarn, Monmouthshire, or Llanrhymny in Glamorgan-shire. His favorite estate in Jamaica was called Llanrhymny after the Welsh village near Tredegar (called Rhymney today). His father was probably Robert Morgan.

8. Pope, p. 65.

9. Ibid., p. 148.

10. Ibid.

11. There is a brilliant description of the Portobello raid, based on a study of the relevant Spanish documents, in Earle, *The Sack of Panama,* pp. 54–90.

12. Ibid., p. 74

13. Ibid., p. 83.

14. Ibid.

15. Sir Thomas Modyford, Governor of Jamaica, noted that the shares of each privateer were half that of the Portobello expedition (ibid., p. 129).

16. Pope, p. 198.

17. Earle, *The Sack of Panama,* p. 237.

18. Taken from the printed apology in later editions published by William Crooke, and quoted in Pope, p. 334.

19. Ibid., p. 246.

20. Ibid., p. 250.

21. Ibid., p. 258.

22. Letter from Lord Vaughan to Sir Joseph Williamson. The letter continues: "Sir Henry has made himself and his authority so cheap at the Port, drinking and gaming at the taverns, that I intend to remove there speedily myself for the reputation of the island. . . ." Quoted by Pope, p. 277.

23. For Hans Sloane's treatment of Morgan see his account in *A Voyage to the Islands of Madera, Barbados, Nieves, S. Christophers, and Jamaica,* 2 volumes (London, 1717–25).

Chapter 4

1. These details are taken from the proclamation issued by Governor Woodes Rogers on September 5, 1720, and published in *The Boston Gazette,* October 10 to 17, 1720.

2. Johnson provides the details of Rackam's story, but see also Black. Black was Archivist of Jamaica for many years and provides some additional information. Johnson's facts are confirmed by the printed transcript of the Trial of Rackam, CO.137/14, PRO.

3. Black, p. 110.

4. Johnson, p. 156.

5. Woodes Rogers' proclamation, *The Boston Gazette,* October 10 to 17, 1720.

6. See news item from New Providence in *The Boston Gazette,* October 10 to 17, 1720.

7. Captain Jonathan Barnet had been issued with a commission to attack pirates by the Governor of Jamaica in 1715. See CO.137/12, no. 78 (i-v), ff 231–235, PRO.

8. In the printed transcript of Rackam's trial, there is a description of the fight in the evidence given by James Spatchears, a mariner of Port Royal (CO.137/14, PRO).

9. Ibid.

10. Johnson, p. 153.

11. The transcript of the trial was printed in Jamaica by Robert Baldwin in 1721. It is entitled *The Tryals of Captain John Rackam, and Other Pirates.* There are two copies bound into the Colonial Office documents relating to Jamaica in the Public Record Office, Kew (CO.137/14, PRO).

12. These details and the quotations which follow are all taken from the transcript of the trial, CO.137/14, PRO.

13. CO.137/14, PRO.

14. Black, p. 117.

15. Details are taken from Edgar J. March, *Sailing Drifters: the Story of the Herring Luggers of England, Scotland and the Isle of Man* (Newton Abbot, 1969), pp. 227–29.

16. Barlow.

17. For a discussion of the role of wives, sweethearts, and prostitutes in the Georgian navy see Rodger (1990 paperback editon), pp. 75–80.

18. See Wheelwright, *Amazons and Military Maids,* a scholarly survey of women who joined the navy and the army dressed as men, which has a comprehensive bibliography.

19. "The Intrepid Female or Surprising Life and Adventures of Mary Anne Talbot, Otherwise John Taylor" in volume II of Kirby's *Wonderful and Scientific Museum* (London, 1804).

20. Quoted by Wheelwright, p. 84.

21. Ibid, p. 141.

22. For a vivid picture of life on board ship in the eighteenth century see Rodger, pp. 60–71; also Barlow, Dampier, and other journals and memoirs of former seamen.

23. Lavery, pp. 200–203.

24. Johnson, p. 212.

25. Rediker (1989 paperback edition), p. 261, note 16.

26. These quotations are taken from the printed transcript of the trial of Bellamy's crew (CO.5/867, part I, PRO).

27. Dow and Edmonds, p. 226.

28. Ibid., p. 227.

29. Johnson, p. 170.

30. CO.323/6, no. 81, PRO. It is interesting to note that at the top of the list of women who signed the petition is the name of Mary Read. Could this be the companion of Anne Bonny? If we suppose that Mary Read was aged twenty-five in 1709 when she signed the petition, she would have been thirty-six at the time of her trial in 1720, which would fit in with her story.

31. Johnson, p. 76.

32. CSPC, volume 1717–18, no. 298, p. 149.

33. There is a brief account in Charles Ellms, *The Pirates Own Book, Authentic Narratives of the Most Celebrated Sea Robbers* (originally published 1837, cited 1993 paperback edition), p. 2.

34. From a dispatch written by Lord Justice Drury, President of Munster, to the Privy Council in London, November 7, 1578. This quotation and most of the details of Grace O'Malley's life are taken from Chambers. This is a fascinating and carefully documented study of the Irish patriot.

35. Anne Chambers thinks it more likely that her nickname was a corruption of the Gaelic "Grainne Ui (Ni) Mhaille" or Grace of the Umhalls: Chambers, p. 55.

36. Ibid., p. 25.

37. Ibid., p. 85.

38. Ibid., p. 93.

39. Ibid., p. 129.

40. Ibid., p. 145.

41. Ibid., p. 150.

42. Two of the most vivid descriptions of life among the Chinese pirates are the journals of two seamen: John Turner, *Sufferings of John Turner, Chief Mate of the Ship Tay Bound for China and their Seizure and Captivity Among the Ladrones* (London, 1809); and Richard Glasspoole, *A Brief Narrative of My Captivity and Treatment Amongst the Ladrones* (London, 1935). Glasspoole was an officer in the East India Company's ship *Marquis of Ely* and was captured off Macau in 1809. The most authoritative account of the activities of Mrs. Cheng and the Chinese pirates of the early nineteenth century is Murray. Professor Murray carried out extensive research on the Chinese documents in the archives at Taiwan and Beijing.

43. Classpoole, p. 127.

44. Karl F. Neumann, *History of the Pirates who Infested the China Sea from 1807 to 1810* (London, 1831), p. 24. This is a translation of Yuan Yung-lun.

45. For a detailed description of the Chinese pirate vessels see Murray, pp. 91–98.

46. Ibid., pp. 143–44.

47. Professor Linda Grant de Pau makes this claim in her book *Sea Faring Women* (Boston, 1982).

Chapter 5

1. For details of the shipwreck of the *Whydah* and the subsequent trial see *The Trials of Eight Persons Indited for Piracy, etc.*, CO.5/867, part I, f 10, PRO; Johnson; and much useful material in Vanderbilt.

2. ADM.1/2242, PRO.

3. Johnson, p. 322.

4. CO.1/57, f 381, PRO.

5. Dampier, volume I, p. 301.

6. Quoted in John Masefield's Introduction to Dampier, volume I, p. 13.

7. Ibid., volume I, p. 126.

8. Rogers, p. 3.

9. Dampier, volume I, p. 184.

10. Exquemelin, p. 278. For full details of the capture of the charts and an assessment of their importance see *A Buccaneer's Atlas,* edited by D. Howse and N. Thrower (Los Angeles and Oxford, 1992), pp. 22, 27.

11. CO.152/12, no. 67 (iii), PRO.

12. Johnson, p. 208.

13. Ibid., p. 209.

14. *The Boston News Letter*, January 14 to 21, 1712.

15. Ibid., January 4 to 11, 1720.

16. Johnson, p. 315.

17. Rediker, Davis, and Middleton.

18. *The Four Voyages of Capt. George Roberts. . . . Written by Himself* (London, 1726). The relevant section describing the encounter with Low is reproduced in Dow and Edmonds.

19. Dow and Edmonds, p. 161.

20. Ibid., p. 168.

21. Ibid., p. 231.

22. *Proceedings of the Court Held on the Coast of Africa*, HCA.1/99.3, PRO.

23. Dow and Edmonds, p. 325.

24. Rediker, pp. 191–93.

25. CO.37/10, no. 10 (ii), PRO.

26. Rogers, p. 207.

27. Exquemelin, p. 100.

28. Ibid., p. 475.

29. *Proceedings of the Court Held on the Coast of Africa*, HCA.1/99.3, PRO.

30. Bruce Ingram (ed.), *Three Sea Journals of Stuart Times* (London, 1936), p. 230.

31. Exquemelin, p. 343.

32. Johnson, p. 168.

33. Exquemelin, pp. 430–31.

34. Johnson, p. 213.

35. Ibid., p. 213.

36. Ibid., p. 211.

37. Burg, p. 110.

38. HCA.1/55, PRO.

39. Murray, pp. 25, 50 and Note 67, p. 191.

40. Rodger, p. 81.

Chapter 6

1. The details of the attack on the *Princes Galley* are taken from: *The Deposition of John Wickstead*. CO.28/18, f 23, PRO; *The Trial of Robert Corp and Henry Wynn*, CO.152/14, f 292, PRO; Johnson, p. 315.

2. CO.152/14, f 292, PRO.

3. Joseph Hiller, the Public Notary at Boston, had a full account of the attack printed in *The Boston Gazette* of August 15 to 22, 1720. See also Johnson, p. 217.

4. Johnson, p. 217.

5. There was a fifth-rate ship and two sloops stationed at Jamaica, two fifth-rate ships stationed at Barbados, and a sixth-rate ship at the Leeward Islands. See *The Present Disposal of All His Majesties Ships & Vessels in Sea Pay*, ADM.8/14, PRO.

6. CSPC, volume 1717–18, June 21, 1718.

7. CSPC, volume 1717–18, no. 787.

8. *The Boston News Letter,* August 12 to 19, 1717.

9. *The Deposition of George Barrow, Master of the Sloop* Content, CO.28/18, f 22, PRO.

10. These figures are compiled from details of pirate attacks in: *Calendar of State Papers, Colonial, America and West Indies;* Johnson; reports in *The Boston Gazette, The Boston News Letter, The Maryland Gazette, The New York Gazette;* and depositions and other documents in the Public Record Office.

11. See *The Boston Gazette,* October 10 to 17, 1720; and CO.137/14, PRO.

12. For details of this attack see *The Trials of Eight Persons Indited for Piracy . . . on the 18th October 1717* (the trial of the survivors of Bellamy's crew), CO.5/867, part I, f 10, PRO.

13. Although there are numerous references to Roberts' attacks in Colonial Office documents, the only description of his physical appearance is in Johnson, pp. 243–44.

14. See captain's log of HMS *Swallow,* ADM.51/954; Captain Ogle's letter of April 5, 1722, to the Admiralty, ADM.1/2242; and *Proceedings of the Court Held on the Coast of Africa . . .* (trial of Roberts' crew at Cape Coast Castle), HCA.1/99.3, PRO.

15. CSPC, volume 1717–18, no. 551.

16. CSPC, volume 1717–18, no. 797.

17. Rediker, pp. 267–68.

18. Quoted from Part IV of Exquemelin (op. cit.), p. 311, and see also p. 309, note 1; and Dampier, volume I, pp. 30, 35.

19. For details see Earle, *The Sack of Panama,* p. 64.

20. Exquemelin, part IV, p. 324.

21. Ibid.

22. CSPC, volume 1712–14, no. 651.

23. CO.152/14, f 289, PRO.

24. ADM.51/954, part VII, PRO.

25. Johnson, p. 326.

26. CSPC, volume 1719–20, no. 34.

27. *The Boston News Letter*, July 15 to 22, 1717. I am grateful to William Gilkerson (op. cit.) for explaining the technical terms associated with weapons.

28. CO.152/12, no. 136 (vi), PRO.

29. CO.152/12, no. 67(ii), PRO.

30. CSPC, volume 1710–11, no. 177.

31. *The Boston Gazette*, April 27 to May 4, 1724.

32. CO.23/13, f 221, PRO.

33. CO.152/12, no. 136 (ii), PRO.

34. *The Last Speech and Dying Words of Richard Luntly, Carpenter Aboard the* Eagle Snow (Edinburgh, 1721). There is a copy in the Caird Library, NMM.

Chapter 7

1. The details of Gow's life are taken from news items in *The London Journal* for February 12, 1724/5, March 6, 1724/5, March 13, 1724/5, March 20, 1724/5, March 27, 1724/5, April 3, 1725, May 29, 1725, and June 5, 1725; and from Johnson; and Daniel Defoe's *An Account of the Conduct and Proceedings of the Late John Gow, Alias Smith* (London, 1725). A limited edition of Defoe's *Account of the Conduct and Proceedings of the Late John Gow* edited by John Russell (London, 1920) has a useful commentary and notes.

2. Defoe, *An Account of the Conduct and Proceedings of the Late John Gow* (ed. Russell; London, 1920), p. 35.

3. *The London Journal*, June 5, 1725.

4. Walter Scott's *The Pirate* was first published in 1821. It was adapted for the stage and proved popular with the theatergoing public in the 1820s.

5. *Deposition of Nathaniel Catling*, CO.37/10, no. 10 (v), PRO.

6. *Deposition of Edward North*, CO.37/10, no. 10 (ii), PRO.

7. CSPC, volume 1720–21, no. 463 (iii).

8. Ibid.

9. *Deposition of Robert Leonard*, CO.152/12, no. 136 (vi), PRO.

10. CSPC, volume 1724–25, no. 102.

11. I am grateful to Richard Pennell for bringing this news item to my attention. For another account of walking the plank, see *The Mariners Mirror,* volume 80, 1994, p. 224.

12. Exquemelin, p. 152.

13. Earle, *The Sack of Panama,* p. 74.

14. Ibid., p. 75.

15. Ibid., p. 79.

16. Exquemelin, p. 155.

17. Rediker, p. 216.

18. Ibid., p. 219.

19. Ibid.

20. Ibid., p. 220.

21. Ibid., p. 225.

22. Dow and Edmonds, p. 325.

23. HCA.1/99.3, PRO.

24. Rodger, p. 227.

25. Ibid., p. 227.

26. News item from London concerning a trial at the Old Bailey, *The Boston Gazette,* August 14 to 21, 1721.

27. *The London Journal,* May 14, 1726.

28. CO.23/1, no. 18, ff 75–82, PRO.

29. CO.23/13, f 221, PRO.

30. Johnson, p. 75.

31. CO.1/57, f 381, PRO.

32. See Backschreider, pp. 412–36.

33. The Rev. Mark Noble, quoted in Moore, p. 223.

34. Rogers, p. 94. Rogers' description of the rescue of Selkirk is reproduced in an appendix to the Penguin Classics edition of *Robinson Crusoe,* edited by Angus Ross (London, 1985).

35. Rogers, p. 92.

36. Ibid.

Chapter 8

1. Dr. Emmanuel Heath, *A Full Account of the Late Dreadful Earthquake at Port Royal . . . by the Minister of That Place* (London, 1692).

2. Letter from Edmund Edlyne, Jamaica, June 20, 1692, quoted in H. J. Cadbury, "Quakers and the Earthquake at Port Royal, 1692," *Jamaica Historical Review.*

3. Letter from John Pike, Spanish Town, Jamaica, June 19, 1692, ibid.

4. Pawson and Buisseret, p. 98.

5. John Taylor, writing in 1687, quoted by Pawson and Buisseret, p. 109.

6. Ibid., p. 119.

7. Quoted by Clinton Black in his book *Port Royal: A History and Guide* (Jamaica, 1970; cited 1988 revised edition), p. 17.

8. Commission and Instructions for Captain Jonathan Barnet, issued by Lord Hamilton, Governor of Jamaica, November 24, 1715. CO.137/12, no. 78 (i), f 231. PRO.

9. Black (op. cit.), p. 48.

10. Pawson and Buisseret, p. 142.

11. Johnson.

12. There is an excellent description of the pirate settlements on Madagascar in Ritchie, pp. 80–86, 112–16.

13. Quoted by Mitchell, p. 192.

14. Rogers, p. 307.

15. Uring, p. 241.

16. Dampier, volume II, p. 156.

17. Jeremy Dummer was the agent in Massachusetts Bay: CSPC, volume 1719–20, no. 578.

18. Dampier, volume II, p. 155.

19. CSPC, volume 1717–18, no. 104.

20. Report to Secretary Addison, November 21, 1717. CSPC, volume 1717–18, no. 220.

21. CSPC, volume 1717–18, no. 64.

22. Details taken from C. E. Manwaring's Introduction to Rogers, pp. vii-xi.

23. Rogers, entry for December 22, 1709, p. 215.

24. Report from Secretary Addison to the Council of Trade and Plantations, September 3, 1717 (CSPC, volume 1717–18, no. 64).

25. Governor Woodes Rogers to the Council of Trade and Plantations, October 31, 1718 (CSPC, 1717–18, no. 737).

26. A full account of the trial is in the Public Record Office, Kew: *The Trial of Ten Pirates at Nassau in the Bahamas* (CO.23/1, no. 18, ff 75–82, PRO).

27. CO.23/1, no. 18, f 81v. PRO.

28. CSPC, volume 1720–21, no. 390.

29. CSPC, volume 1719–20, no. 31.

30. G. E. Manwaring's Introduction to Rogers, p. xiv, note 3.

Chapter 9

1. Letter from the *Milford Galley,* which was present when Woodes Rogers' flotilla arrived at Nassau, printed in *The Whitehall Evening Post,* London, October 18, 1718.

2. Johnson, p. 115.

3. Ibid., p. 307.

4. Ibid., p. 229.

5. Exquemelin, part IV, p. 417.

6. CSPC, volume 1711–12, no. 335.

7. Rediker, p. 228.

8. These figures are taken from notes on pirate attacks compiled from contemporary newspapers, reports from colonial governors, trial documents, depositions of seamen attacked by pirates (in the Public Record Office), and Johnson.

9. For details of naval vessels see: Lyon; Lavery, *The Ship of the Line;* E.H.H. Archibald, *The Wooden Fighting Ship in the Royal Navy, AD 897–1860* (London, 1968).

10. Robert Gardiner, *The Line of Battle: The Sailing Warship 1650–1840* (London, 1992), p. 51.

11. Baker, p. 108.

12. Ibid., p. 110.

13. Ralph Davis, *The Rise of the English Shipping Industry in the 17th and 18th Centuries,* (Newton Abbot, 1962).

14. Arthur Middleton, *Tobacco Coast: A Maritime History of Chesapeake Bay in the Colonial Era* (Baltimore, 1984), Appendix E.

15. CO.152/12, no. 67 (iii), PRO.

16. Johnson, p. 72.

17. CSPC, volume 1717–18, no. 556.

18. CO/152/13, f 282, PRO.

19. CO.152/12, no. 136 (i), PRO.

20. Ritchie, p. 58.

21. *Deposition of James Blois,* February 24, 1718. CO.152/12 no. 136 (ii), PRO.

22. Vanderbilt; Clifford and Turchi.

23. For a study of pirate films and swashbucklers, see Richards; and Parish and Stanke.

24. Quoted by Parish and Stanke, p. 64.

25. Richards, p. 251.

26. Ibid.

27. Flynn (1961 paperback edition); and Thomas.

28. Robertson, p. 34.

29. Rudy Behlmer, *Inside Warner Bros.* (New York, 1985) p. 25.

30. Ibid.

31. Robertson, p. 55.

Chapter 10

1. The details of this example of buried treasure are taken from three depositions in the Public Record Office, Chancery Lane: *Information of Morgan Miles of Swansea,* and *William Doale of Bristol,* and *Joseph Spollet of Devon.* HCA.1/55, f 9, 10, 11, PRO.

2. Ibid.

3. The account of Captain Kidd given here is taken from: Brooks; Johnson; Hill, pp. 113–22; and Ritchie.

4. Quoted by Ritchie, p. 102.

5. Brooks, p. 40.

6. Barlow.

7. Brooks, p. 70.

8. Ibid., p. 71.

9. Ibid., p. 28.

10. Ibid., p. 27.

11. Ritchie, p. 192.

12. Ibid., p. 193.

13. Quoted by Linebaugh, p. 28.

14. Brooks, p. 187.

15. Ritchie, p. 231.

16. Johnson, p. 87. The logbook of Lieutenant Hicks of HMS *Pearl* notes that 732 pounds of bread, and 6,487 pounds of cocoa, "besides whats in cask," were brought back by Maynard's expedition (ADM/L/P32, NMM).

17. A list of items recovered from the wreck of the *Whydah* is in the Appendix of Clifford and Turchi, pp. 205–14.

18. Rediker, pp. 256 and 281.

19. Report from Governor Lawes of Jamaica, 24 August 1720 (CSPC, volume 1720–21, no. 213).

Chapter 11

1. ADM.51/4250, PRO.

2. ADM/L/P32, NMM.

3. Johnson, p. 78.

4. CSPC, volume 1717–18, no. 800, p. 430.

5. Johnson, p. 78. Robert Maynard was made lieutenant on January 14, 1707. From 1709 he was third lieutenant on HMS *Bedford*. He became first lieutenant of HMS *Pearl* in 1716. He was promoted to commodore in 1739, and to captain in 1740. He died in 1750.

6. Letter of Captain Ellis Brand to the Admiralty, February 6, 1718/19, ADM 1/1472, PRO.

7. A letter from Maynard to Lieutenant Symonds of HMS *Phoenix,* the station ship at New York, was published by *The Weekly Journal or British Gazetteer* on April 25, 1719. It is quoted, together with much other valuable documentation, in Lee, p. 233.

8. Johnson, p. 80.

9. Lee, p. 233.

10. *The Boston News Letter,* February 23 to March 2, 1719. The report was brought by a sloop from North Carolina on February 12. The same issue of the newspaper contains additional information from a letter sent from North Carolina on December 17.

11. Lee, p. 234.

12. ADM/L/P32, NMM.

13. An illustrated booklet with the text of the play is available from Pollock's Toy Theatres Ltd., Scala Street, London.

14. CSPC, volume 1717–18, no. 556.

15. CSPC, volume 1720–21, no. 251 (i).

16. CSPC, volume 1717–18, no. 271.

17. CSPC, volume 1717–18, no. 575.

18. Rediker (1989 paperback edition), p. 256.

19. These figures are taken from Pawson and Buisseret; and Constance Green, *American Cities in the Growth of the Nation* (London, 1957).

20. Rediker, p. 256.

21. For an excellent survey of the British government's measures against piracy see Ritchie, pp. 140–54; see also R. Marsden (ed.), *The Law and Custom of the Sea,* volume II (Navy Records Society, 1916); and Gosse, pp. 315–17; and *Statutes of the Realm.*

22. For a detailed account of the trial see Dow and Edmonds, pp. 99–115.

23. Ibid., p. 112.

24. Governor Bennett of Bermuda issued a certificate of pardon based on the wording of the royal proclamation:

To all whom these presents may concern

Whereas His most Sacred Majesty George King of Great Britain France and Ireland by His Royal Proclamation bearing Date the Fifth day of Septr. 1717 and in the fourth year of His Said Majesty's Reign hath been graciously pleased to declare that if any Pirate and Pirates shall by the time therein limited Surrender him or themselves to one of His said Majesty's Principal Secretarys of State in Great Britain or Ireland or to any Govr. or Deputy Govr. of his said Majesty's Plantations or Dominions every such Pirate and Pirates so Surrendering him or themselves as aforesd. Should have His most gracious Pardon of and for such his or their Piracy & Piracys by him or them comitted as more fully and at large appears by the said Proclamation.

These are therfore to Certifye till His Majesty's Pardon can be made out that hath on this day arrived in these His Majesty's Islands of Bermuda and Surrendered himself to me the Govr. and Vice Admiral aforesaid Accordingly.

Given under my hand and Publick Seal of these Islds this   day of   in the fourth Year of His Majesty's Reign Anno Dom 1717/ 18.

CO.37/10, no. 7. (i), PRO.

25. Ibid.

26. CO.137/13 no. 5 (i), PRO.

27. CSPC, volume 1719–20, no. 33, PRO.

28. CSPC, volume 1717–18, no. 556, PRO.

29. CSPC, volume 1717–18, no. 9, PRO.

30. See Lyon; Lavery, *The Ship of the Line;* and Christopher Lloyd, *The British Seaman* (London, 1968).

31. ADM.8/14, PRO.

32. CSPC, volume 1710–11, no. 782.

33. Rediker, p. 49, note 85.

34. Johnson, p. 66.

35. Rodger, p. 98.

36. CSPC, volume 1717–18, no. 64.

37. ADM.8/14, PRO.

38. Captain's log of HMS *Swallow,* ADM.51/954, PRO.

39. John Charnock, *Biographia Novalis,* (London, 1795), volume III, pp. 402–07. See also a useful entry in the *Dictionary of National Biography*.

40. The details of Captain Ogle's search for Bartholomew Roberts and the final battle are taken from the following sources: Captain Ogle's letters to the Admiralty, April 5, 1722, July 26, 1722, and September 8, 1722, ADM. 1/2242, PRO; captain's log of HMS *Swallow* ADM.51/954, PRO; lieutenant's log of HMS *Swallow,* ADM/L/S564, NMM; *Proceedings of Court Held on the Coast of Africa upon Trying of 100 Pyrates Taken by HMS Swallow,* HCA. 1/99.3, PRO; *The London Journal,* April 3, 1725; and Johnson, pp. 232–55.

41. Johnson, p. 224.

42. Ibid., p. 234.

43. ADM.1/2242, PRO.

44. ADM/L/S564, NMM.

45. ADM.1/2242, PRO.

46. HCA.1/99.3, PRO.

47. Ibid.

48. CSPC, volme 1722–23, no. 76.

49. Ibid.

50. The details of this action are taken from Dow and Edmonds, pp. 292–93; and Johnson, pp. 328–29.

51. CSPC, volume 1722–23, no. 606.

52. *The Boston Gazette,* August 19 to 26, 1723.

53. Ritchie, p 152.

54. CO.137/12, no. 78 (i–iii), PRO.

55. Ibid.

56. CSPC, volume 1720–21, no. 288.

57. For details of this action see the report of the Governor and Council of South Carolina to the Council of Trade and Plantations, CSPC, volume 1717–18, no. 730; and Johnson.

58. See *Deposition of Walter Moor of the Sloop* Eagle, CO.152/14, f 259, PRO; Johnson, pp. 315–17; and Dow and Edmonds, pp. 139–40.

59. CO.152/14, f 259, PRO.

60. See *The Trial of Robert Corp and Henry Wynn,* CO.152/14, f 292, PRO.

Chapter 12

1. Griffiths, volume 1, p. 281.

2. *The London Journal,* July 27, 1728.

3. Ibid., 5 June 1725.

4. Report from Governor Hart, St. Christophers, June 1723. CSPC, volume 1722–23, no. 576.

5. Quoted in Dow and Edmonds, p. 327. It is interesting to compare these costs with those incurred in the hanging of Captain Kidd: the Admiralty Marshal charged £4 for the transport in carts to the gallows; James Sherwood charged £10 for building the gibbet at Tilbury; Thomas Sherman charged £3.2s.6d for the gallows and £1.5s.2d to carry the body and hang it in chains; James Smith charged £4 for making the chains (ADM 1/3666, f 210, PRO).

6. From figures compiled by Rediker, p. 283.

7. Quoted by Senior, p. 19.

8. These figures are taken from: contemporary newspapers; reports from the colonial governors in *Calendar of State Papers* and in documents at the Public Record Office; trial documents; Johnson; Dow and Edmonds.

9. *Whitehall Evening Post,* February 17, 1719.

10. CSPC, volume 1722–23, no. 142.

11. CO.5/867, f 10, PRO.

12. Johnson, p. 107.

13. This account of the trial of Roberts' crew is taken from: *Proceedings of Court Held on the Coast of Africa upon Trying of 100 Pyrates Taken by HMS Swallow,* HCA.1/99.3, PRO; and Captain Chaloner Ogle's letters to the Admiralty, ADM.1/2242, PRO; captain's log of HMS *Swallow,* ADM.51/954, PRO; and lieutenant's log of HMS *Swallow,* ADM/L/ S564, NMM.

14. Davis, pp. 240–45.

15. Captain A. Dewar (ed.), *The Voyages and Travels of Captain Nathaniel Uring* (London, 1928), p. 106.

16. Davis, p. 345; and James Walvin, *The Slave Trade,* p. 318.

17. HCA.1/99.3, PRO.

18. Ibid.

19. Ibid.

20. Ordinary of Newgate, *His Account of the Behaviour, Confession, and Last Speech of Capt. Alexander Dolzell* (London 1715). A copy is held at the NMM.

21. Brooks, p. 49.

22. Ibid., p. 50.

23. Dow and Edmonds, p. 112.

24. Vanderbilt, p. 105.

25. Rev. Cotton Mather, *Instructions to the Living from the Condition of the Dead. A Brief Relation of Remarkables in the Shipwreck of Above One Hundred Pirates Who Were Cast Away in the Ship Whido, on the Coast of New-England, April 26, 1717 . . . With Some Account of the Discourse Had with Them on the Way to Their Execution. And a Sermon Preached on Their Occasion* (Boston, 1717). Vanderbilt quotes extensively from this pamphlet (pp. 106–12).

26. There is a detailed account of the last days of Fly and his crew in Dow and Edmonds, pp. 335–37.

27. CSPC, volume 1724–25, no. 102.

28. The poem is quoted by Dow and Edmonds, p. 307.

Afterword

1. For information on modern piracy see: Eric Ellen, *Piracy at Sea* (International Maritime Bureau; London, 1992); Villar; Merchant Shipping Notice no. M1517, *Piracy and Armed Robbery* (HMSO; London, 1993).

Glossary of Sea Terms

after Situated at the back or the stern part of a vessel.

block and tackle An arrangement of pulleys and ropes used to raise heavy loads, and to increase the purchase on ropes used for the running rigging.

boatswain, or **bosun** The warrant officer in charge of sails, rigging, anchors and associated gear.

bowsprit A heavy spar pointing forward from the stem or front of the vessel.

brace A rope used to control the horizontal movement of a square-sailed yard.

brig A two-masted vessel, fully square-rigged on both masts, with a fore-and-aft sail on the lower part of the mainmast.

brigantine A two-masted vessel having a fully square-rigged foremast and a fore-and-aft rigged mainmast with square sails on the main topmast.

broadside The simultaneous firing of all the guns on one side of a ship.

buccaneer The term originally applied to the hunters of wild oxen and pigs on the island of Hispaniola, but was later used to describe the pirates and privateers who plundered shipping and coastal towns in the West Indies and on the coasts of South and Central America in the second half of the seventeenth century.

bulkhead A vertical partition inside a ship.

careen To heel over a ship and clean the seaweed and barnacles from her bottom.

caulk To seal the gaps between the planks with oakum and pitch.

colors The flags worn by a vessel to show her nationality.

consort A vessel sailing in company with a pirate ship; a companion vessel.

corsair A pirate or privateer operating in the Mediterranean. The most famous corsairs were those based on the Barbary Coast of North Africa who were authorized by their governments to attack the merchant shipping of Christian countries.

cutter A small one-masted vessel rigged with a fore-and-aft mainsail, foresail, and jib. In the eighteenth century a cutter usually had a square topsail as well.

deadeyes A round wooden block with three holes for extending the shrouds.

fathom A measure of six feet, used to describe the depth of water.

flagship A ship commanded by an admiral and flying the admiral's distinguishing flag.

fore Situated in front; the front part of a vessel at the bow.

fore-and-aft At bow and stern; backward and forward or along the length of the ship.

fore-and-aft rig Having mainly fore-and-aft sails, i.e., sails set lengthwise and not at right angles to the ship's hull, as is the case with square-rigged sails.

foremast The mast at the front of the vessel.

gunwale The upper planking along the sides of a vessel.

heave to To check the course of a vessel and bring her to a standstill by heading her into the wind and backing some of her sails.

helm The tiller or wheel which controls the rudder and enables a vessel to be steered.

lee The side or direction away from the wind, or downwind.

lee shore The shore onto which the wind is blowing; a hazardous shore for a sailing vessel particularly in strong or gale force winds.

letter of marque A commission or license to fit out an armed vessel and employ her to capture an enemy's merchant shipping. In Britain and her colonies the letter of marque was issued by the sovereign, the Lord High Admiral, or a colonial governor.

mainsheet The rope at the lower corner of the mainsail for regulating its position.

mizzenmast The mast at the stern or back of a vessel; in a three-masted ship the mast at the front is the foremast, the mast in the middle is the mainmast, and the mast at the stern is the mizzenmast.

mounted guns Guns or cannon mounted on wooden carriages.

pink A merchant vessel with a relatively shallow draft and a very narrow stern, variously rigged as a brig, a sloop, or a ship. Some pinks were used by the navy as armed transports. The term also applied to a type of Dutch fishing boat with a square mainsail and sometimes a square foresail launched off the beaches near Scheveningen.

port The left side of a vessel facing forward.

privateer An armed vessel (or the commander and crew of that vessel) which was authorized by a commission or "letter of marque" from the government to capture the merchant vessels of an enemy nation.

quarterdeck A deck above the main deck which stretched from the stern to about halfway along the length of the ship. It was from this deck that the captain and officers controlled the ship.

rail Timber plank on top of the gunwale along the sides of the vessel.

rate **(as in first-rate, second-rate, etc.)** Warships were grouped into six different categories according to the number of guns they carried. In the early eighteenth century a first-rate ship had 100 guns, a second-rate ship had 90 guns, a third-rate had between 80 and 70 guns, a fourth-rate had between 64 and 50 guns, a fifth-rate had between 40 and 28 guns, and a sixth-rate had between 24 and 12 guns.

schooner A two-masted vessel, fore-and-aft rigged on both masts. Some vessels had square topsails on the foremast or on both topmasts.

sheet A rope made fast to the lower corner or corners of a sail to control its position.

ship A vessel with three or more masts and fully square-rigged through-out. The term is also used to describe any large seagoing vessel.

ship of the line A warship large enough to take her place in the line of battle; in the early eighteenth century this ranged from fourth-rate ships of 50 guns up to first-rate ships of 100 guns.

shrouds The set of ropes forming part of the standing rigging and sup-porting the mast or topmast.

sloop A vessel having one fore-and-aft rigged mast with mainsail and a single foresail. In the eighteenth century the term also applied to a small vessel armed with four to twelve guns on her upper deck and rigged with one, two or three masts. For a description of the West India sloops see chapter 9.

snow A vessel similar to a brig with two masts, fully square-rigged on both masts, but with her spanker (the gaff sail at the stern, also called a driver or main-trysail) set on a separate pole or trysail mast just aft of the mainmast.

spar A stout wooden pole used for the mast or yard of a sailing vessel.

square-rigged The principal sails set at right angles to the length of the ship and extended by horizontal yards slung to the mast (as opposed to fore-and-aft rigged).

starboard The right side of a vessel facing forward.

sweep A long oar used by a large vessel.

swivel gun A small gun or cannon mounted on a swivel and set on the rail or side of a vessel.

tack To change the direction of a sailing vessel's course by turning her bows into the wind until the wind blows on her other side.

topsail A sail set on the topmast.

waggoner A sea atlas or volume of sea charts (derived from the name of the Dutch pilot, Lucas Waghenaer, who published a comprehensive volume of charts and sailing directions in 1584).

weigh To pull up the anchor.

yard A long spar suspended from the mast of a vessel to extend the sails.

yardarm Either end of a yard.

BIBLIOGRAPHY

There are more than four hundred books and pamphlets on piracy and privateering in the Library of the National Maritime Museum in London. The Library of Congress in Washington has an equally large selection. The printed volumes of the *Calendar of State Papers, Colonial Series, America and West Indies* contain relevant correspondence between the colonial governors and the Office of Trade and Plantations in London. Reports of pirate attacks and trials appear in contemporary newspapers, and microfilm copies of many of these are held in the Library of Congress, and the British Library's outstation at Colindale. Further details of pirate activities may be found in ships' logbooks, captains' letters, trial documents, and the depositions of seamen and pirate victims which are held in the collections of the Public Record Office in Chancery Lane and Kew. References to the books and documents which I have consulted are given in the notes to each chapter. The following is a selected list of books for further reading.

The Pirates of Fiction

Backschreider, Paula R. *Daniel Defoe, His Life* (Baltimore and London, 1989).

Ballantyne, R. M. *The Coral Island* (London, 1858).

Barrie, J. M. *Peter Pan* (first performance of the play, 1904); *Peter and Wendy* (Barrie's original title for the book version)(London, 1911).

Bell, Ian. *Robert Louis Stevenson: Dreams of Exile* (London, 1992).

Birkin, Andrew. *J. M. Barrie and the Lost Boys* (London, 1979).

Brogan, Hugh. *The Life of Arthur Ransome* (London, 1984).

Byron, Lord. *The Corsair* (London, 1814).

Calder, Jenni. *RLS, a Life Study* (London, 1980).

Colvin, Sydney (ed.). *The Letters of Robert Louis Stevenson* (London, 1895).

Defoe, Daniel. *The Life, Adventures, and Pyracies of the Famous Captain Singleton* (London, 1720).

Defoe, Daniel. *The Life and Strange Surprising Adventures of Robinson Crusoe, of York, Mariner* (London, 1719).

du Maurier, Daphne. *Frenchman's Creek* (London, 1941).

Flynn, Errol. *My Wicked, Wicked Ways* (London, 1960).

Gilbert, W. S., and Sullivan, Arthur. *The Pirates of Penzance, or the Slave of Duty* (copyright performances at Paignton, Devon, and in New York in 1879; London premiere in 1880).

Green, Roger Lancelyn. *Fifty Years of Peter Pan* (London, 1954).

Haill, Catharine. *Dear Peter Pan* (London, 1983).

Johnson, Charles. *The Successful Pirate* (London, 1713).

McLynn, Frank. *Robert Louis Stevenson* (London, 1993).

Marryat, Captain Frederick. *The Pirate* (London, 1836).

Moore, John Robert. *Daniel Defoe, Citizen of the Modern World* (Chicago, 1958).

Parish, James Robert, and Stanke, Don E. *The Swashbucklers* (New York, 1976).

Ransome, Arthur. *Swallows and Amazons* (London, 1930).

Richards, Jeffrey. *Swordsmen of the Screen* (London and Boston, 1977).

Robertson, James C. *The Casablanca Man: The Cinema of Michael Curtiz* (London and New York, 1993).

Rutherford, Andrew. *Byron: The Critical Heritage* (London, 1970).

Sabatini, Rafael. *The Sea Hawk* (London, 1915).

Sabatini, Rafael, *Captain Blood* (London, 1922), and *The Fortunes of Captain Blood* (London, 1936).

Sabatini, Rafael. *The Black Swan* (London, 1932).

Scott, Sir Walter. *The Pirate* (London, 1821).

Stevenson, Robert Louis. *Treasure Island* (first published in serial form in *Young Folks* magazine, October 1881 to January 1882; first published in book form, London, 1883)

Thomas, Tony. *The Complete Films of Errol Flynn* (New York, 1990).

Wardale, Roger. *Nancy Blackett: Under Sail with Arthur Ransome* (London, 1991).

The Pirates of History

Andrews, Kenneth. *The Spanish Caribbean: Trade and Plunder 1530–1630* (New Haven, 1978).

Baker, William A. *Sloops and Shallops* (Barre, Mass., 1966).

Barlow, Edward (ed. Basil Lubbock). *Barlow's Journal of His Life at Sea in King's Ships, East and West Indiamen and Other Merchantmen from 1659–1703* (London, 1934).

Black, Clinton V. *Pirates of the West Indies* (Cambridge and New York, 1989).

Botting, Douglas. *The Pirates* (Amsterdam, 1978).

Brooks, Graham. *The Trial of Captain Kidd* (London and Toronto, 1930).

Burg, B. R. *Sodomy and the Pirate Tradition: English Sea Rovers in the Seventeenth-Century Caribbean* (New York and London, 1984).

Chambers, Anne. *Granuaille: The Life and Times of Grace O'Malley c1530–1603* (Dublin, 1979).

Clifford, Barry, and Turchi, Peter. *The Pirate Prince: Discovering the Priceless Treasures of the Sunken Ship* Whydah (New York and London, 1993).

Dampier, William (ed. John Masefield). *Dampier's Voyages* (London, 1906).

Davis, K. G. *The Royal Africa Company* (London and New York, 1970).

Dow, George Francis, and Edmonds, John Henry. *The Pirates of the New England Coast 1630–1730* (Salem, Mass., 1923).

Drury, Robert (ed. Captain Pasfield Oliver). *Madagascar; or Robert Drury's Journal During Fifteen Years Captivity on That Island* (London, 1897).

Earle, Peter. *The Sack of Panama* (London, 1981).

Earle, Peter. *Corsairs of Malta and Barbary* (London, 1970).

Ellen, Eric. *Piracy at Sea* (International Maritime Bureau: London, 1992).

Exquemelin, A. O. *De Americaensche Zee-Roovers* (Amsterdam, 1678); *Bucaniers of America* (London, 1684); *Histoire des Aventuriers* (Paris, 1686). I have used and cited the edition published in London and New York in 1923, which was edited by W. S. Stallybrass and entitled *Esquemeling, The Buccaneers of America*.

Gilkerson, William. *Boarders Away II: The Small Arms and Combustibles of the Classical Age of Fighting Sail, 1626–1826* (Lincoln, R. I., 1993).

Gosse, Philip. *The History of Piracy* (first published 1932; reprinted in paperback by the Rio Grande Press, New Mexico, 1990).

Griffiths, Arthur. *The Chronicles of Newgate* (London, 1884).

Harland, John. *Seamanship in the Age of Sail: An Account of the Shiphan-dling of the Sailing Man-of-War 1600–1860* (London, 1984).

Hill, Charles. *Notes on Piracy in Eastern Waters* (Bombay, 1923).

Howse, Derek, and Thrower, Norman. *A Buccaneer's Atlas, Basil Ringrose's South Sea Waggoner* (Berkeley and Los Angeles, 1992).

Johnson, Captain Charles. *A General History of the Robberies and Murders of the Most Notorious Pyrates* (London, 1724). There are numerous editions of this book. I have used the comprehensive edition edited by Manuel Schonhorn. This is entitled *A General History of the Pyrates,* and the author is given as Daniel Defoe. It was published in London in 1972 and has extensive notes on the text.

Lavery, Brian. *The Ship of the Line,* volume I. *The Development of the Battle Fleet 1650–1850* (London, 1983).

———. *The Arming and Fitting of English Ships of War, 1600–1815* (London, 1987).

Lee, Robert E. *Blackbeard the Pirate: A Reappraisal of His Life and Times* (North Carolina, 1974).

Linebaugh, Peter. *The London Hanged: Crime and Civil Society in the Eighteenth Century* (London, 1991).

Lloyd, Christopher. *English Corsairs on the Barbary Coast* (London, 1981).

Lucie-Smith, Edward. *Outcasts of the Sea* (London, 1978).

Lyon, David. *The Sailing Navy List. All the Ships of the Royal Navy—Built, Purchased and Captured—1688–1860* (London, 1993).

Marley, David F. *Pirates and Privateers of the Americas,* (Santa Barbara, Calif., 1994).

Middleton, Arthur. *Tobacco Coast: A Maritime History of Chesapeake Bay in the Colonial Era* (Baltimore, 1984).

Mitchell, David. *Pirates* (London, 1976).

Murray, Dian H. *Pirates of the South China Coast 1790–1810* (Stanford, Calif., 1987).

National Maritime Museum. *Piracy and Privateering,* volume IV of the Catalogue of the Library of the National Maritime Museum (London, 1972).

Pawson, Michael, and Buisseret, David. *Port Royal, Jamaica* (Oxford, 1975).

Pringle, Patrick. *The Jolly Roger: The Story of the Great Age of Piracy* (London, 1953).

Pope, Dudley. *Harry Morgan's Way: The Biography of Sir Henry Morgan 1635–1684* (London, 1977).

Rediker, Marcus. *Between the Devil and the Deep Blue Sea: Merchant Seamen, Pirates, and the Anglo-American Maritime World* (Cambridge and New York, 1987).

Ritchie, Robert C. *Captain Kidd and the War Against the Pirates* (Cambridge, Mass., and London, 1986).

Rodger, N. A. M. *The Wooden World: An Anatomy of the Georgian Navy* (London, 1986).

Rogers, Woodes (ed. G. E., Manwaring). *A Cruising Voyage Round the World* (London, 1928).

Senior, Clive. *A Nation of Pirates: English Piracy in Its Heyday* (Newton Abbot, London, and New York, 1976).

Shomette, Don. *Pirates on the Chesapeake: Being a True History of Pirates, Picaroons and Sea Raiders on Chesapeake Bay, 1610–1807* (Maryland, 1985).

Uring, Nathaniel (ed. A. Dewar). *The Voyages and Travels of Captain Nathaniel Uring* (London, 1928).

Vanderbilt, Arthur T. *Treasure Wreck: The Fortunes and Fate of the Pirate Ship* Whydah (Boston, 1986).

Villar, Roger. *Piracy Today* (London, 1985).

Wheelright, Julie. *Amazons and Military Maids* (London, 1989).

Williams, Neville. *The Sea Dogs: Privateers, Plunder and Piracy in the Elizabethan Age* (London, 1975).

———. *Captains Outrageous: Seven Centuries of Piracy* (London, 1961).

Wilson, Derek. *The World Encompassed: Drake's Great Voyage, 1577–1580* (London, 1977).

Index